Anonymus

The robber chieftain

An historical tale of Dublin Castle

Anonymus

The robber chieftain
An historical tale of Dublin Castle

ISBN/EAN: 9783742800459

Manufactured in Europe, USA, Canada, Australia, Japa

Cover: Foto ©Andreas Hilbeck / pixelio.de

Manufactured and distributed by brebook publishing software (www.brebook.com)

Anonymus

The robber chieftain

THE
ROBBER CHIEFTAIN:

An Historical Tale

OF

DUBLIN CASTLE.

DUBLIN:
JAMES DUFFY, 7, WELLINGTON-QUAY,
AND
22, PATERNOSTER-ROW, LONDON.
1863.

THE ROBBER CHIEFTAIN.

CHAPTER I.

PLOT AND COUNTER-PLOT.—CASTLE KIDNAPPERS.

"WHAT a furious, cold, damp, dismal, howling wind this is! What a miserable companion for a night-watch! It is worse than a sullen comrade for a fellow-sentinel, or a cowardly captain for a leader; enough to disgust one with the life of a soldier, and induce him to wish he were back safe and sound again amid the fens of Lincolnshire. What say you, Ebenezer Lawson?—or why have you unloosed your military cloak, and needlessly exposed yourself to this piercing wild blast?"

"Hush! John Elliott. Silence is a portion of the duty of a sentinel. Did not your tongue wag so ceaselessly and so loudly, I would be certain of that, of which I am now but doubtful; for in the midst of your talk, and with the storm blowing around us, I am almost sure that I detected the noise of steps stealthily approaching our post. Look then to your matchlock, and be silent. The postern gate in Dublin Castle is no light charge for either of us."

The speakers in this dialogue were two stout Cromwellian soldiers, who, armed with matchlocks and lighted fusees, had been pacing for an hour in front of the narrow door, which afforded an entrance into that part of the Castle which lay between what was commonly called the Birmingham and the Wardrobe Towers. In front was a fortified wall rising out of the deep ditch, ten feet deep and twenty feet broad, and filled with water from the Dodder; this ditch separated the Castle from a piece of ground that, in reference to the purposes for which it had been formerly used, and the irregular range of buildings that now partially covered it, was then designated "Sheep-street."

The first of the soldiers who had spoken, John Elliott, was a man about six feet in height. His round, bullet-shaped head was placed erect on a large, broad, bulky person. Soft, mild-looking blue eyes, and a good-tempered face, with an open, half-smiling mouth, gave to him the appearance of a farmer who had but encased himself, for a freak, with the iron helmet and breastplate of a soldier.

The comrade of Elliott had been a blacksmith in Huntingdon. Ebenezer Lawson was an inch taller than Elliott, but unlike his companion in figure, face, and deportment; for he seemed to be made up of nought else than cordage-like muscles: his nose, long and sharp, protruded between two small, black, dazzling ferret eyes; his thin lips were drawn in upon a mouth, which seemed to sink back into the face, as if he were destitute of teeth; and the power of relaxing his features into a smile, was apparently an accomplishment he never had mastered.

"What say you, Lawson?" said Elliott, as a ruddy glow illuminated his broad face, whilst puffing new life and vigour into his fusee, "what say you? Some one approaching our post by stealth! Oh, you must dream, comrade! What can any one have to do with us or our post? All dangers are now over. Who is now strong enough to assail us?"

"The Irish rebels," gruffly replied Lawson. "Do not, however, talk; listen, and be watchful."

Elliott remained silent for a short time. At first he stood gazing at his companion, watching every movement made by him; and then perceiving that Lawson went peering round every nook and crevice of the battlements, he imitated the example thus given; and having, by his own examination, satisfied himself that Lawson had made a mistake, and that all his apprehensions were vain, he drew his cloak tightly around him, and approaching his comrade, said: "Lawson, I wish you to answer one question I have long desired to put to you."

"What is it?—be brief, I pray you," answered Lawson, as he laid his matchlock down, and, like his companion, sought to shield himself from the harsh cold night-wind, by drawing his thick over-coat above his mouth and ears.

"What is your reason for always speaking of the people of this country, as if they had done you a personal wrong? Why do you hate the Irish?"

"Because they are rebels."

"Rebels!" said Elliott in amazement—"how rebels! They have fought in defence of their king; we, on the other hand, have fought against him. If the term 'rebel' is to be applied to either, it more justly belongs to us than to them."

"The Commonwealth of England is the supreme sovereign of England, Scotland, and Ireland. The God of armies has already decided that our cause is just, and our claim to dominion rightful: and the Irish having taken up arms against that just cause and that rightful power, are rebels," answered Lawson.

"Be it so. I who have shed my blood, and abandoned home, family, and occupation, in defence of the Parliament and liberties of old England, am not, and cannot be the person to deny that you are right in saying the Commonwealth is the sovereign power in these countries. But still I cannot see why you should have so strong a dislike to the Irish, merely because they are rebels."

"They are Papists as well as rebels," added Lawson.

"Well, it is said by some, that there is no greater proof of piety than an abomination of Popery," continued Elliott. "I have been told to regard Popery as a new-fangled idolatry, and advised to do my utmost to exterminate it from the face of the earth; but that is not a sufficient reason for detesting every one who is so deluded as to be an adherent to the Pope of Rome. Why, I again ask you, have you, what I might call, a personal hatred against the Irish?"

Lawson made no reply to this question in words, but unloosing his cloak, he stretched out his left hand to his comrade.

"Bah!" said Elliott, "that is no just cause for persecuting to the death a whole race. In the same skirmish in which you received a stunning blow and lost two fingers of your left hand, I was unhorsed with a gash in my head, of which I am sure to bear the scar to my grave; but that, of a verity, is no reason why I should carry with me for ever a rankling resentment against the brave, valiant foeman, who in open fight encountered us. Instead of revenging the blow, I would, if I could, render a service to him who inflicted it, and that man, I believe, was Colonel Fitzpatrick——"

Was it a sudden blast of the chill wind that shivered through the frame of both soldiers? Or was it a suppressed whistling sound, like that of the human voice, that made both the English soldiers start from the attitude of repose in which they had been resting, and rush forward to the same point of the wall, and look with piercing eyes down its sides into the ditch beneath? What was it that thus aroused, and so startled them? They could not distinctly tell—they could not positively define the cause, but both stopped, leaning over the wall; and the first to resume the conversation was Elliott.

"I am not suspicious—I am certainly not apprehensive of any danger; but as I am a living man," said the bold-hearted Englishman, "I would swear that in the midst of the fierce gust of wind I heard a person pronounce, and in the Irish manner, and with the Irish accent, the word 'Whisht!'"

"I am sure of it," replied the suspicious Lawson, "There is some one lurking about our post. Would that I could discover him, and I would despatch him with as little remorse as I did the fugitives in the cave near Dundalk, where we smoked them out of their hiding-hole."

"Lawson! Lawson! that was a dire and an accursed deed—one to be, if possible, for ever buried in forgetfulness; never, oh! never to be mentioned but with execration. You forget," continued Elliott, "I was a witness to that transaction; but, thank God! I took no part in it. What injury had those wretched Irish fugitives done to us that they should have been so ruthlessly pursued, and so mercilessly put to death? Of all the actions of our Lieutenant-General Ludlow in Ireland, that was the worst—the most unprovoked, and the most cruel. The Irish rebels, as you call them, were utterly defeated; they had no forces in the field to encounter; their bravest leaders were conquered or slain; or like him of whom we have been speaking—Colonel Fitzpatrick—they had become self-exiled with their soldiers, and transported to other lands. And yet, because our general was told that a few persons were seen lurking or hiding in the hills, he set forth in pursuit of them, and finding that they had withdrawn into a cave, and would not come out nor yield themselves prisoners, he had the mouth of the cave stopped up, and the attempt made, by closing all the apertures to it, and by burning wood around the mouth, to smother the fugitives! And then, when the cave was again opened, and our soldiers penetrated into its deepest recesses, the few who were still living were dragged forth and most of them put to death! Oh! it was a cruel and a barbarous deed.* And what could be the reason for perpetrating it, I cannot even surmise."

"You forget," said Lawson, who appeared to be greatly excited by the strong language of his comrade, "you forget, or you are so fond of Irish Papists, you do not choose to remember, that before those bloody Irish rebels met with their deserts, they were summond to surrender— that refusing to obey such a summons, my brother, Jacob Lawson, upon creeping into the cave, and shooting the first person he encountered, was barbarously murdered."

"There was no barbarous murder in shooting to death a man who had slain another but an instant before. But what I want to know is, why these poor wretches were so beset? or, why did the Lieutenant-General seek to smother

* See Illustration A.—The Death-Cave of Dundalk.

them? or, why, having made the attempt, he did not leave them, or the remnant of them, to the miserable fate to which they seemed to be self-doomed? Why, I ask, was there this merciless pursuit of a scattered band of the fugitive Irish?"

"As you seem to have made a hero of the Irish Colonel, since he knocked you on the head," sneeringly answered Lawson, "I will tell you. I suppose you have heard of the execution of the mother of Colonel Fitzpatrick?"

"Certainly—she was burned alive as a murderess, having been convicted, as I heard, of putting English prisoners to death; and expressing as rabid a hatred of the English as you do of the Irish," replied Elliott.*

"She was justly put to death," observed Lawson. "She knew well what were the rights acquired by us in lawful warfare—that the lands we had conquered by the sword were justly ours; and she was doing her utmost to defeat our claim, and render nugatory our rights. The broad lands, and extensive estates, which formerly belonged to her son, she was endeavouring to retain for her grandson—that grandson she had put out of the way; but the estates were apportioned by our Commissioners to be divided between Colonel Axtel, the Governor of Kilkenny—the same brave man who led the tyrant Charley Stuart to execution—and the nephew of the Lieutenant-General. The latter has promised to give one hundred acres of the best land in the Queen's County to whomsoever will place, living or dead, in his hands the body of the son of Colonel Fitzpatrick. That son is not now more than two years of age. It was believed he was with the fugitives in the cave near Dundalk, most of them a family named Geraghty,

* See Illustration B.—The Execution of Mrs. Fitzpatrick.

and cosherers of Fitzpatrick's foster-family. My brother lost his life in seeking for him. I am engaged in the same pursuit; and you ask me, why I hate the Irish? I have a right to hate them; for they seem to know I am struggling to lay hold on the boy Fitzpatrick, and they appear to take a malicious delight in baffling me, and every other honest Englishman engaged in the same pursuit."

"You hate the Irish—first, because they are rebels—then you hate the Irish, because they are Papists—and lastly you hate the Irish, because they will not place an unoffending infant in your hands, in order that you may become, by the sacrifice of his life or liberty, a landed proprietor in Ireland. Are not these the causes of your animosity against the Irish?" asked Elliott.

"Exactly so," replied Lawson.

"And as a Christian man, Lawson—as a diligent reader of the great book of mercy and forgiveness, do you think you are justified in the sight of God in nurturing such sentiments against your fellow-creatures?"

"I do," answered Lawson. "We are the chosen people of God, and they are idolatrous Philistines; but silence, I pray you, Elliott. There can be no mistake now, there are persons approaching our post."

"Shoulder your matchlock, Lawson. Who goes there?"

"A friend," was the reply that came out of the darkness which enveloped the ramparts of the Castle.

"Advance, friend, that I may question thee," said Elliott.

The steps of a dozen heavily-armed men became now distinctly audible; and when they had approached within thirty yards of the spot where Elliott and Lawson were posted, they were directed to halt, and the person who seemed to be their commander advanced alone and unattended towards the two sentinels.

"Stand where you are, friend," cried Elliott; "until you have announced your name and quality."

"Captain Ludlow, nephew of the Lieutenant-General of the Horse," replied the new comer.

"Advance, Captain Ludlow," said Elliot; "you will find us watchful."

"The Commonwealth relies on the diligence and zeal of such men as you, Elliott," answered Ludlow; "but my present business is with your comrade, Lawson—I would speak a few words with him in private."

"As you wish," replied Elliott; "but before permitting Lawson to quit his post, you will please, Captain, to give me the watchword of the night, so that I may be sure what you have to say to a sentinal on duty, whilst under my command, has reference to the affairs of the Commonwealth."

"You are over-scrupulous, Elliott," answered Ludlow; "but be it as you desire—the word for the night is the name of our present ruler in Ireland—'*Henry*.'"

As the word was thus spoken, there was the sound as if of some movement beyond and outside the ramparts; and the new comer, not less than Lawson and Elliott, started as each seemed to hear the word repeated in whispering accents.

"One would fancy he was in command of raw recruits, and not veteran soldiers," remarked Ludlow; "what stupidity it is thus to repeat the watchword of the night; but I have things more important to do than to chide these armed boors. Come hither, Lawson, I would speak with you."

"Stop, Lawson," said Elliott; "leave your matchlock with me whilst speaking with Captain Ludlow. I cannot permit you to take your weapon from the post you are charged to defend."

"Quite right, Elliott," observed Ludlow; "a good soldier is never forgetful of the most minute points of discipline. Come hither, Lawson, I would speak with you beside this battlement, for I wish to remove you the shortest possible distance from your comrade."

"Humph!" said Elliot to himself, "the Captain thought me over-scrupulous but a moment ago, and he now praises me for my diligence! I must be somehow an impediment in his path, or I should not have his laudation and his censure for the same course of conduct. The captain must have some wicked scheme a-foot—I will keep a watchful eye upon him."

Whilst Elliott was thus communing with himself, Captain Ludlow and the soldier, Lawson, advanced towards the rampart.

"Let us both lean over the wall, and look into the fosse," said Ludlow, "so that there may be the less chance of what we say being overheard by that brute, Elliott, or any of my followers. Have you heard the news from England, and what are the plots now on foot, Lawson, for undoing all the labours of our greatest statesmen?"

"I have heard my fellow-soldiers say," replied Lawson, "that there is the determination to get rid of the Protectorate of Richard Cromwell; that some are planning to restore the old Parliament to its former power, and that the adherents of Charles Stuart are taking advantage of the dissensions amongst the republicans, and seeking to replace him on his father's throne."

"It is true," replied Ludlow—"it is but too true. The fools are fighting with each other, quite forgetful of the fact, that if the royalists are restored, the life of every man who aided, directly or indirectly, in putting the tyrant Charles to death, will be forfeited; and that every acre of land we have acquired by the sword will be restored to the Papists in Ireland and the malignants in England. My uncle Ludlow is for the old Parliament; Fleetwood is for the government of the Commonwealth by the officers; and others, who have acquired name, power, and influence amongst us, are suspected of intriguing with Charles too, for the purpose of placing the sceptre once more within his grasp. What is the feeling of your fellow-soldiers about these plots and intrigues?"

"So far as I have been able to learn," replied Lawson, "they are indifferent as to what is the form of government—whether it be by a Protector, a Parliament, or a Board of Officers; but they are to a man hostile to the restoration of the Stuarts; because they know that restoration would be followed by a redistribution of the forfeited estates amongst the original Irish owners."

"And they are right in their conjecture," remarked Ludlow. "Would! that the officers of the army in Ireland were gifted with the same sense and prudence as the common soldiers. There is Coote, for instance, who is more than suspected of underhand intrigues with officers in Scotland and England, to curse the land again with the plague of monarchy. Fools and knaves as they are, do they suppose a king can ever be forgetful of his father's blood, or pardon any one who has aided in shedding it? And then, looking nearer home, regarding, as every man gifted with the smallest sagacity is bound to do, our own interest, what chance have I, or even you, bound up as we are with Axtel in the retention of the Fitzpatrick estate, what chance, I say, should we have of possessing even a single acre, were there a Stuart king once more crowned in Westminster Abbey? Of what avail all that we have done to gain that land, of your oaths against the old woman, the grandmother of the heir, of your search for the heir amid the corpses in Dundalk cave, of your tracing the boy from hamlet to hamlet, until you at last tracked him to the hostlery in Oxmantown; where I rejoice to tell you he was last night arrested with his nurse."

"And I hope his foster-father and foster-brother also," interrupted Lawson.

"No," added Ludlow, "they escaped through the stupidity of the men sent to arrest the entire party."

"Then, so long as they are abroad," added Lawson, "and the boy is alive, neither your life nor mine is safe, nor is the property secure to you or Colonel Axtel."

"Pshaw!" said Ludlow, "what care I for such miserable wretches, whilst the heir to Colonel Fitzpatrick, the boy Vincent, is, as he is at this moment, a prisoner in the Castle of Dublin; or, as he shall be before the morning sun has arisen, a captive with his nurse on board a vessel, bound with some hundred other Irish boys and wenches for the island of Jamaica, there to work as slaves, and there to die in the course of a few months, as so many thousands of them have already perished in consequence of the heat of the climate, bad food, and over-work.* The soldiers that now attend my orders will be the escort of the boy and nurse from this postern gate to the Custom-house, at the end of Winetavern-street, where now lies the ship, the Anne of Bristol, on board of which will be placed him, who, if he lived, might be the claimant of the estates I now hold. I feel then perfectly secure for the present and the future, had I not reason to dread the consequences of the

* See Illustration C.—Cromwellians kidnapping Irish boys and girls.

disputes now raging between those that the strong firm hand of the great Protector was alone capable of retaining in due subjection."

As Captain Ludlow spoke these words a flush covered his thin pale features, and his weak, fragile, boyish-like form seemed to be shaken with rage and terror, for a sound to which his ear was well accustomed had just reached him, —it was the long piercing cry of a person enduring intense agony. Little more than two-and-twenty years old, his countenance was marked with the haggard lines of senility, and his large grey, greedy eyes, his pursed-out long lips, his thin sharp nose, and his peaked-out chin, gave to him the appearance of an aged and heartless miser. He stamped his high heavy boots with rage upon the stony flag-way, as he muttered in the ear of his associate Lawson:—

"The fools! the dolts! the idiots! They have mistaken my orders. Where we now stand is directly over the torture-room of the Castle; and I requested Axtel to take the boy's nurse there, and by threatening her with the torture to extort from her the secrets of the rebels, the hiding-places of her kinsmen, the plots and projects, if any were known to her, of the loyalists. Instead of threatening, Axtel has actually applied the torture. That was a woman's shriek in her agony. It is a cry such as never can be mistaken for that of a man. I must at once put an end to it. We are ruined—I, at least, am ruined, and all my projects nought, if my uncle hears of this; or if the Protector's brother, Henry, learns we have been misusing, for our private ends, the powers confided to us. Lord Henry Cromwell can endure no abuse, from which he is not to derive a direct personal or pecuniary benefit. I must put a stop to this. Remain here—I will return directly. By your leave, Elliott, I will pass by the sallyport into the

Castle. To put an end to all cavil, I repeat for you the watchword, *Henry.*"

"Pass, Captain Ludlow," said Elliott, as he gave the military salute to the officer, when he had unlocked the postern-gate; and then carefully relocking it, and fastening the key to his girdle, he turned about and said in a loud, and what was very unusual with him, an angry tone of voice:—

"Lawson—Private Lawson—return to your post."

There was no response to the command thus peremptorily given. Elliott looked to the spot where a few moments before he could discern, even in the darkness, the tall form of Lawson distinctly visible. The spot was now vacant!

"How is this?" cried Elliott in amazement. "Can Captain Ludlow have conspired with Lawson to play a trick upon me? Has Lawson slipped into the Castle without my being able to notice him? Oh! that is an impossibility. I am sure I only opened the door sufficiently wide to admit the thin, spare figure of the Captain? But why should they attempt such a prank, when it would entail disgrace and punishment upon both? But what has become of Lawson? When I last saw him he appeared to me to be leaning over the wall, and looking down into the moat. Can he have tumbled by accident or slipped by design into it? For what purpose? The moat is full of water. What am I to do? I dare not, on peril of my life, quit this sallyport, as I do not know the instant persons from within may require to be allowed to issue forth. What am I to do? Holloa! fellow-soldiers, here is my comrade has deserted, or been spirited from his post, I cannot tell which; come, come quickly, I beg you, and help me to search for him."

"Is that John Elliott who is calling for help?" said the

soldier in command of the detachment which had been led by Captain Ludlow.

"It is, it is," replied Elliott, "come hither, I pray you; my comrade Lawson has I fear fallen into the moat, and I cannot stir from this, as I have to watch the postern gate.'

"I am very sorry to hear it, John Elliott," replied the soldier, "but as you obey orders in remaining where you are, so we must obey orders and stop at the place where we have been posted. Captain Ludlow halted us here, with special directions not to advance nor retreat a single step unless he himself issued the command to do so. We wish you well, John Elliott, but we are, like yourself, soldiers, and can obey none other than our officers."

"I would not ask you to do so," rejoined Elliott; "but whilst we are talking our poor comrade may be drowning, for I fear some such calamity has befallen him. But who comes here?" said Elliott, turning round, as he heard the steps of a person approaching from a direction opposite to that in which the Captain's band of soldiers had been posted. "Who goes there?"

"A friend," replied the stranger, on whose head was a trooper's helmet, and whose face was concealed, and his person covered by the long, heavy cloak of a soldier.

"Your business?"

"Admission to the castle by the postern gate."

"The watchword."

"Henry."

"Pass, friend," said Elliott, as he opened the gate, then carefully re-locking it as before, he again fastened the key within his girdle.

John Elliott was a fair average specimen of the country to which he belonged. He was an honest, rough-spoken, right-thinking, and well-intentioned Englishman, more remarkable for good nature than for wit, and for rectitude of purpose than liveliness of fancy. His faults were attributable to the prejudices engrafted upon his mind, not so much by ignorance as by mis-education; and the consequence was, that he had been for a long time struggling in vain to reconcile with each other the statements impressed upon him from his youth with respect to Ireland, the Irish, and the Papists, and his own actual experience of facts to which he was an eye and an ear-witness. This perpetual endeavour of a slow-witted and honest-hearted man to unravel the truth, kept him in a constant state of doubt and perplexity; and hence it cannot be a matter of surprise that when an event, such as has been just described, of the sudden disappearence of a comrade, in a manner alike strange and unaccountable, had occurred, that it should have thrown Elliott into a state of perplexity that he did not know what to do, and not knowing what to do he remained quiescent, and did—nothing.

A full half hour had passed away, and John Elliott still remained standing in the same position, with matchlock in hand, and his left foot resting upon the weapon of his companion Lawson. Thus he stood completely silent, and his faculties in the same state of bewilderment, utterly incapable of unravelling a meaning out of recent events, or of accounting for them, or of finding even a clue to them.

This confusion of thought was at length put an end to by his hearing a loud knocking at the inside of the postern gate, with the repetition, as in hurried accents, of the watchword—" *Henry*."

" Elliott at once opened the door; and then emerged the same stranger who had entered the Castle half an-hour previously. From the manner in which the stranger had his cloak folded over his breast, Elliott fancied he was bearing something bulky concealed beneath it. Whether he so supposed at the moment, or that the notion subsequently occurred to him, he could never distinctly tell; but to Elliott's great astonishment the stranger stepped hastily over to the same point of the ramparts where Captain Ludlow and Ebenezer Lawson had previously been standing, and there, as it appeared to Elliott—for the darkness prevented him from distinctly perceiving anything—he saw, or thought he saw, the stranger divest himself of his helmet and cloak, and then, crossing the battlements, disappear suddenly from sight!

"Holloa!" exclaimed Elliott, at length aroused from his stupor—"There is treason at work here—I must alarm the garrison;" and as he so spoke, he discharged his matchlock, aiming the piece at the only object he could see to fire at—the discarded helmet of the stranger.

At the same moment that the shot was fired, Elliott heard the clamour of several voices at the postern gate, and amongst them was distinguishable the screaming, shrill accents of Captain Ludlow, directing the postern gate to be opened. Elliott flung it wide open, and on the instant Captain Ludlow, his face covered with blood, and his sword drawn, appeared on the ramparts, his pale, distorted visage and haggard eyes being illuminated with the red light of at least twenty torches borne in the hands of his followers.

"Ha! Elliott, have you slain the miscreant?" asked Ludlow, his voice trembling with rage as he spoke—"say yes, and I will reward you with a hundred pounds. I heard the shot. Have you slain him?"

"Slain him!" exclaimed Elliott; "I know not, Captain, whom you mean. A man who gave the word but this moment passed the postern gate."

"Where is he? Where has he gone? In what direction are we to pursue?" asked Ludlow.

"The man I speak of passed direct from this gate to the rampart opposite. He then, I think, cast away his helmet and cloak, and——"

Ludlow stopped to hear no more, but rushing with the men who bore the lighted torches over to the battlements, he caught up from the ground the helmet and cloak of a Cromwellian trooper. For an instant he stopped to examine the helmet, and then startled Elliott and the other soldiers by the exclamation—"Why this is the headpiece of Ebenezer Lawson—his name is written inside— and, oh! horrible! he must have been murdered, for here is the mark of a bullet which has penetrated it. Revenge—revenge—revenge upon the Irish rebels!"

"Revenge — revenge — revenge upon the Irish Papists!" was the hoarse echoing response of the infuriated men who, with torch and matchlock, stood upon the ramparts.

"Where did you say, Elliott, did the murderer cross the wall?" inquired Ludlow.

"The man seemed to me," said Elliott, "to clamber over the rampart at the very place where you are now standing. He did not do so with great agility, as he seemed to bear some burden with him; and as he disappeared, I fancied I heard the smothered cry of an infant."

"You heard aright," answered Ludlow; "the boy thus spirited away is the son of one of the most notorious rebels, and whose transportation for the West Indies had been specially directed by his Highness the Lord Protector. The importance of the boy may be seen from the efforts of his adherents. To rescue him, you observe how Lawson has been barbarously murdered; to rescue him—to take him out of my hands—the traitor, who has just passed through our ranks unscathed, assaulted me in a passage leading from the torture-chamber, struck me to the earth—but why stop wildly talking here when he, the villain, as well as the young rebel he seeks to rescue, may be recaptured. Here, soldiers, use your torches, examine wall and moat, and then pass to the other side; leave not a house in Sheep-street unexplored."

As Ludlow was thus speaking, the whizzing of an arrow was heard, and at the same moment the Captain was observed to fall upon his back, even though the weapon which struck him was repelled by the strength and thickness of his breastplate.

A cry of indignation burst from the Cromwellians, when they witnessed this assault upon their leader.

"The rebels challenge us to the conflict," said Ludlow, as he raised himself from the earth. "Instead of evading pursuit they court it. Look, men, to the other side, and if you can see any living person there, discharge your pieces."

"I think," cried one of the soldiers, "I can discern something lying on the edge of the moat on the other side, that has all the appearance of a human body stretched upon the earth, as if the person so lying were seeking to conceal himself."

"Fire, soldiers, at whatever you can see that bears the semblance of a foeman," cried Captain Ludlow.

A discharge of musketry succeeded this command, and it was followed by a heavy groan on the other side of the moat, whilst, as if in reply to it, there was the flight of a single arrow, which, directed with a better aim than its predecessor, struck slantingly on the cheek of Ludlow, inflicting, as it ploughed its way, an awful and ghastly wound, and dashing him with a cry of agony to the earth, where he lay without sense or motion.

The soldiers gathered for an instant around their fallen commander; but perceiving that the wound, though severe, was not mortal, they eagerly inquired what was to be done.

"In consequence of the disaster that has befallen your leader," remarked Elliott, as he stood upon his post, "I would recommend you to remove him at once to his own quarters, where he can be visited, and his wound tended by his own chirurgeon. I would then advise a file of men to pass to the other side of the moat, and look to the condition of the person whose moans are so plainly to be heard even here. Be the person friend or foe, he should, because wounded, be attended with care."

Soldiers are more accustomed to obey commands than to inquire into the authority of him by whom they are issued; and, therefore, the directions of Elliott were at once acted upon.

Captain Ludlow was removed from the Castle ramparts in a state of insensibility; and a file of soldiers, divesting themselves of headpieces, breastplates, and cloaks, plunged into the moat, and clambered up to the opposite bank, where, in an instant afterwards, one of them was heard thus crying out:—

"Help! help! help!"

"What is the matter?" asked John Elliott, utterly forgetting, in the excitement of so many unlooked-for events, the strict performance of his duty, and rushing over to the rampart where he heard the dismal cry for help.

"What is the matter with you? Why do you cry for help?" asked Elliott.

"Help! help! help!" exclaimed the soldiers on the other side of the moat.

"What, I say, is the matter?" cried Elliott, impatiently.

"Help! help! help! Oh! the dismal sight!" again exclaimed the soldiers.

"What is it? Why do you not speak?" again asked Elliott.

"Ah! poor Ebenezer Lawson!" said the soldier.

"Well—well—well—what of him?" asked Elliott.

"Ah! here he is wounded by the discharge of our musketry. We found his mouth gagged, his arms and legs tied together, and his clothes as wet as if they had been steeping in the Castle ditch for half an hour. We have cut the cords that bound his limbs; we have removed the gag from his mouth; but still he is unable to speak—he has, we know not how many gun-shot wounds in hands, legs, and body. Send us aid to remove him."

* * * * * *
* * * * * *

The wounded man had been removed; the silence of the still night had succeeded to the clamorous cries of infuriated troopers; the followers of Ludlow had dispersed, and John Elliott was left alone and solitary in charge of the postern gate. He paced up and down slowly and solemnly, and as he did so his thoughts untiringly returned to the various events that had passed before him.

"What," said he musingly to himself, "what can be the reason that a young person so exalted in rank, and of such ancient lineage as one of the Ludlows of Wiltshire, should seek out as his associate, and the confidant for his secrets, a person so low in birth as Ebenezer Lawson? What common interest can bind two such personages together? And then, who can that young boy be, for whose transportation to the West Indies Ludlow is so anxious? Is he one of the royal family of England? Oh! absurd—all are too old or too young for an infant with any rightful claim to be associated with them. Then it must be some one that is entitled to large estates in Ireland—probably the head of some clan like that of Owen Roe O'Neill. Lawson said something of a Colonel Fitzpatrick—yes, that must be the case: and then the bravery of the young Irishman—for the person who twice passed me, I marked him well, could not be more than eighteen years of age. What a gallant, glorious, fearless youth he must be! What risks; what peril of life and limb, of death, of torture, of slavery, he exposed himself to for the purpose of preserving a young child that may never live to repay him even with barren thanks! And these things are not only attempted but achieved by the Irish, whom I have been taught to despise and contemn, and that Lawson says he hates—and now that I think of Lawson, how richly he has deserved all that he has received! But how was he spirited away from the ramparts? I hope he may live, if it were only to explain that mystery. Mystery! mystery! what is one's entire life, but an incomprehensible mystery? What this whole live-long night but an almost incredible mystery, in which the only thing that is plain to me, and the only matter of which I am positive sure is, that the headpiece of Lawson suffered no injury from an Irish rebel, and that the bullet that penetrated it was discharged from no other matchlock than that which my own hand grasps. I am sure of that—I am in doubt about everything else—in doubt and difficulty upon all I have heard, and all I have seen. It was I fired at, and shot through Lawson's helmet; that I know, and beyond that I know nothing."

CHAPTER II.

OLD ACQUAINTANCES.

The old tavern or coffee-house, "the Cock," in Cook-street, was for a long time one of the most celebrated houses of entertainment in the city of Dublin ; but at no period was its fame better established, nor its public room more crowded from mid-day to mid-night, than during the last ten years of the reign of Charles the Second. It was the resort of persons of various classes and conditions in life. Courtiers from the Castle, merchants from the quays, wealthy shopkeepers from Castle-street and Dame-street, and the gentry from distant parts of Ireland, all met on terms of perfect equality within its walls, and each could select for himself a small box or compartment, which served the purposes of a private room whilst acting as the host towards those he chose for the night as his associates.

In the large dining-hall of "the Cock" there was thus combined together all the advantages of select society and of general publicity. All sat within view of each other ; but each box or compartment was regarded as a reserved spot, into which no stranger ventured to intrude, unless specially invited to do so by the person who had first taken his seat there.

"The Cock" was not a tavern or eating-house alone; for a considerable portion of the premises was devoted to the purposes of an inn, and hence there might not unfrequently be seen cowering in the darkest corners of its public room persons of an inferior condition in life to those who composed its usual company. These strangers were easily distinguishable, for the most part, not less by their coarse dress, and the humble fare of which they partook, than by their broad Irish brogue—a contrast as great to the pure English spoken by the Castle office-holders, as to the assumed Anglified tones, or bastard English accent of the Anglo-Irish citizens of Dublin.

Upon a warm summer evening in the year 1679, there might be observed sitting alone in one of the boxes of the public room of "the Cock," a small man of middle age, and in whose face or appearance there was nothing remarkable beyond the fact that on his right cheek there was a long, red streak, which seemed to be the trace of an old wound. This man had not, with the exception of the scar upon his face, the semblance of ever having been a soldier. His head was stooped, his face thin and haggard, his large, grey, covetous eyes, which he seldom raised to look around, and his shrinking, timid, reserved manner were the embodiment of a man whose life was devoted to some unmilitary, lucrative pursuit, and in which profit was sought for by every means it could be grasped at. The dress, a plain grey suit of fine cloth, was in accordance with the seeming mercantile profession of the wearer; and the sword he wore, then the indispensable emblem of a gentleman by birth and position, was not in contradiction to it.

This man might be observed (and he was noticed from the moment he entered the coffee-room) to look up from time to time towards the door, as if he were waiting the arrival of some one with whom he had made an appointment. The flagon of claret which he had ordered upon entering the room lay untasted before him, whilst his only amusement or occupation was to twine his fingers from time to time in the well-crisped curling ringlets of the long, jet black, and in contrast to his features, too youthful peruque which covered his head, and flowed down upon his back, neck, and shoulders.

In a box almost directly opposite to this man there was seated alone, and apparently fully occupied with his dinner of a roast fowl and a tankard of foaming beer, an aged, smooth-faced, coarse-dressed countryman, whose full, dark eyes were seldom raised from the table before him, and who, sitting with his face half turned away from the company, and towards the wall, had, by chance or design, thrown himself into a position in which, without seeing the company, he could be certain of hearing the general conversation going on around him.

Truth compels us to say, that if this was the design of the rustic, such was the tone of morals then generally prevailing, that neither the topics that were then fashionable, nor the mode of discussing them, could have tended to his edification or instruction. He might have learned amid sneers, and jibes, and laughter, what vices of the English court had been imported into Dublin, and he might have informed himself what was the nature of the last profane joke, or loose poem, or disgusting ballad, with the habits and previous lives of the most popular actresses or Whitehall belles. All that tavern knowledge which contaminates by communication was within his reach, if he chose to take advantage of the opportunity of acquiring it. It was almost certain that he did not do so, for his manner, his attitude, and his look, were unchanged whilst this vain and wicked prattle was going on around him. Such, however, was not the case when he heard, from the box opposite to him, the words :—

"So you have at length come. I was beginning to doubt that my message had reached you."

The old rustic turned round for an instant, cast one glance at the person thus addressed, and then pulling up around his face the collar of his coarse outside cloak, he looked away from the company, and more directly at the wall than he had done before.

Such was the haste with which the rustic had turned round, that he did not remark that the new-comer had been followed by a stranger, a man in a plain brown suit of clothes, but wearing a sword, who slid unperceived by the person who had preceded him, into a vacant box adjoining that in which the man with the long black peruque was seated.

"So you have at length come. I was beginning to doubt that my message had reached you."

Such was the salutation again repeated by the man in the black peruque.

"Had I known it was to a profane drinking booth you had invited me, I would not have come at all," was the surly reply of the stranger, a gaunt, fierce-faced old man, with close-cropped grey hair, and whose great height was marred by one of his legs being shorter than the other.

"Nay, nay, Ebenezer, find no fault with a place in which the liquor is faultless. I invited you to partake of a stoup of wine, where the claret is super-excellent. King Charles, or the Duke of York, or old Oliver himself, never had finer wines in their cellars than the Cock of Cook-street can justly boast of."

"The wine is good," said the stranger, sitting down, and at one draught emptying the flagon before him. "I find no fault with the wine, but I do with the place in which I am imbibing it. You know well, Edward, it was not to drink wine you asked me hither, but it was to talk on matters of serious import. And what a place is this to talk in? with babblers on one side of you, and for aught you can tell, eaves-droppers on the other. Let me see who are our neighbours. Ah! on your right hand there are roysterers, fitting followers for Ormond, and on the other a gentleman in a brown suit, a tippler, I presume, for he has fallen asleep with his wine half drunk before him. And who is that old tory opposite, whose face is turned away from us? I suspect from his smooth shaven face, and his rustic garb, that he is a Popish priest or prelate in disguise—perhaps a Jesuit; if so, I shall test him before he leaves that spot, or I quit this tavern."

With these observations the old man reseated himsel, and then added: " Now, Edward, speak out your mind. What new scheme have you on hand for increasing your wealth, in which my services may be useful to you?"

" In all my dealings with you hitherto," said the man who had been addressed as Edward, " have you not found me scrupulously exact in the performance of all my promises?"

" Assuredly, yes," replied the old man; " and for very good reason too—first, you could not have carried on your plots without me; and next, you are quite certain that if you had deceived me, I would have pistolled you with as little remorse as if you were a sparrow, instead of being what you are—the nephew of the bravest and best soldier of the Commonwealth—Lieutenant-General Ludlow."

" Hush! hush! Ebenezer," said the terrified Ludlow, " the times are sadly changed, and the less there is now said of my connexion with General Ludlow, one of the late king's judges, the better for my safety and security, both of person and property in this country. My family history is no more to be boasted of than the injury which has lamed you for life, and which you may remember was inflicted by some one who was as anxious to keep the son of Colonel Fitzpatrick in Ireland, as you and I were to have him transported."

"Withered like a bramble be the accursed hand that inflicted that wound," said the enraged Lawson, as his pale, harsh, rugged features were suddenly overspread with the red flush of indignation. "Accursed, for ever accursed, be the villain who inflicted so many injuries in a single night, first basely and coward-like gagging my mouth as I stood on the Castle rampart, then flinging a rope around my neck and dragging me as if I were a dog, down the wall, and through the waters of the ditch, and up the side, and then along the ground, and then binding me neck and heels together, so as to be a conspicuous object for the musketry of the Castle to fire at, making my body a target for the weapons of my friends, and so causing the wound that has lamed me for life. But, oh! I trust, I hope, I may yet encounter the wretch who thus wronged me. There is not a day in the long, long years that have since passed away, that I have not asked of the Lord, that I have not prayed to the God of vengeance, I might be permitted to meet again, and living, the caitiff who so tortured and afflicted me. Oh! that I might but once again meet him face to face, once again look in his fiery black eyes, the glare of which can never pass away from my memory."

Lawson was interrupted in his denunciation of his unknown aggressor by a loud burst of jeering laughter, so loud and so prolonged, that persons stopped to listen to it; and, as is usual upon occasions where men meet for festive purposes, the sounds of hilarity are contagious, and there was a shout, an actual chorus of laughter from all parts of the coffee-room.

The old Cromwellian stopped, confounded and amazed

by this outburst. At length he resumed by saying, " That
poor drunken creature in the next compartment to us has
set the example to idiots like to himself, and they have
imitated his folly; but *every beast loveth its like: so also
every man him that is nearest to himself.*"

" Ebenezer !" said Ludlow, " a public tavern in Cook-
street, a place so near to the Castle walls, is not a fitting
spot on which we should either boast of, or even refer to
our former exploits. We have outlived the times of the
Commonwealth, and the reign of the republicans, and we
must now give way to cavaliers, and king's friends, and
tories, and, if we can, retain in peace what we have won
in war."

" And is it to utter such bald nonsense as that you have
invited me hither ?" asked Lawson, whose angry passions,
excited by the recollection of former transactions, had
not yet subsided.

" Not at all," answered Ludlow; " I have invited you
hither, because, you living in the east, and I in the
south of Ireland, wished to confer with you on a matter
in which we are alike interested,—I mean the retention of
the Fitzpatrick estates. I need not tell you how sorely
weakened is our claim to hold them, by that claim being
united with the valiant Axtel, who suffered as a traitor
for obeying the commands of Parliament, but who, believe
me, was exempted from the Bill of Indemnity, in consequence of the manœuvres of the Irish Papists and rebels,
who wished, as I believe, first to take the Fitzpatrick
estates from his grasp, and next to revenge the death of
the old woman, the Colonel's mother, and the many other
mischiefs he did to the Irish race, when he was Governor
of Kilkenny."*

* Ludlow's Memoirs, vol. i. pp. 340, 341, vol. iii. p. 89.

"I hope you have not summoned me from Drogheda to a wine-shop in Dublin, to tell me that my old colonel was executed a quarter of a century since, at Tyburn," said Lawson, his irritation not yet abated.

"I summoned you," replied Ludlow, "as a man who would prefer the consideration of present dangers to the useless reflections upon past grievances and by-gone offences. I wanted to speak to you of your pecuniary interests, and not of your personal sufferings."

"Then you should have commenced with that topic which you yourself deemed to be of the most importance. It was you, not I, who first alluded to the events of that hateful night, which resulted in maiming me for life," said Lawson, somewhat soothed in manner.

"You forget this hideous scar will not permit the events of that night to pass for one hour from my mind," continued Ludlow. "The same hand that maimed your body, has rendered my face hideous. But to turn now to that which is possible."

"Vengeance is possible to him who has the firm will to execute it," interrupted Lawson. "I live but to revenge! and that revenge I am sure I shall yet inflict upon my aggressor. But go on; wherefore have you wished to speak with me?"

"I have been assured," said Ludlow, "that there are now three persons living, who may claim to be owners of the lands you and I have, since the death of Axtel, divided amongst us."

"A strange division!" observed Lawson; "for every acre of land I have, you possess three."

There was a pause for a few minutes when Lawson made this remark. The thin features of Ludlow quivered, and the red scar in his check assumed a purple hue, as his trembling left hand grasped the hilt of his sword. Whatever were his emotions, they were too strong for utterance, and could not without an exertion be fully mastered. At last he appeared to gulp down the words he was on the point of uttering, and filling out a draught of wine, he hastily swallowed it, and then stretching his right hand across the table to his companion, he said :—

"Pardon me, Ebenezer, if in all our dealings hitherto on this matter, I have only looked at the shares of land as they were originally apportioned by Cromwellian Commissioners between two men, one of whom was a captain as well as nephew of the Commander-in-Chief, and the other who was nothing more than a private soldier in the army. Times have greatly altered since then, and so should be our treatment of each other. Henceforth we shall have share and share alike."

"If I am to be united with you in any plans for the future, that regulation must apply to the Fitzpatrick lands. I should have as much of them as you, as I have equally suffered for them like you," remarked Lawson.

"And so you shall. Let me but see that the other claimants are put out of the way, that my rights are secured, and from that instant the land or the profits of the land shall be equally divided between you and me. To this promise I bind myself, and pledge my honour as a soldier, my truth as a gentleman, and my faith as a Christian."

"But first duly enrolled in a formal deed, with all necessary guards, conditions, and provisoes, such as the skill and learning of our good friend, Tom Edwards, the scrivener of Exchequer-street, can devise," added the cautious Lawson.

"Of course, of course," said Ludlow, in a hurried,

stammering voice. "If you cannot, with all your many years' experience of me, rely upon my word, you shall have my bond."

"Life is short. I do not expect to live for ever, and, therefore, I prefer your written deed to your spoken word," said Lawson. "I have a daughter—an only child; Judith, Captain Ludlow, is her name. I hope to see her yet wedded to one who is like her father, a true friend to 'the old cause.' If I died to-day, she would have but a small part of the Fitzpatrick lands to inherit. Endowed by your deed, she will be the richest republican heiress in Ireland."

"You forget," said Ludlow, "what I have been but this moment saying to you, that between the inheritance which you wish to bequeath to your daughter, Judith, there are now three claimants, and all, I fear, living; and it is to devise with you the best means of defeating those claims that I have sought this interview with you."

"Proceed," said Lawson. "Now that you have agreed to my terms, I am an attentive listener. I feel that we have but one common interest to promote, to maintain, and to defend."

"The first of the claimants who is said to be living," continued Ludlow, "is the original owner, Colonel Fitzpatrick. He, in consequence of an agreement made with my uncle, the general, and those who then represented the English government in Ireland, passed with his Irish regiment from the service of Charles Stuart to that of the King of Spain. It was supposed that he had been slain in Africa by the Moors; but within the last few months a rumour has been going through the South of Ireland, that the Colonel, who must now be a very old man, was captured and made a slave, and has lately been restored to liberty, and was on his way back to his native country. If that report should prove to be correct—if he once lands in safety in this country, he will, of course, get back from Charles II. the lands he lost fighting in defence of the crown of Charles I. You and I must then devise the means of preventing the Colonel being publicly recognized in Ireland."

"I understand you," said Lawson, with a grim smile, as he grasped the hilt of his sword. "There is one sure means of disposing of his claims; but they do not appear to me to be so formidable as you fancy. The Colonel is a Catholic. If he returns he can be charged with being a participator in the massacre of Protestants in 1641; and he, like many hundreds of the Irish Papists, may be so deprived of estates, which are applied to the use and advantage of 'English loyalists,' like you and myself. Though the King is restored to the throne, and the next heir to the crown is an avowed Papist, we have fallen upon times too touchy and too perilous for the King or Duke of York to attempt exacting justice for Irish Romanists. Let me then hear who is the next claimant. As regards the Colonel, he is, in my estimation, by no means formidable—he can be easily got rid of—either by the law, as it is now administered in Ireland; or, if that fail, with still less trouble—by an inch of steel or an ounce of lead. Who is the second claimant?"

"The second claimant," observed Ludlow, "is one, on whose account you and I have already endured insufferable rebuffs and everlasting injuries. It is the son of Colonel Fitzpatrick."

"What!" exclaimed Lawson, "that boy still living to cross my path! I thought he had been got rid of twenty years ago. Have you deceived me respecting him? I believed what you told me concerning him, namely, that, despite of the adherents of his family, he had been tracked out to his hiding-place in the caves of Clare; there, with his nurse and foster-sister, laid hold of, and transported to Jamaica, where, you were assured by a letter from the Commonwealth governor in that island, he and his nurse hath both died within a few months of their being placed within the influence of such a pestilential climate."

"I told you as a truth that which I myself believed to be a fact," replied Ludlow; "but events of which I have lately heard, induce me to suppose that I was wilfully deceived— and that, too, by a person on whose fidelity I supposed I might calculate. The governor of Jamaica was Major Sedgewick—a stout, sincere republican—a man who was persuaded that the late Oliver Cromwell was an inspired and heaven-ordained prophet and warrior; but Sedgewick, with all his republicanism and fanaticism, was, like your former comrade, John Elliott, a very tender-hearted fool; and it is believed, that he took pity on the boy, preserved him from the fate to which he had been doomed, and sent him and his nurse to one of the English colonies on the continent of America, upon condition that they should never return to Ireland as long as he, Sedgewick, lived. Sedgewick has died within the last twelve months; and some of the older tenantry in the Queen's County have been heard to declare that they had seen and recognized the son of the Colonel, and were prepared to support him once he openly claimed a restoration to his rights."

Lawson remained for a few minutes silent. Resting his elbows upon the table, and leaning his head between both his hands, he paused as in profound meditation. At length, raising himself up and casting himself back in his seat, he poured out a fresh draught of wine, and quaffing it off, he spoke, as if in communion with himself, rather than addressing his companion :—

"The boy that I thought dead and gone—alive and in the flesh! All that I have suffered—my distorted limb, my crushed body—cheaply suffered, as I fancied, because rewarded with his death—of no avail! Vincent Fitzpatrick, a grown man, in Ireland, coming to claim from King and Parliament the green fields which for years I have been treading upon as mine own! My toil, my thrift, my watchings, and my wounds to be productive, not of good to myself, but to another—who comes, as it were, out of the grave in which I supposed I had buried him—who comes here to bid me and my child return to England as poor and as despised as the first day I landed—an humble, moneyless, obscure trooper in the army of the Parliament. He comes to claim from me what is dearer to me than life. What mean you, Edward Ludlow, to do with such an adversary? I ask you the question, believing you will respond to it, as I mean to do—with my right arm and my sword."

"I have already remarked to you," said Ludlow, "that in this matter our interests are the same, and we must unite together in defending them. I have not said that the boy was positively living; I have only told you the rumours respecting him."

"They are true," replied Lawson, "depend upon it they are true. No one could have invented such a fiction. They are consistent with the character of Sedgewick. I knew him well, as well as I did John Elliott, to whom you have referred, and of whom I have lost sight for a long time. Know you what has become of him?"

"John Elliott is not only alive," replied Ludlow, "but is now one of the richest citizens of Dublin. The house in which we are sitting is his property; and he has lately become the purchaser of my uncle's splendid old mansion and park at Monkstown; but why think of him when we have matters of deeper import to engage our attention? I have mentioned the report that prevails respecting Vincent Fitzpatrick, because it was my duty, having heard it, not to conceal it from you; but, at the same time, I must add that I am not disposed to attach much credit to it. The people of this country are fond of circulating wild legends and improbable stories, and this is perchance one of them; or it may be one of the deliberate inventions of the arch-villain, Redmond O'Hanlon, and set afloat, like so many other tales concocted by him, for the purpose of annoying those republican holders of land, whom he cannot assail by his gang, and whose persons and properties are beyond the sphere in which he carries on his aggressions."

"The Rapparees, be sure of it," said Lawson, "have nothing to do with these rumours of the re-appearance of Vincent Fitzpatrick. It is, I am sure, a truth, and all we have to do is to render the claim against us abortive, and I can see but one way to put an end to the difficulty, and that is by the sword."

"Be it so," added Ludlow. "Let it be as you say, by the sword, or if you prefer it, the pistol."

Lawson smiled, and winked at his companion.

"But," continued Ludlow, "before you can use either, you must know the haunts of the person to be assailed, what are his means of defence, by whom he is sustained, and by whom protected."

"True," observed Lawson, "and be it the business of both to make diligent inquiry respecting him. Until we have ascertained such facts, it is in vain to discuss further a subject on which both are fully agreed. And now, let me know, who is the third claimant of the Fitzpatrick estates?"

Ludlow did not at first reply to this question. His haggard features were distorted, and his thin, long, bony fingers trembled as they clasped the stem of the goblet before him. "The third," said he, in a low, hoarse voice, "is the most formidable of them all."

"How is that possible?" asked Lawson, astonished, not less at the assertion, than the agitation of the weak, deformed, and withered object before him. "How can there possibly be a more formidable claimant to the land than the original owner, or the rightful heir to that owner?"

"False pleas and fictitious statements may defeat the Colonel and his son," replied Ludlow. "The false plea of 'the Irish massacre' may serve as a bar to the one, false testimony as to the birth and education of the other may brand the heir as an impostor, and so deprive him of his rights, whilst the truthful allegation, which neither will attempt to deny, that they are Papist, will be sufficient to prejudice the Irish law courts, the Castle, and the English Parliament against them. Such, however, is not the case with Kathleen Fitzpatrick."

"Kathleen Fitzpatrick!" cried Lawson, "a woman! who is she? I never heard of her before."

"Kathleen Fitzpatrick," replied Ludlow, "is the niece of him whose lands we occupy. She is the daughter of a younger brother. She has been educated in the religion of her mother—a Church of England Episcopalian. She is, I have heard, the protegee of the Duke of Ormond, and by that powerful nobleman, it is said, her claim to her uncle's estate will be sustained. If these reports be true, our hold upon her uncle's lands is not worth a year's purchase."

"You have devised a scheme for rendering that claim of no avail," said Lawson, with an ominous frown: "let me know what it is, that I may aid it; for here, I admit, my wit is at fault."

"I have, as you say, devised such a scheme," replied Ludlow, "and it is comprised in a single word—marriage."

"Marriage! Marriage!" cried the astonished Lawson. "Marriage with whom?"

Ludlow made no reply in words, but laying his hand on his heart, nodded to his companion.

"Marriage with *you!*" added Lawson, unable to suppress his feelings of surprise. "What age is the maiden?"

"Eighteen."

"Is she in any way deformed?"

"She is straight as a rush, fair as a lily, fresh as a half-blown rose."

"And you propose to unite yourself in marriage with all these perfections?"

"I do."

"And how think you, Edward,—I do not mean to offend you—but how do you suppose will your personal defects, your gashed face, your—I cannot refrain from saying it—hideous appearance, be received by such a young beauty? How can you hope your proposals will be favourably regarded. How can you imagine you will be accepted?"

"I mean to wed, not to woo her," replied Ludlow, whose changing colour showed how keenly he felt the remarks of Lawson upon his personal defects.

"Oh! I perceive," said Lawson, "you contemplate a forced marriage, you're thinking of that which is a frequent practice in this country,—the forcible abduction of an heiress."

"Precisely so," answered Ludlow, "and there are numberless instances to show in Ireland, that many an unwilling bride has in a short time become a dutiful, a loving, and an obedient wife. Be you ready, whenever I may require your presence, with twenty armed horsemen to aid me, and in less than a week afterwards I shall be the husband of the fairest girl and the greatest fortune in Ireland,—of no less a personage than the Lady Kathleen Fitzpatrick, of Gowran Castle."

"Hush! Edward," said Lawson hastily, "you forget you are in a public room; and you speak so loudly you can be overheard. I have, for instance, remarked, that ever since you mentioned the name of a certain fair lady, that smooth-faced, antiquated knave in the compartment opposite to us, has been listening to every word you said. If he has heard all, he bears with him a secret which we cannot allow him to carry out of this room. I will therefore fasten a quarrel upon him."

As Lawson spoke, he filled out a cup of wine, and then bearing it in one hand, and his sword in the other, he approached the seat where the old rustic was apparently still engaged with his dinner, and thus addressed him:—

"Good sir, I perceive you drink beer and not wine. I have, then, to request of you to drink this wine, and at the same time to give as a toast: 'A plague upon Pope and Popery, priests, pagans, nuns, and friars!'"

"Sir, I do not know you," replied the old man dressed as a rustic. "I seldom drink wine; I never do so with strangers; and the sentiments I express are my own, and never dictated to me by another."

"Good sir," sneeringly remarked Lawson, "I suspect you are a Popish priest; I believe you have been playing the spy upon me and my companion, and therefore I propose this toast as a test of your sincerity and loyalty. Now mark what I say to you. If you refuse the wine, I shall scatter it over your person, and if you decline the toast in the very words I have uttered, I shall inflict upon you the bastinado.

"Sir, you thus insult me," meekly replied the rustic, "because you see that I am a man of peace, that I am old, and that I wear no sword."

"But I do," said the stranger dressed in a brown suit, as he stepped from the box in which he had been seated, "and I not only know how to handle it, but also how to use the wine goblet, which this tavern brawler has tendered to you."

As the stranger thus spoke, he snatched the goblet from the hands of Lawson, and flinging the contents in his face, he cast the goblet itself at Ludlow, striking him on the forehead, and as he did so drew his sword, and thus addressed them:—

"Ruffians, kidnappers, and scoundrels! I know you both. I have heard you both mention in a public tavern the name of a lady with whose family I have the honour to be acquainted. Come on, then—one or both—that I may punish you on the spot where such an outrage upon a lady's fair fame has been perpetrated."

Whilst the stranger was still speaking, the huge hanger of Lawson was uplifted, and aimed with a giant's force at the head, in the hope of breaking his guard, and cutting him down; but the blow so aimed was not only vigorously parried, but the keen blade of the stranger slid like lightning along the sword of Lawson, cutting, as it passed, the four fingers of his right hand, and with a roar of agony the huge sword was relaxed from the ruffian's grasp, and fell useless to the earth.

Ludlow in his confusion, was unable to draw his sword before the persons assembled in the coffee-room rushed between the combatants.

"What means this scandalous riot in my orderly house?" inquired the burly, fat, contented, red-faced landlord, as he rushed into the midst of the crowd who separated the stranger and Ludlow, who now stood with drawn swords, glaring at each other.

"Honest John Elliott," said the stranger in the brown suit, pointing at the infuriated Ludlow, and the enraged Lawson, "there are the disturbers of the peace,—there are the shameless brawlers. The old tall man was for forcing one of your peaceful guests to drink wine he did not like, and to propose a toast of which he did not approve; whilst the other, that pale, ugly, ill-looking caitiff yonder, had the presumption to speak in terms of disparagement of a fair lady who, if not known, is, I am sure, highly respected by you. In your absence, John Elliott, I was punishing those vile and scandalous disturbers of the peace?"

"Good Master Brown, I am much indebted to you for your volunteer services on my behalf; but where is the peaceable, wine-hating guest for whose protection you interfered?"

"Where is he? Of a verity," replied the man in brown, "I cannot tell, John Elliott; but here he sat, and here he has deposited a piece of gold to defray the expenses of his dinner, and whatever other refreshment you may have supplied him with."

"I call all to witness, then," added the landlord, "that I stand indebted to that stranger many shillings; but go your ways, good Master Brown, it is not safe your tarrying longer under this roof. A man named Tighe has but this instant called to say he would wish to speak with you at nine, beneath the arch of Dame's gate. I was on the way to deliver you that message when I heard the clash of your sword."

"Thanks! Master Elliott, but look to that vile old Cromwellian yonder. Be assured that good food and rich wine were never wasted on two greater villains than himself and his associate,—the fellow with the scarred face. Farewell."

"Farewell—farewell," said honest John Elliott, as he looked with admiration at the tall figure and vigorous form of the man in brown, as he bounded out of the room.

"Ha! Master Lawson," continued the landlord, as he advanced to the seat on which the wounded man was now resting, and vainly endeavouring to stop the blood which poured out from his hand. "Good Master Lawson, I am grieved to see you so suffering. What an ugly wound it is! permit me to bind it up for you. Ha!" added Elliott, as he examined the gashed fingers, "this is a very awkward wound, indeed! It is to be hoped you may not lose the use of your right hand. How came you to hold your weapon so awry? What a swordsman that Master Brown is! I think he must have learned to fence in Paris; for he has cuts, and thrusts, and parries utterly unknown to us, Lawson, when we were learning the sword exercise. I am now convinced there is no such swordsman in the King's dominions as Master Brown."

"You know this Master Brown, then," remarked Lawson, as he winced with the pain caused by binding up his wounded fingers.

"I know," answered Elliott, that he is Master Brown; but I am not quite sure that I know anything more about him. I suspect, however, more than I know; but I will injure no man by expressing my suspicions."

"Be he who he may, I hope I may once more encounter

him. If I do, one or other will be, before many minutes, no longer a living man," said Lawson.

"And I," added Ludlow, "promise, wherever I again meet him, see him, come in contact with him—were it at the altar itself—my sword shall revel in his heart's blood."

"Pshaw," said Elliott, "to bed both of you—you talk like men overcome with drink. I do not know who Master Brown is; but I strongly suspect you have both seen him before to-day. You have, I believe, encountered him, not once, but twice. Take care of a third combat with the same foe—it may be fatal to both."

CHAPTER III.

RAPPAREES.

"I am afraid, Hannah, we shall never reach home before night. We do not travel more than two miles an hour on these rough and broken roads. Even my good steed Adolphus lags in his pace, although he cannot be more eager for food and rest than I am to be within the shelter of my father's strong-walled mansion, when darkness has succeeded to daylight."

"I have far less fear, mistress, of the perils of the road, than I have of the evil wayfarers to be found on them."

"And so have I, Hannah, and therefore I am for hurrying onward with all speed; for I own to you, I have more confidence in my own courage and your determination, than in the bravery and trustworthiness of the two knaves behind us, whom my father has ordered me always to take as an escort."

The speakers were two young women, apparently a lady and her attendant, such was the contrast in their outward habiliments. The first was in the full bloom of womanhood, her age something between twenty-five and thirty years, her skin brown, her hair of raven blackness, and her eyes, large, full, and dark, shone with a brilliant light which the long, black eye-lashes could not conceal, though they sometimes served to moderate its fierceness of expression. When her full red lips relaxed into a smile, which they seldom did, they were withdrawn to exhibit large, even, and brilliant white teeth, firmly locked together. But that which was the most remarkable characteristic of this young female was her height, and breadth, and bearing; for although she exhibited all the perfection of the female form in her figure, still these were combined with all the muscular power and free, proud, unembarrassed action of a man five feet nine inches in height. Her dress was in accordance with her appearance. Her riding hat, of the finest beaver, was looped up one side with a rich, short, thick chain of massy gold, and from the hat drooped a long wavy plume of black feathers. Her riding dress, confined at the waist with a thick girdle of gold, from which depended a short gold-hilted hunting knife, was in other respects like the military dress of an officer, for around the collar was a thick band of gold lace, which also ran down the front of the entire dress, and the wide sleeves were turned up at the wrist, with broad lace bands, and so displayed the hands covered with white gloves fringed with gold, and the seams on the back worked with gold lace. This proud-looking, haughty-seeming, almost manlike dame, rode a heavy, black war-horse, and whilst she checked his speed with a hand well accustomed to the rein, she also held, as if it were a slight wand, a thick riding whip, the handle of which was heavy with a thick knot of lead, covered over with a shining ball of gold.

The attendant upon this rich, proud-looking young lady, was a plainly-dressed, timid young Englishwoman, who was now living for a twelvemonth in Ireland, and who, having come to the country with a conviction that all its inhabitants were wild animals, was in a constant state of astonishment that she had not yet seen any of them, and was labouring under a perpetual apprehension that the moment she should come in contact with them, she would be murdered.

Behind these two women, and at the distance of about two hundred paces from them, rode two serving men, armed with swords and muskets, and from whose manner, their eager looks, and their timid whispers, as they saw the night closing around them, the young lady seemed fully justified in the remark she had made as to the little reliance to be placed upon them in a moment of danger.

"How like you living in Ireland, Hannah? What think you of to-day's sport?" asked the young lady, wishing to occupy the attention of her attendant, and to relieve, if she could, by conversation, the tedium of their slow and toilsome journey.

"Oh! mistress, I like Ireland so little, that I would wish to be back once more safe in quiet England," replied Hannah. "All the people here seem to hate each other. I do not understand what they are always quarrelling about. We have Roundheads and Cavaliers in England; they have done to one another a world of mischief; but now that the mischief is at an end, and the King has, as they say, got 'his own' again, neighbours do not fight with neighbours. It is not so in this country; they are always squabbling about something or nothing. Even the two men that ride behind us—John Norris and James Brophy—I have seen them draw their knives upon each other in your father's kitchen, and all because Norris maintained that Sir Charles Coote was an inch taller, and a better general than Lord Inchiquin. And then, mistress, as to this day's sport, the horse racing which you wished me to see, I have no taste for such diversions. I do not understand what can be the pleasure in seeing poor brutes whipped, and spurred, and urged to run beyond their speed. I did, indeed, derive pleasure from one thing—it was to witness the admiration you excited, to see so many young lords and brave gallants paying court to you."

A heavy lash from the whip, applied with a vigorous hand to the slow-pacing Adolphus, made him bound forward impatiently, and as a strong wrist checked his rein at the same time, he came rearing up close to the side of Hannah's steed, whilst the impatient mistress said in an angry tone:—

"Silence, Hannah; never so speak to me again. Think you that I am a foolish girl in her teens, and that I do not know how to estimate, at its proper value, the buzzing of such gadflies and blood-suckers. I saw roysterers and gamblers, debauchees, fools and fops, and fortune-hunters, on the race-course, but not one true, honest man, that would prize me for myself, or who would care one pin for me if they fancied I was as poor as you. Nay, of the two of us, you are the better looking woman—fairer, younger than I am, and yet there was not one of these nobles and brave gallants, as you call them, to be commonly civil to you, whilst all their attentions were bestowed on me. And wherefore? Not merely because there was gold on my garments—though that, I have no doubt, was an attraction to spendthrifts—but because it is well known that my father is rich, and that I am the sole inheritor of all he possesses. Were I as destitute of fortune as you are,

Hannah, then be certain that those who bowed the knee before me to-day, would screw up their lips with scorn at me as the low-born daughter of Ebenezer Lawson, the Cromwellian trooper."

"I am not well skilled in the ways of the world," replied Hannah; "but still I cannot but think that the admiration to which you are justly entitled was honestly and sincerely given to you to-day. As to me, I know my position in life too well not to have felt rejoiced, that the slightest notice was not taken of me. A compliment from any one of the group of your admirers, would have been, to a person in my lowly condition, an insult."

"And it is no less an insult to me, Hannah," observed Judith Lawson. "What right had any one of those persons, from the son of the Lord Lieutenant, to the meanest and poorest ensign in the garrison of Dublin, to intrude upon me with his unmeaning compliments? If they respected the daughter of the trooper, as they would respect the daughter of a duke, why not treat the one with the same deference which they would feel compelled to treat the other? What right had any one of them to approach me, but that they knew I was Lawson's daughter, and that I was on the race-course alone, and unprotected? Surely, if I were the child of a lord, or of a gentleman by birth, I would have been allowed to look, safe from intrusion, upon the day's sport; I would not be, as I have been, persecuted with attentions I did my utmost to repel; and this I am quite sure of, that I should not have endured the dishonor of having a wretch, like the infamous David Fitzgerald of Limerick, pursuing me with his noisome flatteries for hours."

"Is the person you call David Fitzgerald of Limerick," asked Hannah, "the tall man with the florid face, flaxen hair, and light blue eyes, and who was so constantly by your side during the whole day?"

"It is—the wretch!" said Judith, indignantly. "I desired Norris to inquire who and what he was; and, according to my man's statement, this Fitzgerald, it appears, is a most infamous character. He has, though young, wasted his fortune on his vices. He has now the reputation of being in high favour with the Lord Lieutenant Ormonde; for he pretends, or declares he has discovered a plot amongst the Papists, and is in correspondence with Lord Shaftesbury and the 'patriots' in England, for the purpose of devising the best means of bringing the conspirators to justice. Meanwhile, he would improve his fortune, by seeking for the hand of Judith Lawson! Am I not right, Hannah, then, in considering myself as degraded, when a wretch so base and vile as Fitzgerald, can, for a moment, seriously believe he is in a position to become my suitor?"

Before Hannah had time to reply to the question of her angry and excited mistress, the voice of one of the men behind them, was heard exclaiming:—

"Hurry!—hurry!—hurry onward, mistress; there are horsemen following us at full speed. The Lord have mercy on us all, if they are Rapparees, and Redmond O'Hanlon in command of them!"

Despite her natural courage, a chill of terror ran through the frame of Judith Lawson, when the awful name of Redmond O'Hanlon was pronounced; for she remembered to have heard her father a hundred times speak of him as the most merciless foe to every one of English birth and descent that had settled and acquired lands in Ireland. Her belief of that well-known, and then most formidable chieftain was, that his delight was in shedding the blood of men, women, and children; destroying the English farms, tumbling down English-built houses, and sparing neither age nor sex when they were purely English.

The mere mention of the name Redmond O'Hanlon was alone sufficient to paralyze all the energies of the young Englishwoman, Hannah; and she would have fallen from her steed to the earth had not Judith caught the fainting girl in her arms, and as she did so she cried out:—

"Here, Norris, take this poor girl and place her in the saddle before you. Do you, Brophy, hold the rein of her horse, and guide it with your own—let both follow me wherever I lead."

Judith having seen these directions acted upon, then turned round in order that she might, with her own eyes, determine whether there was just cause for that alarm which had been given to her and her companions.

Four horsemen were seen advancing at full speed towards the travellers; and a second glance was not necessary to convince the cool and courageous Judith that they were robbers by profession. The nags they rode were rough, wild-looking animals. The dresses of three of the riders were old and ragged; whilst the fourth, who wore a short, red cloak, and had a feather in his hat, was, like his companions, armed with a long gun. The face of the man with the red cloak was covered with a black mask, whilst his companions had thick mustachios and long beards.

The purposes of the pursuers could not be for a moment doubtful, because even whilst Judith turned round to look at them, she saw one of the men stop, deliberately unloose his gun, take a steady aim at her, and discharge his piece.

At the same instant she heard the sound of the shot,

and saw Hannah's horse tumble on the earth, and then struggling in the agonies of death.

"Whatever may befall us," said the gallant Judith, "these villains shall be made to feel we do not fear them. Give me your gun, Norris, and I shall try and unmask the villain yonder."

"For heaven's sake, mistress," said the terrified Norris, "do not shoot at them, or we shall be all massacred."

"Give me your gun, sirrah," cried the enraged Judith, "or I will stab you with my hunting knife."

"Oh! here—take it, take it, and God send you hit nobody. Above all things don't fire at the man with the mask: for I am quite sure it is Redmond O'Hanlon himself," said the trembling Norris.

"If it were Redmond O'Hanlon a thousand times over," said Judith, "I will do my best to unhorse him. It is a poor revenge to kill an Irish garron for the good steed of my father's he has slain."

As Judith spoke, she directed the musket with a fixed and deadly aim at the person who appeared to be the commander of the pursuers, and a shout of joy burst from her lips as the smoke from the piece cleared away, and she perceived that her shot had been followed by the fall of man and horse.

"I am sure I have slain the horse and spared the rider," remarked Judith.

"Heaven have mercy on us!" cried Norris.

"We are all as one as dead men," added Brophy.

"Here, Brophy, load Norris's gun for him, and give me yours to make use of, if I need it," said Judith. "Fools and cowards as you are—do you not perceive these fellows are not in such a hurry following us as they were a few minutes ago. They, like ourselves, have now but three horses at their command; and they will not be so eager to fire upon us when they find we can reply to them with effect."

"Alas! madam," cried Norris, whimpering and trembling, "you are only bringing down on yourself and us the vengeance of men who know not what it is to feel pity for another."

"Then, if such be our assailants," added Judith, "let us at least sell our lives as dearly as we can. The butcher does not spare the lamb, though it licks the hand raised to kill it; but the butcher is not in a hurry to assail the wolf, which he knows will, if he makes one false step, rend him to pieces. Have you loaded Norris's gun, Brophy?"

"Yes, ma'am," said Brophy, winking at Norris, for the purpose of showing that he was deceiving his mistress, whose readiness to combat was no less a cause of anxiety to both than their terror of the gang, whose cruelty they feared would be provoked by her courage.

"Then give me his musket and take back your own; his is the piece to which my hand is best accustomed, and with which I can take the surer aim."

"Alack! alack! this comes of firing shots to alarm the country!" exclaimed Norris, pointing to a narrow path which approached the high road at a right angle, and along which two furious and ragged fellows, armed with guns, were hurrying towards them on foot.

"The odds are against us!" exclaimed the dauntless Judith, whose courage seemed to rise as dangers increased around her. "All that we have now to do is to retreat as best we can; and our only place for making a last struggle is that little slated cabin on the hill-side yonder. Hasten on towards it both of you; I will take the post of danger in the rere."

These commands were at once acted upon. The attendants of Judith rode as men ride whose lives depended upon the swiftness and strength of their steeds. At once they quitted the road and paced along the green fields, and bounded over wide ditches, which an hour before they would not have ventured to look at but with surprise that any one would have the courage to cross them. The high breeding and the solid feeding of their horses served them well on such an occasion; whilst, as impediments to their pursuers, was a long tract of swamp which lay along the wood, and between it and the hill down to the very point where Judith and her companions had first quitted the road, so that the pursuers had to come down to the very point, from which she and her men had started, and then to follow as well as they could with their weak nags over the same fields and across the same ditches. Judith and her followers might by the new course they had taken, have completely escaped, without stopping at the slated cabin, from their pursuers on horseback, had not the assailants been aided by the robbers on foot, who kept at an untiring speed behind them.

"Knock at the door; ask for permission to enter, and save yourselves from those thieves and murderers," said Judith to Brophy.

Her commands were obeyed. The door was opened: and it was about to be again closed, when it was thrown wide open, and the person inside the cabin stepped into the air, and, removing from his head a small black cap, he bowed low to Judith, and said:—

"I pray your pardon, lady; I was alarmed by the appearance of an armed man knocking at such an hour at my humble door. The moment, however, that I perceived he was accompanied by a woman, I knew there was not only no danger to be apprehended, but, perchance, it might be within my poor means to afford relief. I pray you, madam, to enter, and to regard all that you see as your own, for all is at your command."

Judith listened to the words thus spoken to her, but was unable to reply to them. Her own perilous situation, and the danger that threatened her companions, were equally forgotten in the new sense of unmixed admiration for the noble-looking man who stood before her. A diligent reader of her Bible from her childhood upwards, she had never before seen any one in her father's home, in conventicle, or in society, that reminded her of those whom she had admired as patriarchs, prophets, and apostles. But here, and for the first time, she saw a living man, on whose ample forehead, flowing nut-brown hair, commingled with streaks of gray, whose large dove-like eyes, whose perfectly-moulded features, whose sweet smile, and meek look, and noble form, seemed to present him to his fellow-creatures as something more than mortal—as one, whose brows were already illuminated with the light of the pre-sanctified, and who seemed born for no other purpose than to praise God and to win sinners to repentance.

Judith felt, as she looked upon this venerable man, as if she could kneel to him, and entreat his blessing. She felt, as she stood before him, that she at last beheld a human being, whose pure soul had never been stained by one degrading passion, and who had the strength and the will to contemn the world, its wealth, its vanities, its riches, and its terrors.

Awe and wonder benumbed her faculties. She stood as if awaiting a repetition of his words; and she felt, for the moment, that she was unworthy of addressing him.

The old man looked first at her, then at her alarmed

companions, and then at the fainting form of the still insensible Hannah, and casting his eyes on the space the fugitives had traversed, he perceived the wild horsemen and the eager pedestrians who were quickly advancing in pursuit. He cried in hurried accents:—

"Alight, my children! at once alight from your horses, and seek the shelter of my roof. I see that you are beset by the wicked thieves that haunt this neighbourhood. Hasten in, my children, that I may give you such security as well-barred doors and iron-fastened windows can afford.

"I am told, sir," said Judith, bounding from her steed, and aiding her men, as she spoke, in bringing Hannah inside the house, "I am told that the men who pursue us are robbers, and one of my servants assures me that the man in command of them is the notorious footpad, Redmond O'Hanlon."

"You have been misinformed, my child," replied the old man, as he bolted the windows and barred the door, "Redmond O'Hanlon is not a footpad, nor have I ever heard of his employing the men under his command as common highway robbers. The villains who pursue you are not, I am sure, the adherents or the friends of Redmond O'Hanlon."

The conversation of the old man and Judith was rendered inaudible by the loud shouts and exulting cries of the robbers, as they captured the horses of the travellers—a capture that was rendered particularly precious by the seizure of Judith's horse, with its silver bit, and velvet saddle-cloth fringed with a deep border of thick-worked heavy gold embroidery.

"I hope," said the old man, "that these unhappy men may be satisfied with the prize they have already taken; and that respect for me will induce them to leave you in peace within my dwelling."

"I fear them not, sir," replied Judith, " while I hold this gun and have strength to use my hunting-knife against them."

" Better to suffer wrong than to shed blood, daughter," said the old man. " Your strength and skill would be a poor defence against those savage men. My words may be of more avail than twenty swords. If these wicked men will not listen to me, then place your confidence in God, and be certain He will not desert you in the hour of need."

As the old man ceased from speaking, a shot was fired outside, and a loud clatter, caused by the beating of the butt ends of muskets, was heard at the door. This was followed by the cry of "The prisoners, the prisoners, we demand the delivery of the prisoners, their weapons, and their purses."

" Lie down, my children, on the ground, lest those men should fire in through door or window. I will, with this lady, proceed up stairs and parley with your assailants from an opening in the roof."

When the old man had thus addressed the trembling domestics, he led Judith, who still bore the musket with her, to the roof.

"Conceal yourself, my child," he said, "from their view. As to me, I fear no harm they can do me. If I am about to meet death in trying to save life, then do not weep for me; but wish that you may one day partake of that happiness which is the sure reward of all who, for God's sake, lay down their lives for the benefit of their fellow-creatures."

" What would you ?" said the old man, as he pushed aside the boards that concealed the opening on the roof, and stood full in view of the assailants. " What would you ? or wherefore have you attacked this house, in which none are to be found but peaceful travellers ?"

"Give up the prisoners, deliver our prisoners, we want their weapons and their purses," cried two or three persons in the same breath.

"Let one man speak for all," said Judith's venerable host. "I wish to hold parley with none but your leader."

"I am their leader," said the man with the mask, whom Judith had already unhorsed.

"I know you not, sir," said the old man.

"But I know you, most reverend sir," replied the masked man in an insolent tone of voice; "and it is probable that, before long, you will know more of me, and much more, too, than you would ever like to have heard."

"That I think, sir, is by no means improbable, should I ever hear anything at all about you," said the old man, with a gentle smile. "At present I wish to know, why you have knocked at my door, and by what right you claim persons under my protection as your prisoners?"

"I claim them, most reverend sir, by the plainest, simplest, and most indubitable of rights—the right of the strong hand," answered the ruffian. "Mine is the stronger, and those you call your guests the weaker party. However, I am disposed to compromise this matter with you. All I ask for my men are the weapons and the purses of your guests; whilst, for myself, I shall be content with a single prisoner—the person who fired at me; and that person, I am well aware, is Miss Judith Lawson."

"And that person," said Judith, trembling with rage when she heard her name thus publicly mentioned, "will die sooner than yield herself your prisoner. She fired at you once before, intending only to slay your horse; but now she aims at your heart, with the intention to rid the world of a base thief and a cowardly villain."

As she spoke these words the musket she held was

directed at the man in the mask; but the lock snapped, and no report followed, and as Judith, in her vexation, was about to cast the useless weapon from her, she felt her arms clasped from behind, and a cord ran through them pinioned her elbows close together, and a broad, red-faced, foxy-bearded man, whose breath was fetid with the fumes of usquebaugh, grinned at her, as he peered up in her frowning eyes.

"What a wicked, wilful Penthesilea!" the rude captor cried, in a bantering voice. "Achilles wept because he had, unconscious of her personal charms, slain a beautiful virago; but here is a Queen of the Amazons who would slay the suitor who is risking life and limb to make her his wife."

"Unhappy, fallen, and degraded creature, forego your ribald jests," said Judith's host. "I hear the shouts of your brutal confederates in the rooms beneath, as they rifle the peaceful travellers. I suppose it is you, taking advantage of the knowledge you formerly had of these premises, have betrayed to thieves and villains the private and secret entrance to a home in which you were once hospitably received."

"My Lord! my Lord! drive not an unhappy man to despair," said the ruffian, whose jeering tones were at once abandoned, and whose coarse voice became husky with deep emotion. "If I am a fallen and a degraded creature, as you say I am, remember who it was that was the first cause of my fall, who cut short the career to which I had devoted myself, and who prevented me from entering a profession for which I had prepared myself by days of labour and nights of study."

"Miserable man!" replied the venerable personage who was thus appealed to; "blame not me, but your own vices, your own bad habits, your own evil propensities, as your worst and direst foes. It was my duty to watch over the fold of which I was the shepherd; to take care that no wolf should ravage my lambs. I could not permit you to take vows that you had not the strength to keep; I could not allow you to become a stumbling-block and a scandal to those for whose salvation I was responsible. Repent, repent, Murfey, if you can; and, as you hope for eternal life, abandon your evil courses and your wicked companions. Perhaps you hear now, for the last time, heaven's warning voice calling you to repentance. You have time given to you to-day—wait until to-morrow, and time may be for you no more."

"Too late, too late!" cried the unhappy, desperate man, who had been addressed by the name of Murfey; "your public denunciations have rendered me a reprobate and an outcast. I am now the associate of your enemies, and I warn you, my Lord, to look to yourself. I am not the only man upon whom your blighting excommunication has fallen. I am but one of many determined to avenge such excommunications by the shedding of your blood. You have warned me. Well, I now warn you;—fly from this land before another month has passed away. Neglect this warning, and the wishes of your many enemies will be fulfilled; and your blood be on your own head. You gave me not one hour for sorrow or repentance, I give you a month to look to your own safety."

"I care not for the wrath of man, whilst performing the will of heaven," replied the old man. "I care not for your threats nor for the wicked machinations of those whom I have cut off from the discharge of duties they were unworthy to perform. Here then I will remain, until it pleases God to remove me—ever prepared to submit to His holy will, and my only prayer, that I may be deemed worthy to close a life of suffering by receiving the Martyr's Crown."

"I will stop to talk no longer with you," said Murfey. "I must obey my commander's orders, which are, to deliver up to him this Amazon, who would slay a man with as little remorse as she kills a dumb beast. The other prisoners, my Lord, will be left to your guardianship. I now part from you—most probably for ever—but, in so doing, I repeat my warning to you, the only friendly warning you shall ever receive from me. It is this: quit your present habitation at once—fly from Ireland with what speed you can. Neglect this warning, and then be as sure as that you hear my words, that your enemies will triumph over you, that an ignominious death on the scaffold will be inflicted upon you, and that what you so boastingly say you pray may be bestowed upon you, will assuredly be given to you —and that is, a Martyr's Crown. Such, I say, is your doom, already planned and contrived for you; as surely your doom as that my name is Edmund Murfey, a degraded student in divinity, and that your name is Oliver Plunkett, titular Archbishop of Armagh, and Primate of all Ireland."

CHAPTER IV.

AN ABDUCTION.

For some hours Judith had been on horseback. Tied by a thick cord to the person who rode before her, and her arms still bound, although the bonds had been so relaxed as to allow her hands to touch each other, she rode on silently and sullenly, never condescending to make a single reply to her captors, from the moment that she was a prisoner, and that she had been deprived of her hunting-knife and riding-whip.

As Judith thus rode she perceived that the cavalcade that watched her was led by the man with the mask; that the number of her guards, as they advanced upon the road, seemed to increase; and that messengers from time to time hurried up, and departed after a few minutes conversation with him who seemed to act as the commander of this expedition.

Judith concluded, from all she witnessed, that her captors were apprehensive of coming into collision with some force hostile to their own, and that secrecy, not less than expedition, was necessary to secure success to their enterprise. Her courage, which had never abated, received new strength and vigour when the appearances around her led her mind to this conclusion; and she was, therefore, watchful to avail herself of any opportunity that might present itself to enable her to effect her escape.

The moment, she fancied, had at length arrived for making such an attempt, when, after riding for a few hours in the night, she perceived her captors unexpectedly pause, and that the masked man at the head of the expedition rode suddenly up to her.

"I wish, Mistress Lawson," said this man, "to shorten your journey by some hours. I can do so by passing direct through a village that lies on our road; but I cannot venture to make my way through it, unless I have your promise that you will remain silent, that you will not alarm the inhabitants by your cries, nor seek in any way to make your escape from us."

Judith looked scornfully at the man, but made no reply.

"I must have an answer," said the man. "I have no other object in proposing this to you, than to save you a toilsome journey. Escape from us is now an impossibility."

"Villain!" replied the enraged Judith, "I will enter into no terms with you. Do your worst—I defy you; all I require is but to know the name of my cowardly oppressor, in order that I may vow eternal enmity against him."

"Foolish girl!" replied the man, with a scornful laugh, "think you I would have commenced such a project as this, without securing the means for making you my own —mayhap my slave, not for a day nor a year, but for life. You have defied my enmity—Idiot! the time, I trust, will come when you shall be my loving mistress, and most dutiful wife."

"I am your prisoner, sir," observed Judith, "but the day and the hour may not be distant, when we shall stand upon terms of greater equality with each other. Should that day ever arrive, then you shall be made to fear, not a woman's tongue, but a woman's hand; but until then I will not degrade myself by exchanging another word with you."

"Oh! spirit of Penthesilea, look down upon and pity me," said Murfey, who rode in front of Judith. "Compassionate a creature who is tied to such a man-eater; for had you, Amazonian Queen, been at all times so piteously obdurate, poets would never have feigned or fancied you could, under any circumstances, have became the mother of Cayster."

"Peace! babbling drunkard," added the excited Judith, "peace! you who have exchanged the pastoral care of the holy Prelate we have parted from, to become the pander of a miscreant who fears to show his face to the helpless woman he has grossly injured. Peace! you, upon whose hot forehead rests the burning brand of an excommunication your own vices have provoked."

The bitter words of Judith told with a fearful effect upon

the unhappy man, Murfey. A sickness, as of death, came upon him; his limbs trembled, and his head reeled, and he would have fallen from his horse, dragging his female companion along with him, had not her hands, so far free as to grasp him, held him on tightly to his saddle."

"Here!" she exclaimed, "look to this drunken wretch. So far is he from being competent to take care of me, he is unable to hold himself straight on the animal he bestrides."

"Woman! woman!" cried Murfey, arousing himself as these opprobrious terms were applied to him; "what devil has possessed thee, thus to rouse up an evil spirit against thee? Oh! how true were the words of the wise man: '*The stroke of the whip maketh a blue mark, but the stroke of the tongue will break the bones.*' Woman, your foul language has made of me your mortal enemy for life."

"Wretch!" replied Judith, "you have profaned the holy words of Scripture by quoting them. Remember what the same Scripture says of you, and of persons like you: '*The manners of lying men are without honor, and their confusion is with them without ceasing.*' You have belied your promises to your God; and what can you hope for the remainder of your miserable existence, but reproach and contumely from men—from women as well as men, from children as from women. Drunken fool! who have sold your birthright for a mess of pottage, ponder upon these words of Scripture, when you threaten that you will be, for the future, a worse enemy of mine than you are at this moment, and when no word of mine had been uttered to provoke your enmity—'*As an arrow that sticketh in a man's thigh, so is a word in the heart of a fool.*'"

"Reply not, Murfey, to our lovely, fascinating prisoner," said the man in the mask. "At present she is unduly excited; the time, however, will come, when she shall treat you as one of my most honoured guests, with a smiling face fill your flagon for you, and coax you to troll out a merry catch for her. Our present business is to hurry her to her destined home. It is her own fault if she find the way longer and wearier than I would have it for her. Onward, my men, march."

The party proceeded in silence for four hours, and the darkness of night was beginning to yield to the first grey tints of morning, when Judith fancied that she could recognize in such portions of the landscape as were discernible, features that reminded her of the neighbourhood of Dublin. She would have felt certain she was correct in her surmises, but that she saw, or supposed she saw, a building in the distant gloom which resembled a small fort or castle; with two low flat towers; and such a building was utterly unknown to her. Whilst her mind was thus occupied, her attention was excited by new sounds, that made her heart bound with hope and exultation. It was the regular tramp of a small body of cavalry, which seemed to be crossing directly at some distance the high road that her captors were travelling. Her hope was that her captors might be perceived by the commander of the cavalry, and that this circumstance might lead to her release, and the punishment of her aggressors. The hope thus entertained seemed to be on the point of being realized, for the cavalry had halted, and the persons who held Judith a prisoner challenged by them.

Judith observed the leader of her party at once ride forward towards the cavalry, and as he did so, she was sure he had put off his mask, and drew forth a large piece of paper or parchment, and as he advanced, open it for the inspection of the officer.

Judith was unable to hear the following brief conversation which passed between the captor and the officer:—

"Who are you, sir?" said the commander to her captor, as he advanced, "and by what authority is there an armed band of men on the king's high road, at this hour of the night?"

"This, sir, is my authority—my name, office, and duties are explained in it," replied the captor.

"Bring hither the lanthorn, Sergeant," said the captain of the cavalry, as he took in his hand a long piece of parchment on which there was a large official seal.

"You are, sir, I presume, the person named in this document?"

"I am."

"I see this is an order in Council issued in England, and authorizing you to call upon the Irish government, magistrates, and all persons in civil or military authority here, to aid you in the business for which you have been despatched to this country—in arresting prisoners, and collecting evidence with respect to the horrid Popish plot. Very well, sir, I have no right further to question you. I presume you have here a prisoner in custody. May I inquire the name?"

"I must not tell it, sir. All I can say is, my prisoner is a lady of high rank—a notorious Papist—and was arrested by me last night in the dungeons beneath the Archiepiscopal mansion of the Popish Bishop of Armagh, having been sent to Ireland by Pere La Chaise, the Popish confessor of the King of France, to devise the best means for destroying by poison our blessed Protestant king, his most gracious Majesty, Charles the Second."

"Sir," said the captain of the cavalry, "I reverence you for your zeal. I feel honored in having spoken with you; I regard you as one of the saviours of the country, as one worthy to be associated with that great and good man, the Rev. Doctor Oates. If any additional assistance is required by you, I and my men will be most happy to be at your disposal, and to act under your orders."

"I thank you, valiant sir," replied Judith's captor; "but the force at my command is fully sufficient. I shall be most happy, however, to bring (if you will be so kind as to mention it) your name under the special notice of the Privy Council in England. Lord Shaftesbury, Lord William Russell, and divers distinguished Protestant patriots, will be delighted to learn that the army in Ireland corresponds with them in zeal, and sympathises with them in their hatred of Jesuits, and their horror of the savage Popish plots."

The captain of cavalry was enchanted to hear those words. "Most worthy and excellent sir," he replied, "I hope you may, amid your many glorious avocations in discovering and bringing to punishment all the dark conspirators in the hellish Popish plot, bear in mind before the Privy Council in England, that one of the most ardent supporters in this country of such illustrious, benevolent, generous, kind-hearted, and disinterested Protestant patriots, is your humble servant, Captain John Jones, Captain in Colonel John Jones's dragoons—son to Major John Jones of the Popery-hating regiment. Be so good, patriotic sir, as to remember me—to mention my name as Captain John Jones, of Lickspittle Hall, in the County of Monmouth."

"Farewell, sir; be assured that from this day forth I will ever bear impressed upon my memory, and in letters of brass, the-always-by-me-to-be-honoured name of Captain John Jones, of Colonel John Jones's dragoons, Captain John Jones, of Lickspittle Hall, in the County of Monmouth."

Judith watched with an anxiety that amounted to agony

the incidents that marked the preceding dialogue. She saw the captain of cavalry reading the document placed in his hands, and she could perceive, as the light shone upon his person, that he bowed lowly and humbly before the person who had presented it. She observed the same humility in the officer's entire bearing from first to last, whilst her captor stood haughty and erect as if he was addressed by an inferior. She then observed these two persons part from each other, and as the tramp of the cavalry horses, when they resumed their march, reached her ears, she was no longer able to conceal her feelings, but shrieked aloud—" Help—help—help—rescue, soldiers, a lone woman from the hands of highway robbers."

The officer of cavalry halted his men as the shrieks of Judith reached his ears; but he did so, it appeared, only to give his followers a new order, and in its execution to prove to her how vain was an appeal to him or them.

" God save our Protestant King from his Papist enemies! Long live the saviours of the country—Doctor Oates and the other discoverers of the hellish Popish plot."

Judith was utterly astounded by the inexplicable incidents of which she was an eye-witness. Here was she, the daughter of a man of great wealth, a peaceful traveller on the common high road, assailed by a band of robbers, captured, borne about the country as if she were a malefactor; and when she at last has met with a body of soldiers, whose duty it is to protect her, and preserve her from insult and outrage, she finds her appeal for assistance disregarded, and as far as she could understand them, cheers given by the King's troops for highway thieves and audacious ruffians.

Never, not even for a single moment, had Judith's stout heart, up to this time, felt one pang of terror; but when she beheld a scene for which she could not account, and

found that her captor possessed an influence such as she
could not fancy would be exercised even by a prince of
the blood, her firm hand for the first time trembled, her
spirits sank, and she could not refrain from thus communing with herself:—

" What can be the meaning of this? The commander
of the King's troops to bow down before a common robber,
for up to this time I have never thought of the wretch in
command of the base villains about me but as a robber.
Is that his real character, or does he but assume the profession of a highwayman to carry out his wicked designs?
Then what can be these designs? I tremble to think of
them. The wretch has already threatened me with a
slavery for life. There is but one description of slavery
existing in these countries, it is that of the poor drudging
wife who knows and feels that her husband is her greatest
enemy, her worst and most unpitying of tyrants. Then
who is there, possessed of such influence as this man
manifestly wields, who desired to sue for my hand, and
might not calculate upon being received in my father's
house as a welcome suitor? The ambition of my father is
well known: his desire to see me united to a man of rank
and title is notorious. But I dream; no nobleman, no
man of rank, would be base enough to descend to such
vile means as this wretch has resorted to, for the purpose
of winning the hand of one whose father is, like mine, of
the humblest condition in life. My suitor, or rather my
captor, must be a man whose deeds are as base as his
origin, perhaps a hanger-on of the Duke of Monmouth who
has been sent to this country to procure a wife with a large
fortune. Such a person might, through the Duke of Monmouth, and his grace's influence with the army, find, as
this villain has done, a captain in the cavalry to counten-

ance his scheme, and to promote it under the pretext he was sustaining the interests of the No-Popery pretender to the throne. If I be right in this conjecture, then I can attach a fitting signification to the shouts of the troopers, which otherwise would be as unintelligible as the ravings of a madman. Of one thing, however, I cannot have the slightest doubt, that this outrage has been committed upon me because I have the reputation of being an heiress, that I am one to be added to the many who have been persecuted under the sham name of 'love,' and the profession of the profaned vows of marriage, in order that he who has so degraded the daughter, may claim to be the possessor of her father's wealth. The villain who has speculated upon making me such a victim to his sordid craving for wealth, little knows the woman he has to deal with. Better death than give him the chance of such a victory; but better his death than my own, whilst at the worst I am prepared to purchase with my own life the sacrifice of his."

As Judith's thoughts thus hurried through her mind, and that she was beset with doubts and surmises as to the past, the present, and the future, she permitted her horse to be guided on with the party that hitherto had accompanied her. She offered no further resistance by word, or action, or even look; but watched attentively every peculiarity in the ground she travelled over; she stored up in her memory every trifling incident that might serve, should the opportunity occur, of making her escape.

As the daylight was dawning, she found herself and steed crossing a wooden bridge into the narrow gate of a small fortress; and, as the gate closed behind her, she was certain she heard the noise of machinery lifting up and removing the bridge over which she had passed a moment before.

Judith, without a murmur, permitted herself to be lifted from her horse; and she followed, without remark, the degraded Murfey, as he mounted a narrow winding stair, which led to an apartment that appeared to her to be at the top of the fortress. This apartment was a large round room to which there was a single window.

"There," said Murfey, pointing to a narrow doorway, there lie your bed and dressing-room. Here is wine; there bread. The Brass Castle, for such is the name of your present abode, can afford you no better nourishment to-night. In the morning the Governor will wait upon you, and then he will hear what are your wishes; and then, perhaps, you will learn from him what are his commands; and, it is to be hoped, for your own sake, that you will at once put them in practice."

"I did not intend," said Judith, "ever again to address you; but, remembering the words of the good man who spoke to you but a few hours ago, believing from the address to you of that gentleman you called Archbishop Oliver Plunket, there was a time in your life, when the remembrance that you had a mother—and, perhaps, a sister—would have stirred your heart with generous emotions, I cannot refrain from entertaining the hope that you do not utterly forget what you once were—that so much of the sacred character of a clergyman still clings to you, that you will think it is not fitting I, a young woman, should be, as I am here at present, alone, unaided, unprotected; but that, if it be possible, I may be permitted to have with me the society of one of my own sex—no matter how old, how aged, or how decrepit—so that she be a woman."

The jibing manner and leering expression of an habitual drunkard, which was on Murfey's face as he entered the apartment and spoke to Judith, was changed at once by her address; and when she alluded to his mother, this unhappy man raised his hands to his face, as if he wished, unperceived, to wipe away the tears that filled them. He did not immediately reply to Judith's address, but paused for a couple of minutes as if he desired to couch his refusal in the softest terms possible.

"A woman to be in the same room with you: it is a reasonable request—but under present circumstances, and at this hour of the night, impossible to be complied with. I will not, however, be forgetful of it; and if I can it shall be acted upon, although, truth to say, I never heard but of one woman being admitted into the Brass Castle, and she is such a nuisance that it is considered a holiday every time she takes her leave of it. Have no fear, young woman, for yourself for to-night at least. You may perceive this room has strong bolts on the inside. I do not say it would not be possible to break into it, these bolts notwithstanding; but no one could effect such a purpose without making a noise that would rouse the dead. For to-night, I repeat, you are perfectly safe. You will be in no danger until you see my friend; and then it will depend upon yourself whether you will live together like cat and dog, or be as happy as most married people are; and such happiness, so far as I have remarked, consists in this, that husbands and wives love one another a little and hate one another a great deal. Again, I say, have no fear for to-night. What you have now to do, is to lock me and all other intruders out. You may be sure that I shall do what is my business on the outside, and not only lock, but so far as iron bonds can attain the purpose—treble chain you in. There is wine; there is bread; there your sleeping room. Think over the events of to-day, and prepare yourself for to-morrow, by being a mild, meek-tempered young woman —that which I would say, judging of you by your behaviour this day, you never can be. *Bon repos!*"

CHAPTER V.

A CAPTIVE AND A JAILER.

Judith Lawson had never known a mother's tenderness, and had never been controlled by a mother's watchful care. She could not remember to have seen in the house in which she had been reared any one but her father, whose will was more powerful than her own; and that father had never exercised his power in contradicting her whims as a girl, or her wishes as a grown up woman. The natural goodness of her heart had alone prevented her from being a despot at home and a tyrant amongst the crowd of dependants and flatterers she met with when she went abroad.

All her life she had done as she pleased, travelled where she liked, and dressed as her fancy dictated. She had been her own absolute mistress, and up to this time had met with no one who ventured to lay the slightest restriction upon her actions. But now, in the course of a few hours, in the short revolution of a single day, she found herself, unconscious of any fault, and without the intention of doing the slightest wrong to any living being, not only deprived of her liberty, but a captive in an unknown prison, and in the power of persons of whom her only knowledge was that they seemed to be the basest, meanest, and most brutal of mankind—flagrant thieves and audacious felons, who lived by plunder, and would not hesitate at the perpetration of murder for the accomplishment of their wicked purposes.

The change was so great, so sudden, and so unlooked for, that she felt her faculties were incapable for the moment of comprehending all its consequences. She was as one who has received an awful wound, and whose senses are so stunned by the shock, as to be unable to feel at once the agonies which the injury inflicted is sure to produce. Pain and suffering are to come—sure to come—with rest and reflection.

And so it was with Judith. She mechanically bolted the door of her chamber the moment that Murfey had left her, and then flinging from her the richly plumed, gold-laced hat she had worn during the day, she cast herself upon the bed, dressed as she was; and whilst endeavouring to think over the incidents of the day, a deep, heavy, almost apoplectic sleep, fell upon her, and the sun was high in the heavens, and there was a loud, incessant knocking at the door, before she again awoke to consciousness, or that she could be so completely aroused as to be capable of comprehending either where she was, or what had befallen her.

"Had my knocking remained two minutes longer without being noticed, I should have called up Murfey and the other vagabonds below, with sledge-hammers to break open the door, and see whether you had been mad enough to try and make your escape, or wise enough to try and put an end to yourself."

Such were the words addressed to Judith as she opened her chamber-door, and admitted him who uttered them.

The new comer was an old, a very old man. His head was completely bald. There was not a particle of hair upon any part of it; but a long white beard of thin, straggling hairs covered his mouth, chin, and breast. His eyes were large, and staring, and the eye-lids blood-red, as if they were in a constant state of inflammation, and their painful expression of incessant greedy, pitiless, watchfulness was rendered almost appalling by the deep red shaggy eye-brows, as if the last remains of vigour in that wasted human frame were concentrated and retained in the old man's keen powers of observation. The body was lean and fragile, and the legs of the old man trembled beneath him, as he slowly hobbled from the door to the table, and there deposited a basket and an earthen pitcher, which he carried in long, bony, and talon-like-fingered hands.

"There," said the old man, seating himself in a chair by the side of the table, as if he were fatigued with his journey up stairs, and tired from waiting at the door for Judith's awaking; "there, young woman, is your breakfast,—fresh bread, new milk, and a roast fowl. Few prisoners fare so well as that. I never knew but one, and that was a gentleman ordered for execution. Instead of milk, however, we gave him wine. That and a glass of usquebaugh, which I handed to him, put him in heart, and he died like a hero in four hours afterwards, singing a jolly stave two minutes before the hangman put the noose around his neck."

Judith looked at the old man with anxious interest. She was so accustomed to find all who approached her hitherto willing to fulfil her wishes, that she could not suppose the person before her would refuse the request to aid in her escape, when she knew that whatever reward she promised, her father would readily and joyfully pay. Up to this time, however, she had been unaccustomed to converse with any one in the humble position and miserable garb of the old man before her; and that which presented itself as the greatest difficulty to her mind, was how to address him so as not to give offence,—to enlist his sympathies, and, if she could, not to offend his feelings.

F

With these intentions, she stood waiting to see if the old man would renew the conversation—say something to her, to which she could respond in a cheerful spirit; but to her astonishment she perceived that the old man sat still in his chair; never looked up to her; seemed absolutely unconscious of her presence, or rather was so absorbed in the contemplation of some ideas of his own, which, by his death-like smile, appeared to give him satisfaction, that he was alike forgetful of her and of the place in which he was at that moment seated.

Judith, wearied by his silence, and of watching the play of his hideous features, as he sat mumbling and smiling before her, at length addressed him:—

"You speak to me as if I was like the gentleman you allude to—one of your prisoners. Do you consider me to be a prisoner?"

"Anan!" said the old man, awakened from his reverie by the sound of her voice, and his faculties awakened to their usual watchfulness, "say over again what you have already said to me. I do not completely comprehend you."

Judith repeated her question for the old man.

"Do I consider you to be a prisoner? Of course I do—a prisoner of state; otherwise you would not be here. If you were a common malefactor, you would be in Newgate."

"But I have committed no crime," said Judith:

"I never knew a prisoner to admit that he or she *had* committed a crime. They are, if you believe them, all innocent; they all plead 'not guilty'; but still juries convict, and judges condemn, and the hangman ties up to the gallows those innocents, who all have said, as you say, each for himself or herself, 'but I have committed no crime,'" and as the old man spoke thus, there was a chuckling triumph in his hoarse, cracked voice.

"I say," added Judith, with a slight trembling in her

voice, as she remarked the pitiless manner of the old man, "that I have committed no crime; I am so conscious of my innocence, that I cannot even guess wherefore I am deprived of my liberty. Can you tell me of what crime I am accused?"

"I am not the governor of this prison," answered the old man. "If I was, I should know what was stated in the warrant under the authority of which you have been placed here a prisoner. I am nothing more than a menial in this gaol; and my business is not to ask what are the offences of those who are in custody, but to attend them, as I am now attending upon you, and to take care that they do not escape."

"Then it is a matter of indifference to you whether I am innocent or guilty," said Judith.

"To be sure it is," replied the old man. "What is it to me, whether you are innocent or guilty? I am not the better for your innocence, nor the worse because of your crimes: all I have to do with you is to watch you, and if I found you escaping from this room, and had no other means of preventing you, of slaying you, which in this case I would do with as little remorse as I would crush a spider that lay beneath my feet."

Judith looked in the old man's face. It was obdurate, hard, and pitiless—or rather it appeared to her as if he had a pleasure in saying what he could not but know was calculated to pain her feelings. She reflected for a few minutes, as to what was the best course of proceeding with him, and then resumed the conversation:—

"I like your candour," said Judith; "for it emboldens me to say out bluntly both what I think and what I wish."

"Say what you you please," said the old man, with a malignant grin: "you shall find me a patient listener."

"Do you think it would be possible to escape from this place?" asked Judith.

"Yes; if those who had the care of the prisoners were disposed to aid in their escape," responded the gaoler.

"Have you ever helped any one to escape?"

"Never."

"Can you suppose any case possible in which you would aid in any such plan?"

"I can—many cases."

"Tell me one—but one on which you would run such a risk," said the anxious Judith.

"Suppose," said the old man—"suppose that which I hope will never happen, that our Irish hero, Redmond O'Hanlon, was brought into this place a prisoner, that his limbs were fettered with gyves, and that a thousand pounds were offered for his safe custody until the day of his trial—suppose, I say, this was to happen, and that I alone was his caretaker, then I would, if there were no other means, undo his gyves with my teeth, I would spurn the gold of his captors, and with the outpouring of every drop of blood in my body, I would aid him,—I would die, or I would effect his escape."

"Brave old man!" said Judith, "I honor you for what you have just spoken. Now, listen to me. You have mentioned a thousand pounds as the sum you would refuse rather than keep Redmond O'Hanlon in prison. Aid me in flying from this prison, and the moment I reach my father's house, the sum you have mentioned shall be given to you in golden coin."

The old man clasped his thin arms with his long bony fingers, as if he were hugging himself with delight, whilst Judith was speaking to him. At length he started up from the chair on which he had been, up to this time, resting, and pointing to it, he nodded his head to Judith as if he desired her to take the seat he had just quitted.

"I have a few words to say to you," said the old man, "upon which, it is probable, you will have to ponder over for some time; but, in order that I may be sure I do not cast away upon the desert air what has been for years festering in my heart, I wish to be quite sure as to the person I am speaking with. Is not your name Judith Lawson?"

"It is. I am glad you know it; because you must be sure that what I promise I have the power to perform," replied Judith.

"Are you not Judith Lawson, the only child of Ebenezer Lawson, at one time a Cromwellian dragoon, and attached to the army acting at a particular period in the North of Ireland, under the special directions of Lieutenant-General Ludlow?" asked the old man, in a voice that became shrill with intense emotion.

"I am," replied Judith, "the daughter of that same Ebenezer Lawson; and I am certain, from the observations I have heard constantly made by my father, that he was at one time engaged with the army in the North of Ireland, under the command of General Ludlow."

"Thank God! thank God! that I am right," said the old man, as he dropped on his knees; "thank God! that in one case, at least, the evil deeds of our oppressors should be retorted on them. Now, listen to me, Judith Lawson, daughter—only child of Ebenezer Lawson," added the old man, as he with difficulty raised himself from his knees and stood erect before her; "hearken to my words, Judith Lawson; for they are as true as Holy Writ: if every hair on your head was a diamond, if your whole body could be transformed into gold, and that diamonds and gold were tendered to me to aid in your escape—and that escape from the most lingering and torturing death that the wit and malignity of man could devise—I would scorn to touch your gold or to handle your diamonds. I would leave you to your doom; I would not stir a step to save you from perdition. And would you know the reason why, Judith Lawson? It is because you are the daughter—because you are the only child of Ebenezer Lawson—because you are the light of his eyes, and the joy of his heart. Unhappy, miserable, God-abandoned young woman! you know me not, and it is most probable that your cruel and remorseless father never heard my name, and yet I am his victim. And when you tell me that you have committed no crime, and would provoke my pity in your behalf by assuring me you are innocent, what is my reply to you? That I committed no crime; that I too was innocent, and yet your father—yes, your father, Judith Lawson—without the slightest provocation, with no wrong done to him, with no insult offered to him, slew my wife, my sons, my daughters, and tried to slay myself——."

"Who are you, sir? how come you to make such vague and terrible accusations against my father? I do not understand what you are speaking about," said the indignant Judith, believing that the old man was raving in his dotage.

"Oh!" said the old man, with a withering sneer, "Ebenezer Lawson's daughter has been so tenderly nurtured, that she has never heard of the exploits of her gallant father in the neighbourhood of Dundalk—she never heard of the smothering of a number of the miserable Irish fugitives in a cavern to which they fled for safety." -

"Old man! old man!" said Judith, deeply moved by

the jailers excited manner; "you speak in parables to me: I have not the slightest notion what are these circumstances to which you are referring."

"Then you shall not be another moment in ignorance," said the jailer. "You have asked to know my name; I will tell it—Gerald Geraghty. It was once well known; and, I may add, that no act of mine, or of my family, had brought discredit upon the good fame of our ancestors. We took up arms to defend life, and home, and property. In that conflict we were defeated, and the soldiers of the English Parliament were laying waste the land with fire and sword, sparing neither youth, nor age, nor sex. We—that is, my family, my farm-servants, and myself—betook ourselves to a cave, in the hope we might escape that general slaughter to which all were then doomed by the republicans. In that cavern we were joined by others, who, like us, wished to save life, and to avoid a cruel death; and amongst others that fled to our retreat was a poor family, distant kinsmen, having with them, it was said, a foster-child, the infant son of Colonel Fitzpatrick, of the Queen's County. I know not whether it was the report of that child having escaped those who thirsted for its blood that attracted attention to our desolate hiding-place; but the fact was, that in a few days the iron-coats of Ludlow were around us; and most conspicuous amongst those ruthless men were your father and your uncle. By your uncle my brother, whilst guarding the mouth of the cave, was slain, and by my hand was your uncle shot, as he was forcing his way over the dead body of my brother. Then followed a deed of cruelty, such as was never before practised amongst Christians. The cave was closed, all the outlets stopped, and wood was burned around us, so that we might be slain with the stifling smoke—and many were so stifled;

and then, the cavern was entered by your father; and then, with his own hand, he slew my wife, the mother of my children, and my daughters—they were younger and fairer than you, Judith Lawson—dear to me as you are to your father; and then he slew my sons; and then, when he understood who I was, he spared my life; because he said he wished to give me life, as life would be a greater pain to me than death: and he was right; for he so doomed me to years of misery, and grief, and hopeless affliction. He forgot one thing, however," added the old man, with a malignant smile, "that in permitting me to live, my life might be so prolonged, that I would yet see the vengeance of God fall heavily on our oppressors; and it falls heavily on him to-day, when I can say to his daughter, that I could aid her to escape from a fate worse than death, but that, on the contrary, I will not move a finger to help her; that, instead of speaking one word of comfort or consolation, I should tell her, as I now tell you—live—live to be degraded; live and despair."

As the old man spoke these last words he hurried from the room, and in a moment afterwards Judith heard the heavy chains locked and bolted on the outside.

The strong mind and firm nerves of Judith were completely broken down for the moment by this outburst of vindictive passion and undying enmity. It would be difficult to determine whether the proud-hearted, high-spirited young women was most shocked or astonished by the accusations preferred against Ebenezer Lawson, by this obscure and half-witted menial, who called himself Gerald Geraghty.

Judith Lawson loved her father, and that love was repaid to her by an affection that demonstrated itself in every possible form in which wealth can exhibit its power.

In Judith's eyes her father was without a fault; his roughness, his coarseness, and his vulgarity of manners were unnoticed, and had never raised a blush in her cheek; because she was too fond of him to see any defect in his deportment, as she could discern in his gaunt features no ugliness. In her estimation, her father was the best, the bravest, and the greatest of mankind; because to her he had been always the most affectionate. If she could detect a fault in him, it was that he was too fond of her, and that fondness made him ambitious of seeing her united in marriage with some person of high rank, of illustrious name, and of boundless wealth. Such an ambition was, in her judgment, allied to noble qualities; it was, in itself, a pledge of a life of stainless honor, and nursed as it had been for the purpose of exalting her, she could not but love her father the more for the indulgence of such a sentiment, even though she herself neither sympathised with, nor responded to it.

But now, if she was to believe what the spiteful old man who had just left her had alleged, how was her idol shattered! how was that father, hitherto so loved, so cherished, and so venerated, degraded in her estimation! and what henceforth must she think of him! Not such as he had been, the brave but humble soldier, exalting himself by his achievements and his talents, and acquiring at the same time fortune and fame. *That* was the father she had loved and honored; but what was *this image* which wicked Gerald Geraghty would substitute for such a demi-god? A brutal, bloodthirsty, cowardly cut-throat; a wretch not only making war upon women and children, but a miscreant stabbing helpless infancy, and growing girlhood, and matron beauty, and defenceless old age; imbruing his horrid hands in the blood of fugitives, and acting the part of a cannibal, and smothering his fellow-creatures in their last refuge, the caverns of wild beasts!

Judith forgot her own griefs in the contemplation of these accusations against her father, and when knocks were next heard at her prison door, they remained for a long time unheeded.

CHAPTER VI.

COURTLY SUITORS—A QUARREL.

It was mid-day, and the warm rays of the fervid summer's sun diffused their heat around, and made it felt beneath the deepest shade of the thick-growing, umbrageous trees, under which was seated, or rather reclined against the trunk of an old oak, a young maiden, whose right hand listlessly held a fishing rod, from which a line depended into an adjacent but disregarded stream. The face, the form, and the dress of the maiden alike demonstrated her youth and her rank. Exquisitely fair, with delicately-formed features, a pinky blush in her cheeks, and her hair one bright mass of yellow flaxen ringlets, which descended to her shoulders, Kathleen Fitzpatrick did not, with her frail form, and broad-leafed girlish hat, and snow-white dress, appear at the first glance to be more than fifteen years of age. Those who spoke with her, but more especially those who came but for the brief time within the influence of her full, bright, sparkling, luminous blue eyes, were made to feel that Kathleen Fitzpatrick was some years older than she looked; that her thoughts were not those of a giddy girl, but that her heart and her head were worthy of a noble-thinking and generous woman.

She could not be said to be sitting idle, even though the pursuit with which she was apparently engaged did not occupy her thoughts. She seemed to have cast her line into the lazily-running stream that flowed at her feet, in order that she might employ her hands, whilst her thoughts were absorbed with other subjects; and it might be surmised that the subjects of the thoughts which engrossed her mind, were to be found in an open letter that lay on the ground beside her.

"What a strange story!" exclaimed Kathleen, at length speaking aloud her thoughts. "I know of no romance which has contrived such strange and unheard-of adventures as are to be found within the few pages of that letter. The playwright who could invent such a tale, would soon find his piece hissed off the stage for venturing so to outrage all notions of probability. There is nothing more marvellous in the *Seven Champions of Christendom*, nothing more improbable in William Shakspeare's *Winter's Tale*, nothing less like the real occurrences of life in one of Massinger's tragedies. And yet, if I am to believe the writer of this letter, not only are the statements there made literally true, but the hero of all these incredible adventures is my own first cousin—a Mr. Vincent Fitzpatrick—a gentleman that up to this time was in my estimation dead, buried, and consigned to 'the tomb of all the Capulets' years and years before Kathleen Fitzpatrick was born. If this be true, I am glad of it; if false, the pretender will soon be exposed. In either case, I must admit I have a woman's curiosity to see the individual who, whether rightfully or wrongfully, bears or assumes the name of a Fitzpatrick. I marvel as to the new-comer; considering his years, and I suppose size, we cannot say '*welcome little stranger;*' but I must own I am truly curious to know whether this new claimant has those remarkable family features of which my good aunt, Lady Diana, is always speaking—namely, the full, blue, Fitzpatrick eye, and the flowing, yellow, flaxen, Fitzpatrick hair, and short, upper, proud, Fitzpatrick lip,—features, as she boasts, of our pure Norman descent. Heigh ho! this world is all vanity!"

"Ay—all—all vanity; vanity and vexation of spirit, of outward shows, and bare-faced shams; such, for instance, as a young lady pretending to be occupied with rod and line, and ensnaring innocent fishes, when the fact is, her head is thinking how she will worry the heart-strings of the poor wretch she has already hooked, and the proof of whose capture lies in the open letter by her side."

Kathleen Fitzpatrick bounded to her feet, as these words were addressed to her; and looked with merry eyes and a smiling lip on the accomplished young gentleman who had given utterance to them.

The new-comer was dressed in the very height of the fashion, although it might be objected to him that his habiliments were better suited for the drawing-room than the open air. On his head was a long brown wig, which fell in full large curls over both his shoulders and down his back. His coat with wide short sleeves, and broad full skirts, as well as his long waistcoat with large pockets, were composed of thin, fine, light blue cloth, richly garnished at borders and button-holes with silver-lace; his white silk stockings were rolled over the knees, and his thin, high-heeled, dazzling polished shoes were decorated with buckles which glittered with diamonds. At his left side was a white-sheathed, silver-hilted, thin sword; and in his left hand, nearly concealed beneath the thick, rich fold of Brussels lace, was a small hat furnished with short white feathers, and looped up at one side with a band of silver-lace, which was fastened with a star of brilliants.

"My Lord of Arran," said Kathleen with a joyous laugh, " your words were those of an unbidden intruder, but your presence is that of an ever-welcome guest."

" Bird of the forest and bloom of the rose !" replied the gallant nobleman, " your words are as sweet as the notes of the nightingale, but in your wicked eyes is the mockery of the cuckoo, and the mischief of a magpie."

"You smother me with compliments, my Lord," said Kathleen; "we poor peasants in the country must not, if we would be wise, and avoid a fall, venture to run a tilt of words against you, Castle courtiers, who have the first retailing of all the old jokes exported from the mall, or Hampton Court, or Whitehall, to the banks of the Anna Liffey."

" Wood-nymph of Ossory !" answered Lord Arran," you have charms such as Lely never painted, because he wanted such an original to inspire his fancy and give truth to his pencil. You possess what they have not in London—Irish beauty, Irish wit, and Irish virtue."

"Thanks, my Lord, for your good opinion ; but bantering apart for the moment—if I were silly enough to believe that compliments universally addressed to every new face were solely invented for my benefit, and particularly and individually to be applied to myself, then circumstances have lately occurred which would give a semblance to my belief in my perfections. The very letter to which your lordship refers might be taken by me as the proof I was somewhat of an extraordinary person,—at least, if that letter speaks the truth, I have, most undoubtedly, very extraordinary relations."

"Was I right," said Lord Arran, his merry manner and joyous voice suddenly changing, "in saying or supposing that any one had the audacity to address a love-letter to you?"

"Any one!—*the audacity!*—to address a love-letter to me," said Kathleen, her voice also changing, and her face reddening. "What mean you, my Lord, by such language? How come you to assume a guardianship over my actions, or to pronounce without my permission an opinion as to the conduct of others, before you had ascertained what were my feelings towards them? By what right do you claim such a position in respect to me?"

"Pardon me, lady, for a warmth of expression which I feel was not justifiable, and the only palliation for which is the deep interest I take in the most trivial matter that may effect either your peace or happiness," cried Lord Arran, abashed by the spirit and independence Kathleen had manifested.

"My Lord Arran," said Kathleen, moved, not less by the humility of his manner than the apparent sincerity of his language, "of all the personages for whose acquaintance I am indebted to the kindness of my aunt, there is, I frankly tell you, not one in whom I am disposed to place greater confidence than yourself, nor upon whose opinion and judgment I would be more disposed to rely."

Lord Arran bowed humbly before the young lady, and there was a flash of triumph in his eyes as he advanced towards her to take her hand; but Kathleen stepping back, waved her hand, as if she wished to apprize him she had not yet done speaking:

"And my reason, my Lord," she continued, "for giving to you this preference—my reason for referring to that open letter at my feet, is, like my preference for you, beyond all

others, grounded upon this fact—that you alone of all the
men I have seen here, are the only one who has not persecuted me with insincere admiration, or with bare-faced
declarations of love, or unmeaning proposals of marriage.
You have, up to this time, been all that I would wish a
friend to be—frank, merry, and open-hearted, with no
fulsome adulation on your lips, and no insulting glances
in your eyes. I have, consequently, felt no more reserve
with you than if you were a woman of my own age.
Thus have I always thought of you, and so have I ever
esteemed you; and my pain, my resentment, was keen
indeed, when I fancied but a moment ago that you were
about to assume a different position with respect to me.
I am glad to see I was wrong; and there is my hand as
a proof of my full and complete reconciliation with you.'

Lord Arran accepted the small, white-gloved hand thus
tendered to him, and scarcely touching it with his lips,
he resumed the conversation in the same bantering tone in
which it had been first commenced. He desired as speedily
as he could to reinstate himself in his former position with
the fair Kathleen, certain that if he did so she would of
her own accord put him in possession of the contents of
the letter, which she had alluded to in such a strong
manner as to arouse feelings of jealousy in his heart.

"Wherefore," said Lord Arran, smiling, "was the fair
Florisibella absent from the sports of last Monday? All
the fashion from all parts of this poor province, by cour-
tesy called the kingdom of Ireland, were present at the
Races. Even my grave father, weighed down as he is
with affairs of state, was a looker-on. There were but
two illustrious individuals absent,—the gay and beauteous
widow, Lady Diana Massey, and her rusticated niece, the
peerless Kathleen, the wood-nymph of Ossory."

"The wood-nymph's aunt can alone solve your question," replied Kathleen. "The wood-nymph herself was absent for this good reason, that she now hears for the first time that there was to be such a grand assemblage of rank and fashion, and no doubt of beauty. With your lordship's taste and judgment upon such points, I should like to know what was the name of the belle that attracted most of observation, and, of course, admiration, on such an important occasion."

"Ho! ho!" said Lord Arran, bursting into a loud laugh. "Upon one point I can, without a moment's hesitation, reply to your inquiry,— that is, the name of the belle whose appearance attracted most observation. Only fancy, my innocent Florisibella, a young lady upon a war-charger; only fancy that young lady as tall as a trooper, and with a face as brown and as handsome as the very finest of his late highness Oliver Cromwell's picked life-guards; and then, only fancy this conspicuous, almost marvellous dame in a semi-male and half-female attire, dazzling with gold, and a stout hunting-sword by her side; and then only imagine yourself riding by her side; and you can fancy one of the most marvellous contrasts ever witnessed; for she is dark as you are fair, and she is stout as you are fragile."

"Excellent, my Lord," replied Kathleen, amused by this description. "You have given me what I did not ask for, a portrait of the most remarkable belle on the race-course; but you have not given me what I desired to know, and that is, the name of this most extraordinary creature."

"The name, the name!" said Lord Arran, as if he were trying to recollect. "Egad! that is true, I have failed in performing the task I undertook; the name of this wonderful young dragoon of a woman was, if I mistake not, Lawson; yes, I am quite sure it was Lawson."

"Lawson!" said Kathleen, in a tone of surprise.

"Yes, Lawson," repeated Lord Arran. "Oh! now I remember all about her. Her name is Judith Lawson, a young woman, it is said of large fortune, the only child of a certain Ebenezer Lawson, formerly a trooper in the army of Parliament, and who, like so many other worthless fellows that came to Ireland with Oliver Cromwell, has acquired estates and riches which belonged to better and honester men than themselves."

"Ebenezer Lawson! are you quite sure that you remember the name aright, and that the female you describe is his daughter?" inquired Kathleen, her voice trembling slightly as she put this question.

"Perfectly certain, my peerless—but, good heavens! what is the matter? or how come you to be so agitated, or what interest can you have in persons so far beneath you in every way?" asked Lord Arran, his bantering manner at once turning into seriousness, when he perceived that Kathleen changed colour when he persisted in asserting his certainty as to the name of Lawson.

"My Lord, I pray you to read this letter," said Kathleen, "and let me know what you think of its contents."

Lord Arran took up the letter, and at once commenced reading it. Kathleen watched him with intense interest, as he proceeded in perusing it. At first she observed him to smile with contempt, as he read the first page; then the smile of contempt was followed by a flush of anger; his eye-brows raised as if with surprise; then he stopped, turned back the pages he had read over, re-read them again and again; and exclamations of astonishment and surprise burst from him. Having concluded the letter, he slowly folded it up, and addressing Kathleen, said :—

"There are so many things in this letter so strange, so unexpected, and so surprising, that I really feel myself unable to advise you respecting it, without first seriously reflecting upon its contents. Leave me, then, here alone; I shall follow you in a few moments to the house, and there tell you what I think respecting it."

"Be it as you wish," said Kathleen, as she turned to depart.

"One word before you go," said Lord Arran; "have you as yet shown this letter to your aunt, or communicated its contents to her?"

"I have not had either the time or the opportunity to do so," answered Kathleen. "It was placed in my hands not one hour ago, whilst seated in the same place in which you found me."

"And by whom was it delivered?" asked Lord Arran.

"By an old man," said Kathleen, "who first asked me for alms, then inquired my name; and upon being assured I was the person for whom the epistle was intended, instantly quitted me."

"It is well," remarked Lord Arran; "and now may I ask this favour from you, that you will not speak to your aunt about this communication, which is in one respect valueless, because anonymous, until I have given you my opinion respecting it?"

"The favour is a slight one," remarked Kathleen, "and easily granted. Your lordship will find me in the drawing-room; my spinet is in prime order, and I have lately had some Parisian sonatas, on the merits of which I would wish to have the advantage of your lordship's taste and judgment."

No sooner was Lord Arran alone, than he drew forth the letter which he had already disparaged as anonymous; and again he read it over, slowly and deliberately, from the first word to the last.

"Of what vast importance are the contents of this letter to me!" said Lord Arran, his first thoughts showing that with him, as with the great bulk of mankind, the first primary consideration was his own personal and pecuniary interests.

"The writer of this letter appears to me to be an honest man, at least to believe sincerely what he states so positively.

"If the writer were a knave, he would not venture to refer to so many circumstances, a mis-statement in any one of which would convict him of wilful roguery.

"What, then, do his statements, as they affect me, amount to?

"That Kathleen Fitzpatrick is not what I supposed her to be; what my father believed her to be, when he encouraged me to win her affections.

"Kathleen Fitzpatrick, instead of being what I supposed, one of the largest fortunes in Ireland, is solely dependant for a dowry upon the good feeling of her aunt, a lady so young in years, and so jovial in disposition, that the great probability is, she will marry again.

"It is well I have not committed myself with any formal declaration of love—with any regular proposal of marriage; and if I had," said Lord Arran, with some bitterness of feeling, and stings of selfish vanity—"remembering what happened to-day, there is a chance that the son of the Lord Lieutenant would have been rejected by a portionless country girl!

"As it is, I am free, and I can cast back my eyes upon the past without reproach. I can, therefore, as a disinterested person, look to the circumstances disclosed in this letter, not as they reach me, but as they touch the interests of Kathleen.

"Rich or poor, she is a lovely girl, and is worthy of having a friend, though I cannot sacrifice myself, my position, and my prospects, by becoming her husband.

"If I believe this letter-writer, there are two persons, either of whom being living, she has not the smallest claim upon the property to which rumour had declared her to be entitled.

"Either of these claimants, as a matter of course and right, will dispossess her.

"And yet, let me think; if her claim be, as I fear it is, without a shadow of foundation, or a probability of success, how comes it that there is some dark undescribed conspiracy against her—a conspiracy in which that other girl's name is mentioned, in which the tall, black-looking Amazonian's father is a participator? or how is it, that my father, the Lord Lieutenant, an actor in the affairs of Ireland for the last forty years, who must have known old Colonel Fitzpatrick, and must have heard the strange story of the son; how happens it, that he, so grave, so reserved, so cautious, so far-seeing, and so prudent, should have recommended me to seek for this young girl's hand, because with that hand would be transferred to her husband the richest lands and the finest fortune in Ireland? There must be in all these inexplicable combinations of circumstances some state secret, which I have not the experience to comprehend, nor the wit to fathom.

"One safe conclusion as regards myself I can deduce from it all, and that is, to be guarded in my advances—not to commit myself by word or look with Miss Kathleen Fitzpatrick: to act as the young lady herself has already told me she wishes I should conduct myself—that is, as a very well-behaved young gentleman—not to act the lover, but the friend.

"With the knowledge I have of the maiden's expectations, it will not be necessary to repeat the warning; at least, I shall consult my father before I turn another compliment to her beauty.

"Heigh ho! I wish she had the fortune she was represented to possess; for after all, I find I love her more than I wish; and that she has got such a hold upon my affections, that I shall not be able, without a long and painful struggle, to shake her off.

"Fore God! I love her too much to wed her to the worst of all kinds of penury—poverty and a title.

"I will sacrifice for her everything but myself; rather than make her my wife, without a fortune, I will endure the pangs of absence, the pain of regret, and many long nights of inconsolable sorrow.

"Here are noble generous resolutions. I must watch myself, or I shall never have the strength to keep them.

"Meanwhile, what advice should I give to this fair maiden with respect to this anonymous letter?

"To treat it seriously, or as a fabrication?

"If I desire her to look upon it in a serious light, then I must also advise her to show the letter to Lady Diana; and the instant she finds any danger threatens her niece, or herself, through her niece, then she will—I know her well—at once fly to England; and so deprive *me* of these thousand agreeable *tête-a-têtes*, and of the chance of becoming the husband of Kathleen, supposing Kathleen should eventually become possessed of a great fortune.

"On the other hand, if I treat it altogether as a fabrication, Kathleen is too shrewd and sharp-witted to be blinded by me. I should lose the confidence she now reposes in me.

"What, then, is to be done? To say that the matter is not so serious as that it is necessary to alarm her aunt about it; but that one useful lesson may be drawn from it—to be more cautious for the future; not to go abroad; never to venture outside the park-walls without a strong armed escort, and to allege as a reason for this, an unusual attack of nervousness caused by the alarming reports she has heard of the fearful exploits of Redmond O'Hanlon. Yes, that will do; and meanwhile I have the advantage of possessing a secret in common with the enchantress Kathleen, a circumstance of no slight importance, should subsequent events render it desirable for me, and beneficial as regards herself, that I should publicly become a suitor for her hand. Yes, that will do; and now for the fair Kathleen, and a sonata in the drawing-room,—an excellent whet for one of the amiable Diana Massey's luxurious dinners."

Lord Arran was thus thinking upon his future plans, as he advanced towards the mansion, when he suddenly found his steps arrested by a fashionable and handsome dame, who seemed approaching to the middle age, and whose mature beauties were on the present occasion heightened by the hectic flush in her round cheeks, and the more brilliant light in her jet black eyes. "Oh, my Lord, my Lord!" she cried, in a voice of alarm, " what a horrid country is this we live in! better to be a man than a woman in Ireland. They do not run away with men, and they do with women. Oh, the horrid Irish!"

"The difference in Ireland between men and women," said Lord Arran, smiling, "is this; the men capture the women, but the women act with still greater cruelty, for they not only captivate the men, but sometimes kill them with their cruelty."

"My Lord of Arran, this is no time for jesting," said

Lady Diana Massey. "I have been informed but this moment of a frightful case of abduction; and you must have seen, no later than last Monday, the lady upon whom this awful outrage has been perpetrated."

"An abduction—on Monday last—I must have seen the lady. I entreat of you, Lady Diana, speak more plainly; for at present, all I can say is, that I am utterly at a loss to comprehend the cause for your alarm."

"The lady I allude to is, as I am informed, a Miss Judith Lawson—a person of low birth, but large fortune."

"Judith Lawson!" exclaimed Lord Arran. "Why, she has been before now the subject of conversation in this very spot. Strange that a name before unthought of, or unknown, should on a sudden be mixed up with events that may affect the whole future course and action of a life. What of Miss Judith Lawson, for I certainly did see her at the race-course on last Monday?"

"I have just received a letter," said Lady Diana, "in which it is stated that Miss Lawson was, on her way home, attacked by Redmond O'Hanlon's gang near Drogheda; that her female attendants, and her two male-servants, who were in waiting upon her, were robbed of their horses and money, but not otherwise injured; whereas Miss Lawson has been carried off, and, it is now supposed, concealed in some of Redmond O'Hanlon's hiding places—but what will become of her no one knows, and no one can ever guess. She may be detained to become the hundred-and-first wife of O'Hanlon, or she may be retained for the purpose of being sold to some poor royalist, on account of her large fortune; or she may be merely kept in safe custody for the purpose of extorting for her release a large ransom from her father, who is reported to be enormously rich. Whatever be her destiny, one cannot but pity the fate of the poor girl, and shudder to think what would become of one if the like chanced to be their own lot. What in the world, for instance, would become of *me*, my Lord, if I were to find myself made the hundred-and-second wife of Mr. Redmond O'Hanlon?"

"That you would find Mr. Redmond O'Hanlon for once in his life telling the truth," said Lord Arran, " and on his knees making, if you required it, his solemn oath, that his hundred-and-second wife surpassed in beauty all the hundred-and-one charmers who had preceded her."

"Oh! it is all very well for you men to joke on such a subject; but for a poor, lone, and not very old woman as I am, the thought of such a terrible termination to one's career is enough to freeze the very soul in one's body with terror. I at least," said Lady Diana, " will not submit to it; I will not stay a week longer in this abominable, inhuman, woman-persecuting country. Before I am two days older, Kathleen and I shall be on our way to England. On Saturday next, your lordship will, I expect, be bidding us farewell, at the Ring's End, from which the passenger-vessel takes its departure."

"Can you be really serious, Lady Diana, in thinking of flying from Ireland, because a young woman of low birth has been run away with, and, for aught we know, run away with by her own consent, and in accordance with an arrangement to which she was a consenting party; for such things I do, with all my respect and veneration for the fair sex, assert have happened from the days of Helena of Lacedæmon down to the present hour? Why, my good lady, I have seen the damsel by whose rumoured misfortune you would guide your own destiny. As a gentlemen, I am bound to say I saw nothing to her discredit; but as an observer of mankind—ay, and of womankind too—I would say, judging of her by her appearance, her flaunty dress, her bold mien, and her saucy face, she is exactly that description of an Helena who would not run away from a Theseus, in order that she might be forced afterwards to choose a drivelling Menelaus for a husband. Nature does not write with a true hand, if it has not stamped upon face, feature, and figure of Judith Lawson the courage of a soldier, with the form of a woman. Be certain that the man who ran away with that lady against her will must, if he had common sense, have made his own will, before he ventured upon so perilous an enterprise. There was no abduction, be certain, in the case of Miss Judith Lawson. It was a runaway match, and called—for the purpose of saving the lady's honor, and to reconcile her father to a misfortune—an abduction."

"Well! well! what stupid and lying fables are circulated about the plainest facts," sagaciously remarked Lady Diana Massey. "It must be as your lordship says. It was no abduction at all, but a runaway match, for which all the preparations had been, no doubt, made before the young fugitive appeared on the race-course; and, I dare say, that Mr. Redmond O'Hanlon, upon whose broad shoulders every misdeed that occurs in Ireland is fathered, had no more to do with the abduction of Miss Judith Lawson, than he had with the flight of that naughty lady who ran away with one of your ancestors, an ill-behaved King of Leinster."

"I repudiate the connexion with MacMurrough, although I cannot undertake to vindicate the reputation of the celebrated chieftain, Count Redmond O'Hanlon, who, whatever his faults, his errors, and his crimes, cannot be denied to be, both by birth and education, a gentleman.

We, Lady Diana, who can claim for ourselves purity of blood, and noble descent, should be the last to deny those advantages to one's enemy, when he is rightfully and justly entitled to them. My father, I know, would willingly see Ireland well rid of Redmond O'Hanlon, whether by rope or gun—by stratagem, the law, or open force; but, saying so much against that notorious partisan, I am bound also to say, from all I have heard of the Count, that he would not, for the world's wealth, demean himself by a marriage with one whose birth was so low, or rather so sordid as that of Judith Lawson. But I hope," added Lord Arran, "I have said enough to change your determination as to leaving Ireland; that you will remain, as you have done here, in perfect peace and security, and, occasionally, I hope, more frequently for the future, gracing my father's court with your presence."

"No, my Lord," said the lady, gravely shaking her head, "you have not changed my determination, for it has not been hastily adopted. I have, for some time past, been thinking of carrying it into execution, and the incident we have been speaking of has but served to provoke its sudden announcement, and speedy fulfilment. We are not sufficiently protected where we are. I am not old enough to be the sole protector of one so young, and fo fair, and of such wealth as Kathleen will, when she comes of age, be mistress of. Affairs in Ireland, the state of anarchy into which society has been cast, and from which even the wise and prudent administration of your father, the Duke of Ormonde, has not yet been able to extricate it—the insecurity of life, of property, the frequency of such a crime as that of abduction,—all are warnings to me to betake myself to England as a place of safety, of security, of peace, of repose, of——"

"My dear lady," said Lord Arran, in a much more grave tone than he had yet addressed her, "have you well considered the step you are about to take? Have you considered not merely the condition of Ireland, but the state of affairs in England at this time? You say that life and property are insecure in Ireland. Are you aware that, at the very time we are speaking, neither life, nor property, nor liberty are secure in England?"

"My lord, you astonish me," exclaimed the amazed Lady Diana. "No security for life, nor property, nor liberty in England! What do you mean?"

"Simply what I say," replied Lord Arran. "Has not your ladyship heard anything from your friends of the Popish plot?"

"To be sure I have," replied the lady. "I have heard that some vile impostor, a notorious swindler, named Oates, combined with other persons, already convicted of vile offences, have been concocting an improbable tale, in which all sorts of incomprehensible and impossible falsehoods are blended together; and I have heard that a fanatic named Dr. Tongue, and that notorious turn-coat, the Republican Ashley Cooper,—the same base man who sat as a judge, and condemned to death men who had been participators in his own crimes of high treason against the late King—I have heard that these persons have been disturbing the public mind in England with tales of terror about what they call 'the horrid, hellish Popish plot.' But how does that affect me? or why should such a lying tale be of the smallest interest to me, neither I nor my niece being Roman Catholics?"

"Lady Diana Massey," said Lord Arran, in tones of deep solemnity, and showing by his manner that he was deeply affected by what he said to her, "I pledge you my honor as an Irish peer, that if you repeated in England the words you have just spoken to me, had you thus ventured so to speak of the Rev. Dr. Oates, or Mr. Bedloe, or the Rev. Dr. Tongue, or my Lord Shaftesbury, or expressed but a thousandth part of the doubt you have uttered to me as to the truth of the accusations now made against the Roman Catholics, you would, most probably, be torn to pieces by the mob, you would certainly, if you escaped with life for the moment, be conveyed to the most fetid dungeon in Newgate, and most probably be tried at the next sessions upon a charge of being a participator in 'the horrid, hellish Popish plot,' and whatever Oates might invent and swear against you, and that Bedloe would swear and corroborate, would be believed by judge and jury, though you had a thousand witnesses to contradict them, and you would, before three months had passed away, be convicted and executed as a traitor. There is not a man of common sense in England who does not think as you do of Titus Oates and his confederates; but at the same time, there is not a man of common sense who would place himself in the hands of his enemies, by expressing aloud what in his heart he believes respecting them, their perjuries, and their plot. England is, at this day, labouring under the fever-heat of a popular mania, and a universal delusion, and that mania and delusion are now comprised in the same words—' the horrid Popish plot'—a ' plot' in which the accused are the victims, and 'the accusers' the real conspirators; but upon the whole story, the application is this—that true or false, credible or incredible, possible or impossible, it all comes to a case, where the multitude are taken captive in their imaginations, and have no longer any other rule, measure, will, or liking, than what they draw from the dictate of their 'leaders.' And who are their leaders? A fanatic madman, named Tongue, a canting knave, Titus Oates, and an unbelieving hypocrite, Shaftesbury, of whom it has been most justly, truly, and aptly said, that 'he was as good a Protestant as any one can be supposed to be who could atheistically call the *New Testament* the *new cheat*.' I may add, that to give these several leaders or concoctors of the Popish plot their due, there has been 'nothing wanting to their purposes that either fraud, industry, confidence, or hypocrisy could furnish.' And you, Lady Diana, propose to exchange the comparative quietness of Ireland for the purpose of plunging into the midst of the sanguinary tumult that now pervades all parts of England. I tell you, in all sincerity, that with your outspoken honesty, you could not calculate upon a day's safety or an hour's repose in England. As yet we are free to speak what we think of the Popish plot; but how long we may be so is more than I can venture to promise. That the attempt is making to extend the flame to this country, I am certain; for I see the proofs of the pressure upon my father by the proclamations he has been issuing against Popish priests, bishops, and Jesuits. Better, however, for you to live in a land governed by him, than to place yourself in the power of the English Privy Council, and within the reach of a warrant signed by Shaftesbury, or of a declaration corroborated with the ready and corrupt oaths of an Oates, a Bedloe, a Prance, or a Dangerfield."

"Oh, dear! oh, dear!" cried the now-terrified Lady Diana, "how numberless are the anxieties and how great the dangers that beset a poor woman who hast lost her husband! What a sad thing it is to be a widow!"

"Excuse me, Lady Diana, for differing in opinion from you," said Lord Arran; "but at present you are much safer as a Protestant widow, than you would be if your first husband were still living, and you never had been a widow; for he was a Roman Catholic, and his wealth and position would have rendered him an object of suspicion, and you, as his wife, would be involved in the same danger to which he was exposed."

"Then your lordship's advice to me is to remain in Ireland," said Lady Diana.

"Decidedly so," answered Lord Arran; "but as your ladyship honors me by asking my opinion as to the course you should adopt, I would take the liberty of recommending to you, considering the state of this country, how its roads are beset with highwaymen, and how many men of desperate fortunes are to be met with in every province, that neither you nor your niece should ever venture abroad unless attended by an armed escort, on whose vigilance and courage you could rely."

"I will do exactly as your lordship suggests," replied the lady; "but I have detained you too long in the open air; let us proceed towards the house."

"Honor me by resting on my arm," said Lord Arran, as he walked onward with the lady; "and now as your ladyship has so favoured me with your confidence, and as you cannot but be conscious how deeply I am interested in all that affects yourself and the honor of your family, I would take the liberty of asking if you have ever heard a rumour of Colonel Fitzpatrick and of his son being both still living."

"They are idle rumours, my lord," replied Lady Diana; "they are the vague and baseless visions of the Irish peasantry, who are attached with a child-like truth and fidelity to the ancient owners of the soil, and who, wishing the Colonel and his son were both living, have readily circulated an idle tale, as if it were an undoubted fact."

"Is there any possibility of your ladyship being mistaken?" asked Lord Arran, with an anxiety he could not conceal.

"Not the slightest," replied the lady. "If the Colonel, or the Colonel's son, were living, I should be the first to hear of them. There is no reason why either should conceal from me the knowledge of his existence. On the contrary, I ought to be, and I am sure I should be, the very first person to whom such a communication would be made. But supposing an impostor in the case—supposing some knave desired to set up a false claim to the property, then the last person he would wish to see or to communicate with would be myself; because I must be, beyond all others, in a position to detect the imposture."

Lord Arran's heart bounded with delight, as he heard these positive declarations from Lady Diana. He walked on for some time in silence, considering within himself whether the present was not a most propitious moment for avowing himself a suitor for the hand of Kathleen; and it was with the intention of leading to such a declaration, that he thus resumed the conversation:—

"I have heard such rumours as I have referred to; but henceforth I shall know how to treat them, or any one venturing to support them. I hope that the time, the place, and the opportunity may be afforded to me, when I may meet face to face either the person calling himself Colonel Fitzpatrick, or the son of Colonel Fitzpatrick, and on the instant I will denounce such persons as knaves, and publicly brand them as impostors."

As Lord Arran gave utterance to these words, he felt himself struck suddenly and sharply on the cheek, and at the same instant perceived that the blow was inflicted by a glove that had been flung at him. As he did so, he perceived a man standing within a thick clump of trees and close-set bushes, which he had just passed. His assailant, he perceived, was a tall, fair-complexioned young man, in the riding dress of a gentleman of the day, and that he stood with one hand grasping his sword, and the fingers of the other hand to his lips, as if challenging him to a combat, and at the same time warning him to be silent.

Such was the interpretation Lord Arran put upon the incident that had just occurred; and therefore, concealing as well as he could his emotions from the lady, he walked on leisurely with her for about a hundred yards, and trying to occupy her attention with a conversation so vague, that he could not tell the substance of it when it was over, he stopped suddenly, and said, "I beg your ladyship's pardon, I wish to return for one of my gloves which I dropped in the park; I am sure I know the very spot where I can find it again."

"One of your gloves, my Lord!" said Lady Diana; "your lordship is labouring under some delusion; why, you have, at this moment, both your gloves on your hands."

"Oh! true, true," replied Lord Arran, stammering and confused, "but the glove I wish to find again is a riding glove. There are some circumstances connected with it, which would cause me great grief if I could not recover it. I pray your pardon, Lady Diana, I shall be with you again in ten minutes."

Lord Arran, as he spoke, hurried back to the spot where the glove was still lying. Before he could reach it his assailant advanced from the clump of trees in which he had been concealed, and taking up the glove stood there, holding it in his hand, and awaiting his lordship's approach.

A thrill of surprise passed through his lordship's frame, as he regarded the stranger, a man about thirty years of age, and in height nearly six feet, with broad shoulders and well-knit frame, alike indicative of great strength and activity. It was not, however, the stranger's manly form and noble bearing that excited the surprise of Lord Arran; but it was his likeness in features to Kathleen Fitzpatrick, and beyond all things, in his long, flowing, flaxen, yellow ringlets, which covered his shoulders, and in his luminous large blue eyes.

"I presume, sir," said Lord Arran, "you are the owner of the glove, which was flung at me."

"I am," replied the stranger; "and by my hand it was cast at you."

"With the intention of insulting me?" said Lord Arran.

"Yes," answered the stranger; "I repelled an insult with an insult."

"Insult you, sir!" said Lord Arran. "I never saw you in my life before this moment."

"An offence can be more strongly conveyed by words than looks," remarked the stranger.

"You are aware, I presume, from your appearance, of the consequences of what you have done," said Lord Arran, and his colour slightly changed as he spoke.

"Certainly—and ready on the instant to encounter them," answered the stranger, laying his hand on his sword.

"Not here, sir—not now, at all events," replied Lord Arran, "for here we would be liable to interruption. You compel me, sir, to embark in a quarrel that cannot be appeased without bloodshed: I have a right to know that I risk my life with an equal."

"I did not, until this moment," said the stranger, with a somewhat scornful voice, "suppose that a Butler would bear a blow from an inferior: that an offence given would level all distinctions, in the estimation at least of the offended party. But be satisfied, my Lord, although I do not bear a title, I am, as a gentleman, your equal."

"And your name is——" said Lord Arran, eagerly,

"Vincent Fitzpatrick," replied the stranger.

"Well, Mr. Vincent Fitzpatrick, meet me in the park to-morrow evening at five o'clock, with one other person to vouch for you as the person you describe yourself to be, and then we shall cross swords with each other."

"Be it so," replied Vincent Fitzpatrick; "but as it is not your lordship's convenience to dispose of this quarrel at once, and where we stand, may I venture to suggest, that mutual friends may arrange for us both the time and the place where they and we may be secure from that interruption of which you are now apprehensive."

"Very well, sir," answered Lord Arran. "Let me know where you are to be found, and a friend shall wait upon you."

"The hotel in Cook-street, of which a man named John Elliott is landlord," said Vincent, as he turned away from Lord Arran.

"This is no impostor," said Lord Arran to himself. "There can be no doubt he is what he calls himself. His look—his very voice, are the same as his cousin's. His quarrel is a just one; but then he has struck me, and that blow must be avenged, and can alone be wiped out with blood. Would! it were not so; but the laws of society are inexorable; and before to-morrow's sun has set, he or I shall be one of its victims."

CHAPTER VII.

RETRIBUTION.

"WELL, Ebenezer, what tidings of your health to-day? How goes your wound? Still suffering pain?"

"The pain is nothing, Ludlow; what most effects me is the loss of strength, the inevitable result of the awful medicines with which I have been drenched."

Such was the address, and such the response, with which Ludlow and Lawson saluted each other, upon the former visiting the chamber in which the latter lay—an upper room in "the Cock" hotel and tavern in Cook-street, and from the window of which there was a view of the city-wall, the river, and the green fields of Oxmantown, on the opposite beach. The room itself was a very small one, barely sufficient to hold the bed in which Lawson lay, the chair on which Ludlow sat, and a table, on which were arranged a few phials of medicine. The room was boarded on all sides, and it appeared to be one of many small rooms, which had been, like the boxes in the coffee-room, made out of one large apartment, by being divided from each other by thin partitions.

Here lay Lawson; his right-hand swathed with linen bands, and his cheek, more pale and haggard than usual, showed that he had gone through much bodily pain and weakness in the course of the last few days.

"I had hoped to find you better and stronger," said Ludlow, as he clasped the outstretched left hand of Lawson within both his own; "I had even hoped I might have found you out of bed, and able to bestride a horse for some hours; because, in all my experience of men, whether soldiers or civilians, I never knew one, where an enterprise, requiring courage and skill, was to be undertaken, upon whose strong hand and cool head, I could place such unhesitating reliance as Ebenezer Lawson."

"Reserve your compliments for those who attach value to them," sulkily replied Lawson, his brutal temper irritated by the pain of his wound, and the weakness of his body. "I am as God made me, a sure friend, and an unrelenting enemy. Instead of speaking of me, tell me of yourself, what you have done, and what you are prepared to do."

"I have had the house and park at Palmerstown, where Kathleen Fitzpatrick resides with her aunt, beset with spies day and night; I have ascertained the number of domestics, male and female, in the house; I have found out in what part of the house are the sleeping apartments of the ladies; I have discovered what are the habits of all in the house; their time for going forth and returning home; the time spent by them in the park, and I have also ascertained that the only person of consequence who is a constant visitor at the house, is Lord Arran, the second son of the Lord Lieutenant."

"What age is the second son of the Duke of Ormonde?" asked Lawson.

"Five-and-twenty."

"And unmarried?"

"Yes."

"Then be sure," said Lawson, "that the cunning sly old fox, the Duke of Ormonde,—he who never yet did anything for King or Commonwealth, but with a view to his own interest,—has marked out Kathleen Fitzpatrick cas a wife for his son, Lord Arran. Our wily old Lord Lieutenant is as proud as Lucifer; and rest assured, he never would consent to his son marrying a woman without a title, unless she had fortune sufficient to purchase a coronet."

"I care not what may be the schemes of the Lord Lieutenant," observed Ludlow, "provided my simple plan of abduction be crowned with success, and of that——."

"Have you ever seen Lord Arran?" said Lawson, suddenly, and interrupting his companion, as if some new idea had occurred to his mind.

"I have, very often," answered Ludlow, unable to guess at the reason why Lawson put the question.

"Then you can tell me whether it is true or not the statement I have often heard, that he is one of the finest men of the day; that he was remarkable for his manly beauty and noble figure, amongst the best-looking courtiers of Charles the Second?"

"I never heard him so spoken of," said Ludlow; "but I can state, of my own knowledge, that I never yet saw a finer face, or a more graceful figure with a man."

"Indeed!" said Lawson, with a bitter smile. "It is very generous and very candid in you to say so, at the very moment that you are contemplating to become the husband of a young lady, who must have eyes to see as well as yourself, and yet to whom this Lord Arran has been paying his addresses, as a lover, and in exchange for whose perfections, you purpose to bestow upon her, not rank, nor a title, but your own deformities. Look in the mirror, Ludlow, and tell me did you ever gaze at a face more calculated to excite a woman's aversion than your own?"

Ludlow started up, as if every word that Lawson uttered was a spark of fire, and that each burned into his flesh as it reached his ear. His first impulse was to stab his companion as he lay prostrate before him, but a second glance at the huge and gigantic man who thus taunted him, restrained his wrath, and inspired him, if not with fear, at least with prudence. He restrained the rage that inflamed his heart, and then, in broken accents, which ill concealed his excited feelings, he thus addressed Lawson :—

"Why do you say those things to me, Ebenezer? We have in this matter but one common interest. Here is the bond, signed, sealed, and duly attested, in which I bind myself, under heavy penalties, to share the Fitzpatrick property, both what I now hold and what I may afterwards acquire, equally with you."

"Let me look at the bond," said Lawson, stretching forth his left hand. "Hold it open for me, in order that I may with the greater ease and facility master its contents."

Lawson sat up in the bed and examined the document, clause by clause, with all the scrupulous and verbal accuracy, and watchful caution of a practised lawyer. He then folded it carefully up, and pushing it under his pillow, said with a tone of contented joy, which was the very opposite of his sulky demeanour hitherto :—

"You have, I think—I am almost certain, acted fairly and honorably, at least by me, Edward. Why did you not show me this precious parchment at first? Had you done so, I would not have made the remarks which have given you offence. Not, however, that the objection to your personal appearance is one of slight moment. It is a difficulty in *our* way—for now I am heart and soul with you, and I look upon your project as my own, upon your success as my success, upon your failure—if you should fail—as a great and grievous loss to me. Tell me, then, what is your project? I promise you, without knowing it, my full and hearty co-operation."

"I propose to carry out my old plan—to take away Kathleen Fitzpatrick from her aunt's house, by stratagem if

I can, and by open force, if stratagem should fail me," replied Ludlow.

"And having carried her off, where do you propose to place her for safe custody?" asked Lawson; "for some days must elapse between her abduction and the completion of your project by marriage."

"Well," answered Ludlow, "a degraded parson—an old chaplain at Whitehall, when Cromwell sat there as King, and called himself Protector—I have hired his services for the day; and it is my intention to take him with me, and by his means to have performed the marriage ceremony, or what will answer my purpose as well as if the same ceremony were performed in the King's Chapel in the Castle."

"An absurd project!" observed Lawson, "and one that would be sure to fail. What! do you think you could marry Kathleen Fitzpatrick, as if she were a common gipsy, in the middle of the high road? No, no. You might be pursued—in all probability you would be interrupted, and the lady snatched from your hands, in the same state of safety as if you had never laid hold of her. What you have first to do, is to have prepared a safe place to retreat upon, a place with which you have no connexion, a place in which the lady's friends would never think of seeking her or of finding you, suppose by any accident you were suspected of being a participator in the outrage upon her person. I can, without a moment's reflection, suggest a better place than yours; for here I have the means to aid you. What think you of carrying the young dame to my house? You know how lonely is its situation, how few ever resort to it."

"Take her to your house!" repeated Ludlow, musing over the unexpected proposition just made to him.

"Yes, take her to my house," added Lawson. "You

are aware the only mistress it possesses is my daughter Judith. I can easily invent an excuse—a trip for a few weeks to England, for example—to induce her joyfully to abandon the place for as long a time as you may want it. Take my word for it, many days will be required to reconcile a young lady, who expects to be married to Lord Arran, to the change of accepting in lieu of such a lord, one of your age and appearance, as a husband."

"I am more disposed for open force and undisguised violence. In such a case as this," said Ludlow, "I never expect to win the lady's love; all I am struggling for is the possession of her fortune."

"I admire your sentiments, and, in this case, entirely approve of them," observed Lawson. "The desire of a brisk young fellow to revel in a lady's fortune is an excuse for any rudeness of which he may be guilty. At the same time, the less there is of open force and undisguised violence, the better; not that I object to them, you will observe, if they are indispensable—that is, if they are absolutely unavoidable. But say, do you approve of my plan for carrying away the lady to my house? because if you do, I will on the instant write a letter to Judith, directing her to come with her waiting-maid, and the two men especially devoted to her service, at once to Dublin."

"Pardon me, Captain Ludlow—forgive me, comrade Lawson, for intruding upon your private conversation," said the robust landlord of "the Cock," as he entered the room, his broad, honest face now clouded by an expression of grief that he did not desire to conceal. "Excuse me, I say, for thus breaking in upon you; but there is at this moment a rumour circulating amongst the company below stairs, which is of such deep interest to one of you, that I could not refrain, even for a moment, communicating it, in the hope that he whom it most deeply concerns, may be in a position to contradict it."

Ludlow and Lawson looked at each other in mute surprise, and both nodded their heads to Elliott to proceed.

"I fancied," said Elliott, wishing to break the intelligence he had to tell, as well as he could, "that I heard my former comrade, Lawson, say, as I opened the door, he was about to write to his daughter."

"Yes, I did say so," replied Lawson.

"And where," asked Elliott, "were you about to address a letter to her?"

"To my own house in the country," answered Lawson, as yet without the slightest suspicion of the evil tidings that were about to be conveyed to him.

"And when did you last hear from her?" said Elliott, trembling as he put the question.

"Upon last Saturday, when she wrote, amongst other things, to say, she was going to some grand festival at which the Lord Lieutenant was expected to be present."

"Alas! alas! my poor old comrade!" said Elliott bursting into tears.

"What mean you, John Elliott?" exclaimed Lawson, bounding up in the bed. "Speak out—speak out; has anything happened Judith? has she broken an arm, or a leg, or is she dead—dead—dead? Speak, I say, out at once, or you will drive me mad; you see I am cool; I am collected; I am calm; I can say, I suppose, that Judith, my beloved Judith, is dead—dead; and yet you see I am firm, very firm, John Elliott. Speak out, man; say the worst at once; say she is dead, and there's an end on't."

"Would! that I could say she *was* dead," replied John Elliott; "she is worse than dead."

"Not dead! and yet worse than dead," said Lawson,

his faculties so benumbed that there was a long, solemn, and fearful pause between every word he uttered. "Not dead — and — yet — worse—than—dead," he repeated. "What can he mean? Why must grief be tortured with riddles? John Elliott, as you hope for salvation, as you always had the character of an honest man, speak out in plain language the rumour respecting *her*." The wretched man's voice trembled, for he felt he had not strength to pronounce the name of Judith—" Repeat, I entreat of you, whatever you have heard of *her*, in the very words they were told to you."

"Well, then, so adjured, my poor comrade," answered John Elliott, "I will tell you what I have heard; but though I believe it is not all truth, there is, I fear, too much truth in it for your peace of mind."

"Speak on—speak on," said Lawson, scarcely able to articulate the words with his parched lips, and his voice choking in his throat.

"The topic of conversation in the coffee-room," said Elliott, "is your daughter—Judith."

"My daughter become the town-talk? O God!" cried Lawson, sinking back upon the pillow. "But proceed, John Elliott; you see I am calm—very calm—very, very calm, and so patient!" and as he so spoke, he gnawed the sheets between his teeth.

"It is said that your daughter, in returning from the races with her tire-woman and two men-servants, was attacked upon the road near Drogheda, by Redmond O'Hanlon and a large band of armed Tories and Rapparees; that the tire-woman fainted; that the two male-servants fled, or were in collusion with the leader of the gang, O'Hanlon; that Miss Lawson defended herself bravely, that she shot two of the assailants, and would have killed

Redmond O'Hanlon himself, but that one of her servants gave her an unloaded, instead of a loaded musket."

"My own brave daughter! my gallant, high-spirited, generous, and courageous Judith!" exclaimed Lawson. "Go on, Elliott, for as yet you have told me nothing but what is grateful to me to hear."

"Ah, I wish my tale stopped there," added Elliott; "but, alas! I must proceed. Your daughter and the servants were taken prisoners by O'Hanlon's gang. The servants were robbed and sent away otherwise unharmed: not so with your daughter."

"What mean you, Elliott?" cried Lawson, as Elliott here paused, as if to recover breath, before he proceeded. "What mean you? Assuredly they did not maltreat her, they did not commit any act of cruelty upon her, because she had courageously defended her life?"

"I cannot tell you what they did with her, comrade," replied Elliott. "I have told you all that is known. What is certain is, that your daughter has been carried away a prisoner by Redmond O'Hanlon's gang; and the rumour is, that the abduction was a long time planned, because she is known to be your only child, and because it is said she has a very large fortune, and it is now supposed she never will escape, if she escape at all with her life, but by accepting some thief or murderer, or follower of O'Hanlon's, as a husband; and, therefore, nought but degradation or dishonor awaits her——But good heavens! Captain Ludlow, aid me in holding this unhappy man in his bed. Alas! alas! he is going stark, staring mad. Help! help! help there below stairs! help! help! or this poor distracted father will destroy himself."

CHAPTER VIII.

A RENEGADE.

Upon both sides of the small apartment in which Ebenezer Lawson lay, and in rooms not larger than his, there were, at the moment of the outburst of rage and agony described in the last chapter, three persons. In one of the rooms Vincent Fitzpatrick and the individual John Elliott had called "Mr. Brown," and in the other, sitting alone, the old man who had sate opposite to Ludlow and Lawson in the coffee-room, and in the attempt to insult whom, Lawson had received the wound which now confined him to his bed.

The cries of Elliott for "help" did not induce any one of these three persons to respond to his call; for it so happened that in both rooms had been heard much of the conversation which had preceded Lawson's maniacal demonstrations of grief, rage, and despair.

Instead of aiding Elliott, or rendering the smallest assistance to Lawson, Vincent Fitzpatrick and his friend remained in their room, and the old man descended to the coffee-room.

"What villains these are!" said the old man to himself, "and yet what miscreants are they victims to? Strange that the very weapon which Lawson was employing to destroy the peace and happiness of another's family, should be turned against himself, and the misery and despair to which he was about to consign his neighbour, should have overwhelmed himself, and converted his stable homestead into a mass of ruins. I was right in sending an anonymous letter to Kathleen to put her on her guard against both Lawson and Ludlow. I must now address to her another, recommending to her never to stir outside the house, or at once to betake herself to England. I must afterwards see if I cannot contrive the means, either here or in England, to bring about an interview between her and Vincent; and on the success of that interview, I look to the restoration of the fortunes of the Fitzpatrick family. Meanwhile, I must endeavour and ascertain who are the persons who have run away with Lawson's daughter. I strongly suspect that the strange story which John Elliott last night told in the coffee-room, of the boasting young Welsh captain, and the arrest of some French woman, as a partaker in an Irish Popish plot, has something to do with this abduction. I must see Elliott again, and try if I cannot detect those wretches in the commission of their rank crimes. It is impossible this delusion as to the Popish plot can be much longer maintained, whilst every fact, tending to show the wickedness of those who have promoted it, can but serve to its speedier explosion. That which these plot-makers are aiming at is as plain as light to my eyes: they are seeking to deprive a good and brave prince of his inheritance, to exclude my friend, my patron, and my benefactor, the Duke of York, from the throne, and the ultimate object aimed at is, the promotion of that which they call '*the good old cause,*' the cause of crime, of anarchy, and tyranny—the re-establishment of a republic in England and Ireland. In fighting against those anarchical principles, I have suffered much, lost much, and am prepared to lose my life. My opponents, to attain their ends, have stopped at the commission of no wickedness; they have employed against my last sovereign all the arts that the demon himself could suggest, and to deprive the future king of his rightful crown, they are now invoking, from the very dregs of society, the vilest and most abandoned wretches, and by flagrant perjuries, sending the innocent to death, and bedewing the very Gospel itse with blood! The courts of law, which ought also be courts of equity, are converted into so many shambles; 'for an oath may be good in law, and yet carry a man to the devil on the point of conscience.' So writes to me about this 'concocted Popish plot,' my honest old friend, Roger L'Estrange; and how just are these his remarks as to the popular delusion existing with respect to that plot: 'TREACHERY was called *truth and faith;* SLANDER was only *liberty of speech;* PERJURY was hallowed by the lips and credit of a king's evidence; FORGERY (if detected) was but a *mistake;* REBELLION, a true Protestant association; A SHAM NARRATIVE passed for the discovery of *a damnable, hellish, Popish plot,* and the people were stirred up and instructed to hate and *persecute* the Papists, in despite of the *evangelical precept,* that bids us love one another; SUBORNATION was authorized under the name of *reward;* MURDER was recommended, under the varnish of *public justice.*'— These are the views of an honest, sincere, truthful, and conscientious English Protestant, upon the present persecution of us Catholics; and how just, also, are his opinions as to the manner in which this persecution against them has been moulded, managed, and directed! 'As to the time the faction had the ascendancy of the government, and the multitude bore down all before them like a torrent, the *witnesses* led the *rabble,* the *plotmongers* led the *witnesses,* and the *devil himself* led the *leaders;* for they were to pass to their ends through *subornation, perjury, hypocrisy, sacrilege,* and *treason.*

"Yes," continued the old man, "that is the truth, the plain, simple truth; treason is at the bottom of all this business, and for the sake of promoting that crime, every other is committed. It was so in the old rebellion, which ended in the decapitation of Charles I. That rebellion was popularized in England by denunciations of Popery and Irish Papists, and false accusations against my countrymen, of having stained their hands with a ' general massacre' of Irish Protestants. And now the same arts are renewed, and again we, the Catholics, are victims, and suffer by the sacrifice of our lives, and the spoliation of our properties, and all this upon false accusations which have not, in themselves, even the semblance of truth. Our present sovereign is despoiled of his prerogative, and his successor is sought to be debarred of his rights; and in the name of a republic, the reign of Cromwell, the reign of the thirty tyrants, ' of Cromwellian major-generals,' is sought to be reimposed upon the British dominions.

"But that which I see," added the old man, "that which is plain to every candid and impartial mind, the multitude will not see—they cannot discern; for they are blinded by passion, by ignorance, and by prejudice. But will it be always so? I hope not, I trust not, and the best and surest means of putting an end to it is, to do that which I am now doing—to follow the villains into their private lives, to see how they employ their time, and how they are turning to their own selfish purposes, and converting to their own wicked ends, the power which they are now permitted to exercise. It is well that they practise against each other the same arts that they have employed for our destruction. And now then, if possible, to trace out the perpetrators of the abduction of Lawson's daughter. Drawer," said the old man as he entered the coffee-room, "tell your master I would wish to speak with him, the first leisure moment he can spare me."

"Master Elliott," said the old man to the host, "I was engaged writing on a matter of some importance to myself last night, when I heard you telling of some curious discovery with respect to an Irish Popish plot, in which, as I fancy, a Welshman had some concern. I did not pay much attention to the matter at the time; but I have since been thinking about it. Perhaps you would let me know the particulars; and, whilst you do so, aid me in drinking some of your own excellent claret, which would, in my judgment, do credit to the table of the *Grand Monarque* himself."

"Your very good health, sir," said John Elliott, willingly complying with the invitation thus given to him.

"You are one of those guests I most reverence; for you are a good judge of a good glass of wine. My wine comes direct from Bordeaux, and as it is sent to me, it is so served to my customers. I charge a high price; I have, I avow it, not only a fair but a large profit on what I sell; but that which I buy is sold in the same condition in which it reached me—the only difference between the article as it was manufactured from the vine, and as it is disposed of by me, is the time it has been in my cellars."

"And that is an improvement," added the old man, smacking his lips, as he tasted the claret. "But what of this strange story you were telling last night?"

"Between ourselves," said John Elliott, winking his eyes, and speaking in a lower tone of voice than usual, "my own opinion is it is a very foolish story; for, in my soul, I do not believe there is one word of truth in the whole Popish plot, either English or Irish, from the beginning to the end."

"Nor I either," observed the old man.

"This is not the first Popish plot spoken of in my time.

I have been now living in Ireland for more than thirty years, and have acquired some knowledge of its people, and sure I am, poor fellows! that what has been the cause of most anxiety to them has been, not to destroy their neighbours, but to make out bread for themselves and their children. Thus, from my own experience, I would say there is nothing to be found in the Irish plot, but as many lies as there are false men to swear them; and as to the English plot, I judge it from the character of one of the witnesses—Bedloe—and of him it can be truly said, that he is ' a fellow known for a blasphemous, atheistical wretch; a thief, a cheat, and, in fine, a scandal to the very alms-basket.' But, bless you, sir," added Elliott, still speaking in a low tone of voice, " that which I say to you, under the rose, I dare not for my life speak aloud. Knaves, who know I said nothing but the truth, would aid fools and fanatics in tearing my house down about my ears, because I had spoken that truth aloud."

"I know, as well as you," said the old man, " the danger of the times; and, therefore, whilst I admire your sentiments I respect your prudence. But tell me, I pray, the strange story in which the Welsh captain was a hero."

" The person you ask about," observed Elliott, " is a young captain in Jones' dragoons. He is like most Welshmen I have ever met with, as remarkable for the dulness of his wit, as the liveliness of his fanaticism; and, therefore, is prepared to believe as a truth, whatever can be said to the dishonor of his neighbour—provided that neighbour be an Irishman or a Papist. Ever since the Popish plot was first spoken of in England, he has been maintaining there must be, at the least, two Popish plots in Ireland; and for this reason, that there are twice as many Papists in Ireland as in England: This firm persuasion of his has, it seems, by his own account, been fully corroborated by an incident which occurred whilst he was patrolling at night around Dublin. He asserts that, whilst so engaged, he met a large armed party; and upon challenging them, he was shown by their leader a warrant from the Privy Council in England, to arrest persons in Ireland accused of being parties to a Popish plot in this country. He says that the party he stopped had a woman in custody—an emissary from France, who was arrested in the very act of conspiring with the Catholic Archbishop of Armagh as to poisoning the King; but with that stupidity and dulness so characteristic of his countrymen, he can neither remember the name of the person set forth in the warrant of the English Privy Council, as being authorized to make arrests in Ireland, nor can he tell to what jail it was stated the prisoner was about to be removed; nor can he describe the person of the prisoner, for he declares he never saw her. At the Castle, nothing is known of any such circumstance. It is certain no such prisoner has been brought there to be lodged in the Birmingham Gate-house, or any other tower; nor is there any such prisoner in Newgate. What is supposed to be the fact is, either that Captain Jones, the person who has sent such a story afloat, was drunk the night this circumstance is said to have occurred, and dreamt it, or that some of his companions, knowing his madness about a Popish plot, have played a practical joke upon him. That Captain Jones believes it to be true is certain; for he has been for the last two or three days besieging the authorities at the Castle, and it is said, has written to Lord Shaftesbury, and other 'patriots' in London, to send him a warrant, in order that he may go down to the country, and arrest the Popish Archbishop, on the charge of being a prime mover in the Popish plot. Ah!"

exclaimed John Elliott, looking up as he spoke, "there is a person just come in, who may give you, if you will condescend to sit and speak with him, some substantial and real information as to this matter; for he, whilst drinking at a late hour here last night, was bragging and boasting, and contradicting persons about it, when repeating the rumour, as if he knew more of the subject than anybody else: shall I invite him to join us?"

"Do you mean," said the old man, "that drunken red-faced fellow in shabby, thread-bare black clothes, who does not seem to have yet got rid of last night's debauch? He looks to me as if he were nothing better than a cast-off and degraded parson."

"More probably," added Elliott, "a degraded and renegade priest."

"You jump to the conclusion," said the old man, laughing, "that a fellow so base and so contemptible must be a bad priest, because you are a Protestant; and I, on the contrary, because I am a Roman Catholic, set him down as a bad parson. Thus, our prejudices influence our opinions, and make us jump to (what further inquiry may prove, in both instances) wrong conclusions."

"No," replied John Elliott, "it is not so in this instance at least; for my main reason for concluding that drunken fellow to be a degraded, renegade priest is founded upon the fact, that he never stops abusing Catholic bishops, and never ceases complaining of the powers vested in them, and of the cruel enforcement by them of ecclesiastical discipline over the inferior clergy. The subject is not one a Protestant parson would think of discussing."

"And the topics are such as a bad priest would be sure to dilate upon," added the old man. "Ask the fellow hither; we may as well, in seeking for information, look for the pearl of truth under the slimy oyster-shell which encloses it, if that fellow's heart can enclose the jewel, and there be any human means of reaching it."

"Then you must order in a quart of usquebaugh. Nothing less potent can reach his heart through his stomach. Claret would chill him into silence," said John Elliott.

"Let us have the usquebaugh, and the man to swallow it," said the old gentleman.

Elliott rose from his seat, invited the new-comer to accompany him to the bar, then gave him a glass of usquebaugh, which was readily accepted, and then taking a full quart and three glasses, he asked the new-comer to aid him and another gentleman in drinking it.

"The usquebaugh is matchless; I would be a brute to refuse you," replied the new-comer.

"Allow me, gentlemen, to introduce you to each other. This, sir, is Mr. ——, Mr. ——, I forget your name sir," said Elliott to the new-comer.

"I wonder at that," said the new-comer.

"Why so?" said Elliott.

"Because you never knew it; and how you could forget what you never knew, passes my knowledge in logic and moral theology," answered the stranger, whom John Elliott's glass of usquebaugh, with the prospect of drinking more of it, put into excellent spirits. "But not to keep you longer in doubt about it, my name is Murfey —Edmund Murfey, at your service. An honest man's son's name, at all events."

"Thank you, Mr. Murfey," said John Elliott. "This, sir, is Mr. Edmund Murfey, and Mr. Edmund Murfey this is——"

"Smith," said Murfey, observing that John Elliott stopped at the name.

"Smith!" said the old man, smiling; "you are quite right Mr. Murfey—I am called Smith."

"See that now," said Murfey, "see that now—see how I could tell the gentleman's name, though I never saw him before. I have travelled a deal, Mr. Elliott, and have seen a great deal of the world, but I never yet met an Englishman, and was at loss for his name, and called him 'Smith,' that I did not find I was right. His name is Smith, you see; and now I bet you a pint of usquebaugh that I guess his Christian name."

"Done!" said John Elliott.

"Done!" said Murfey, "and done again, and done over again; for it's you that was done this time, mine host. The gentleman's Christian name is 'John'—'John Smith' is his name, in full—that is the name he is *called* by. Ain't I right, sir?"

"Quite right; I am, as you say, Mr. Murfey, *called* John Smith."

"Hand me in my pint of spirits," cried Murfey, jubilant with exultation; "I'll take that before I touch a drop that is in that quart bottle. I like to begin with my own honest earnings, before I quarter myself on the contributions of strangers. That has been my way through life. I first spent my own fortune; and never until I had gone right through it, did I think of helping my friends to get through theirs; and the Lord be praised! I have got on wonderfully in life, by succeeding in both ways. But here comes the usquebaugh. My heart's weak this morning, after last night's booze; but I have the courage to face a pint, at all events. Here, mine host, is your health, and may you never have worse liquor in your house than this; and may you always be as sure that others will pay for their drink, as that you will have, in this instance, to pay for mine. And here, too, sir, is your very good health; I respect you for your impartiality, because you decided in my favour. Your health, Mr. John Smith; and although you are an old man, the worst wish I have for you is, may you live until there is no one to bury you."

"Let the fellow drink as much as he pleases, and as quickly as he likes," whispered John Elliott to the old man; "we shall the sooner learn all he has to tell, and the sooner get rid of him."

"I think," said Murfey, as he laid down the vessel containing his beloved usquebaugh, "I think I ought to be able to take the conceit out of that pint in five more offers. I drank your health, Mr. Elliott, in the first, and I had the bad manners to join Mr. John Smith along with you. Forgive me, gentlemen; but I was in such a hurry to get at the *aqua vitæ*, that I stumbled over my politeness. Well, here's to mend my hand, and here's to your health alone, Mr. John Smith, and may you never die until I wish to be at your wake! and that, I can tell you, will be some day that will never come neither before nor after Christmas.

"Well, now that I have thought of my friends, I may as well have a word to say to my enemies, and I ought to have something to say to the latter, for there is more of the one than the other on my hands at this present writing. Faith, as to my friends, you could fit them into a sentry-box, and there would be room for more, and plenty of space to spare; whilst as to my enemies, they are like buttercups on a May morning, past counting. So here goes— 'Confusion to all my enemies in general, rich and poor, great or small, alive and kicking, or dead and rotten. Confusion to them one and all! Amen. *A yiernah!*

"There's my third offer at the pint, and a brave, strong pull I made of it.

"And now, gentlemen, for the worst, greatest, cruellest, unkindest, vilest, and wickedest of all persecutors, the bad man who took the bit out of my mouth, when I was a Divinity student; the cruel bishop who won't let one of his priests as much as say boo to a goose; the antiquated, mitred, bad politician, who is always throwing cold water on the fires of patriotism; the proud prelate who is for impeding, and thwarting, and annoying in every way, every fine-hearted, free-and-easy young levite that is speechifying to the people upon Sundays, holidays, and week-days, about battling for nationality, pure republicanism, and boval raptations. Here is, I say, this horrid instigator and proud enforcer of ecclesiastical discipline; and from all my heart, and with all my heart, and with all the cockles of my heart, I wish death and destruction to you, Oliver Plunkett, Archbishop of Armagh, and once, to my great grief and sorrow, my own bishop. It's you have been the ruin of me, and the least I can say is ruination, high hanging, and a windy day to you, and the likes of you; for Ireland never will be peaceable until it is well rid of you, and of all your sort, and all your backers, and all your understrappers.

"There is the fourth of my pint gone, and by dad it's I that quaffed it fairly, for I have hardly left a drain for my last toast.

"Here it is :— it is the speedy downfall of all proud men and women, and of the women particularly; because one woman is worse than ten men, and one woman's tongue can do more mischief than an army: and so it was from the beginning, from the unlucky hour that Eve wheedled that old omedhawn, Adam, into eating an apple, down to

Monday night last, when of all the *sasseraras* that ever a poor man got, I got from a shrew of a girl, and all merely for taking her to——But, hush! hold your prate, Ned Murfey; for you're letting the cat out of the bag. Stop your mouth with a drop of drink, and drink confiscation and extermination to the *colleen dhu* in solemn silence.

"There, gentlemen, is the fifth and last offer, and you see I have finished the pint. Its contents have disappeared like last year's snow. And now, Mr. Elliott, whenever it is convenient for you to hand me over that quart bottle, I will be after filling myself out a glass."

Elliott and his companion watched with curiosity, if not with interest, the proceedings of this desperate toper. They observed the sudden change which this hurried swallowing of strong liquors produced upon his face, appearance, and even language, and how quickly the geniality and fun which pervaded the man's conversation, and gave his tongue volubility, was changing into vapidity, and sinking down into dogged and sullen obstinacy.

"I am glad to see, Mr. Murfey," said Elliott, "that you relish my usquebaugh. What do you think of it?"

"It is nectar, sir," answered Murfey, as he quaffed off another glass. "The ancient pagans described their heroes as drinking wine; but they reserved for their heathen gods something better than wine, and they called it 'nectar,' and 'nectar' is Greek for 'usquebaugh.'"

"*Nectar* Greek for *usquebaugh*," said the old man, "I never knew that before."

"Did you ever drink usquebaugh before, sir?" asked Murfey.

"No, never."

"Then go on drinking usquebaugh, and you will be astonished to find how much it will improve you. When you have drunk half as much as me, it will be well for you if you know half or quarter as much as I could teach you."

"I have not the slightest doubt, sir, of the profundity of your knowledge, or the extent of your acquirements," remarked the old man, bowing to Murfey, who received the compliment with drunken gravity and solemnity; "but what surprises me is, that you should be so reluctant to impart the information you possess to others. A good scholar should be like a large cask of generous wine, always on draught, never bunged up."

"Sir, I honor you for the metaphor," stammered Murfey. "Ask what question you please, and I will answer you."

"You stopped a minute ago," observed the old man, "as you were on the point of telling us the name of the young woman who gave you dire offence on a recent occasion. I own to a strong curiosity to learn the name of that particular individual of the weaker sex, who was able to excite such angry commotion in the generous heart of a great scholar and an illustrious divine like Mr. Edmund Murfey."

"Cease firing, John Smith! No flattery, Mr. Smith! I confess to being a scholar, I deny being a divine. What I might have been, I will not say; but cruel Oliver Plunkett could tell; for it was jealousy on his part of my superior talents that made him put me under ban. And now you want to know, Mr. John Smith, the name of the young lady who on last Monday night, of all days in the year, put me in a passion. Ah! then, if you wait there, Mr. John Smith, until I tell you the name of that fiery young vixen, you will be found sitting on the same spot where you now are until the day after the day of judgment. But to tell the truth, now, John Elliott, did I do what this old chap says I did? did I directly or indirectly say one blessed word about a young woman having put me in a horrid rage last Monday?"

"You did, indeed, Mr. Murfey, distinctly allude to some such person," replied John Elliott.

"Why, then, more shame for me, and as a punishment, I fine myself to drink off another glass of usquebaugh. There it is—gone! paid the fine the very minute it was inflicted. Is not that honest, Mr. Smith? Is not that astonishingly honest, Mr. Smith? Isn't that superlatively honest, Mr. John Elliott?"

"Honest! you are the perfection of honesty, Mr. Murfey," said Elliott.

"Not a bit of it," answered Murfey.

"You are too honest," said the old man.

"Cease firing, John Smith! Ain't it the hardest thing in the world for a man to be honest? then such being the case, how on earth could a man double the quantity of an impossibility? Answer me that logically, and metaphysically, and theologically," said Murfey, hiccupping in a drunken triumph.

"You are too learned for me to enter into a controversy with you," said the old man.

"I should think so. I should like to see the man from Oxford or Cambridge who could hold a candle to me when I'd try to trip him up with Aristotle in Greek, or Thomas Aquinas in Latin."

"I think you are quite right," said John Elliott, "not to tell the girl's name, or perhaps I ought to say the name of the young lady."

"True for you, John Elliott; and a real young lady, too, by fortune," said Murfey.

"And birth," added Elliott, slily.

"Little said is soon mended," said Murfey, with a drunkard's cunning wink.

"Very proper, and very prudent, and very discreet, indeed!" added John Elliott. "Ah! Mr. Murfey, I wish all men were, where the names of ladies are concerned, as prudent as you are. It is not so; for here has been a young officer—these military men are always boasting they are great favourites with the ladies."

"Not so great as the parsons," said Murfey; "for the parsons gets as wives, all the women with fortunes they choose to ask for; whilst, as to the officers, they are treated as dolls, sure to amuse the young ladies for an evening, and then are thrown aside, or forgotten, in a corner. If I cared for women—and I don't, no more than for the dirt of my shoe—then I would sooner be a poor Protestant curate, with my little white band and my shabby black gown, and my skimping Geneva cap, than an officer with all his gold-lace, feathers, boots, and spurs. As for me, one woman's tongue (it is still ringing in my ears) is, I think, enough to disgust a whole barrack-full of men, against the sex for ever and a day."

"And yet, though so provoked against that one woman with a wicked tongue, you will not mention her name," said Elliott.

"Never," said Murfey. "If I do, may I never drink anything stronger than table-beer for the remainder of my life."

"See here now, Mr. Smith," said Elliott, "see the honor and bravery of an Irishman, where the fair sex is concerned."

"The less we say about 'fair' the better," said Murfey. "Anything more unfair than her remarks upon me, I never heard. Some of her words are sticking in me like so many pins; and when I am fast asleep, give me a prod in the conscience that starts me up, and keeps me awake for hours afterwards. But still, you see, the more I am vexed with her, the more I wont mention her name, and that, too, for a reason I have."

"Ah! I wish all men were like you," said John Elliott. "Not so, however, with that officer I was telling you about, who has been talking of a young lady he met last Monday night, and who was taken prisoner at Archbishop Plunkett's, and that they were carrying her off to prison."

"Whew! this is more and more of it. I fine myself another glass of usquebaugh for listening to you—for it is you, you cunning thief of the world, that's trying to get round me, and to tell you that this is the same girl as that girl that we have been speaking of all the time."

"And is it possible it is the self-same person?" asked Elliott.

"To be sure it is; and now, Mr. Elliott, and you, too, Mr. Smith, do not be bothering yourselves, nor losing your time any longer, trying to make me drunk, and so getting the *Colleen Dhue's* name out of me. First of all, I would drink ten men like the two of you, blind, and stand up myself from the table afterwards as sober as a judge; and next, I dare not tell the name—and I'll whisper you the reason why, *it is a hanging matter to mention*. It has to do with the Popish plot, and I am a King's evidence to the plot, and so you had better let me alone the two of you, or maybe the devil would put it into my head to swear you had been tampering with me as a witness; so let me alone, I tell you. I fine myself another glass of usquebaugh for stopping so long with you.

And so good-bye, landlord, and good-bye, you, sir, who call yourself, or are called John Smith."

"Come! come! not so fast, Mr. Murfey," said John Elliott, catching hold of the toper by the skirts of his shabby black coat, and so dragging him back into his seat again. "Mind you, Mr. Murfey, I am an Englishman, and, what is more, as good a Protestant as yourself."

"Faith," replied Murfey, "if that's all you have to say for yourself, that you are as a good a Protestant as I am, then I can tell you that when you go to kingdom come, Luther will disown you, and Calvin turn the back of his hand and the sole of his foot against you."

"But, Mr. Murfey," said John Elliott, "I want to show my respect for you."

"Do you really now, Mr. Elliott?"

"I do, indeed, Mr. Murfey."

"Very well, then, give us another glass of your usquebaugh."

"Another glass of my usquebaugh!" exclaimed Elliott, as in a rapture of enthusiasm. "Another glass of my usquebaugh! ay, Mr. Murfey, and another quart of my usquebaugh, and a dozen quarts of usquebaugh to the back of that again. Call for what you like, regard this house as your own, its larder and its cellars are alike open to you. All I regret is, that the house is so full I cannot offer you a bed. What, Mr. Murfey, is it that I possess, and that you may not command? Are you not one of the King's evidence to the horrid, hellish, Popish plot, and is it not the duty of every Englishman to sustain, support, and cherish you?"

"Are you in earnest, Mr. Elliott?" said Murfey, "or are you only making game of me? Because, if you are in earnest, it is the best joke I ever heard ; and if you are joking, depend upon it I will make you sup sorrow for your fun."

"Am I in earnest ?" cried Elliott, as if astonished at the question. "Just listen to me. Here, Thomas—you know, Mr. Murfey, Thomas is the head drawer at my inn —here, Thomas, this is Mr. Murfey, and whatever Mr. Murfey orders in this house, you are to bring him, and never send him in a bill."

"Yes, sir," replied Thomas.

"The proof of the pudding is in the eating," said Murfey. "How much is a magnum, Mr. Elliott ?"

"Two quarts, Mr. Murfey," answered Elliott.

"Very well! you, Thomas, fellow, bring me a magnum of usquebaugh," said Murfey.

"Yes, sir," said Thomas, hurrying off, and in an instant returning with a gigantic bottle.

"Uncork that, my man," said Murfey.

"Yes, sir."

Murfey filled, with a steady hand, a glass from the huge bottle ; then smelled, with a knowing look, the liquid ; then tasted it ; then smacked his lips, and exclaimed with rapture—"Better liquor I never tasted, as fragrant as a a rose, as strong as steel, and as pellucid as the honey of Hybla. And now, Thomas, my tight fellow——"

"Yes, sir."

"Mind, whenever I order it, you are never to stop bringing me one of the same sort."

"Yes, sir."

"And take particular notice, my red-nosed Ganymede, that you are not to charge me anything."

"Yes, sir."

"Because, if you do I will never pay you. Whenever

I say I won't pay, you may depend upon it, I'll keep my word."

"Yes, sir."

"And mind you, Thomas, you are not to ask me to settle my bill for this nectar."

"Never, sir."

"Yes!" exclaimed Murfey, as he clasped the monstrous bottle in both hands, and kissed it fervently with his lips. "*This* is nectar, the real nectar, ambrosial dew, compounded by those tight-waisted wenches, the Muses, at a favourite unlicensed still of their own on the banks of the Pactolus. Mr. Elliott, I had little notion that an old Cromwellian true-blue, and blue-mouthed trooper like you, could have half the goodness in you that I see you have. May I never sin, John Elliott, but I honor you, and I reverence you, and if I outlive you, and have the money to spare, I will erect a monument to your memory, as a pattern to all tavern-keepers."

"I am a true-born Englishman, that is all, Mr. Murfey," said Elliott; "and, as such, it is my duty to show my esteem for a gentleman who is so good as to become a King's evidence to the horrid, hellish, Popish plot."

"Oh! then, it's I am the real King's evidence," said Murfey; "it's I that have the story to tell. You would hardly believe all I know about the same Popish plot; and it would make the hair stand as stiff as so many pokers on your head, if you were to hear all I have to say of and concerning that same identical plot."

"Dear me!" said Elliott, "I almost tremble to think of it; but I fear, Mr. Murfey, you do not like the liquor in your magnum. Why, you are five whole minutes without tasting a drop of it."

"Then more shame for me to be losing my time," said

Murfey, as he quaffed off another glass. "Not relish this liquor, did you say? Ah! if I were as fond of virtue as I am of it, I would live a recluse, and die in the odour of sanctity."

"And so you can tell great things about the horrid, hellish, Popish plot," said Elliott, fearful that the man who sat beside him would become stupidly intoxicated before any material fact would be elicited from him.

"Great things indeed!" said Murfey. "Nay, they are marvellous things. Now, what think you, John Elliott, and what think you, Mr. John Smith, who, I must say, are as bad a fellow as I ever sat in company with, for you never open your mouth, either to utter a word or swallow a drop."

"I beg your pardon, sir," said the old man, "but I drink as much as you do."

"Drink as much as I do; the Lord pardon you for so belying your neighbours! *you* to drink as much as *me!* why you might as well say that a pinkeen drank a much as a whale; or that a pint bottle could hold as much as a hogshead. Why, sir, you haven't the capacity to drink as much as I do. And then what a vulgar word you use: 'drink!' I don't 'drink,' sir—I 'imbibe;' beasts 'drink.' The flowers imbibe the dews, and are redolent of odours; rivers imbibe the streams, and enrich the land; the ocean, the greatest toper of all, imbibes streams, rivers, and the rains from heaven; and then it tumbles about always, always, and for ever, just as a man who has got his skin-full of usquebaugh. Never say *drink*, John Smith, always use the word *imbibe;* it is a delicate scholarly phrase."

"Or what think you of the word *swill*, Mr. Murfey?" asked the old man.

"Swill; very good, indeed; I approve of it highly; and I honor you for the phrase, Mr. Smith. Here's your health, wishing you had kept such good company as myself at an earlier period of your life; because it is plain if you had, your society might have been made pretty tolerable to Divinity students, who love capital liquor. Here's your health, John Smith; I never would have thought of proposing it, but that you suggested the word 'swill.' *Swill* rhymes to *fill*. 'Pon my veracity, it is a very nice word indeed!"

"But you were, Mr. Murfey, about to say something of the horrid, hellish, Popish plot," observed Elliott impatiently.

"Ah! then, John Elliott, is it trying to inveigle me you are, with your kimmeen tricks?" said Murfey, his suspicious temper excited for the moment, despite the enormous quantity of raw spirits he had been swallowing. "You want me to tell you, what I have made up my mind to tell the King and the Parliament; but I won't, not a blessed word that you can make any meaning out of, will I say to you. But at the same time your usquebaugh is too good for a man to be cross with you, and therefore I will say this to you, and just too in the way I was going to say it to you, when old John Smith, who never stops talking, interrupted me. Now what do you say, John Elliott, or what do you say, John Smith, to this? shut your eyes and open your ears, while I put these few interrogatory questions to you. What do you say of a man who intends to swear that a certain great man in the north—I name no names, mind you—but a mighty great man in the north entirely; a bad-hearted man, too, he is, and has been my persecutor, and took the bit out of my mouth, when I was going on for Holy Orders; what do you think, or what do you say to such a man letting me into his secrets, and telling me of a plan by which the King of France was to land seventy thousand soldiers, horse, foot, and dragoons, bag, baggage, and artillery, in Carlingford Bay——"

"Carlingford Bay!" exclaimed Elliott, unable to suppress his surprise. How were they to get there? or how could a fleet sufficient to convey such an army enter Carlingford Bay?"

"Hush!" exclaimed the old man, "let him go on without interruption, or we shall never be able to fathom this villainy."

"I said Carlingford Bay; I said that, and will stick to it, and what's more, I'll swear it," said Murfey; "that was the very place the great man in the north—I name no names, mind you—proposed to me to have sixty thousand men landed. Don't you see, John Elliott, that the cunningness of the plot consists in determining to do what is impossible, and proposing to land at a place that is inaccessible. And what is more, this great man in the north—I have not, and I will not mention his name—until he is safe in Newgate; but what he told me was this, that the Duke of York was bringing all those Irish and Spanish soldiers, fifty thousand of them, no less, to cut the throat of John Elliott and all like him in Ireland, as if they were so many pigs, instead of being, as they are, church-going Protestants; and didn't this great man in the north also say to me——"

"But," said John Elliott, tiring of what he regarded as the drunken fancies of Murphy, "I do not see what the French lady who was arrested on Monday last has to do with all this horrid, hellish, Popish plot."

"Ah! I see what you are driving at," said Murfey; "you want me to tell the name of the *Colleen Dhu*— but I won't. All I will say to either of you is this, that I am prepared to swear I was in France, and that I was talking with the French King and his Majesty's father confessor about this same plot ; and that it was as much as I could do to prevent the two of them from making me a Duke or a Cardinal, whichever I liked best, to promote this plot; but instead of doing any such thing, I said to the French King in French : ' What a gallows bosthoon you must take me to be, to suppose I would give up my chance of being an English bishop in Ireland, to become a dirty, trapseeing, beggarly bishop in France, or an old battered, red-stockinged Cardinal in Italy. *Mon-a-mondhoul*,' says I to the King's confessor in French, ' but I would sooner be a cow-boy in the Bog of Allen in Ireland, than a captain of dragoons in the Louvre in France'—and so I would, too. May this blessed liquor be poison to me, if I don't speak the truth !" added Mr. Murfey, his tongue stammering, and his utterance becoming nearly unintelligible.

"Very interesting, indeed," said the old man; " but as you have seen Louis XIV. and the Pere La Chaise, perhaps you would let us know the appearance of both. I have often wished to ask the question of some one who had conversed with them."

"With all the pleasure in life," added Murfey, as he half-spilled a glass of usquebaugh in the attempt to convey the contents to his lips: "Louis XIV. is a great tall man, six feet six inches in height—I measured him, and I can swear to the fact ; he always wears a crown of gold on his head, and is never to be seen without a long sharp knife in his hand, which he carries about for the purpose of cutting off the heads of the Protestants. As to Father La Chaise, he is—and few but myself know the fact—an Irishman ; he was a school-fellow of my father's, and his real name is Father Ignatius O'Callaghan ; and the reason he is called

Father La *Chaise* is, that he is so enormously fat he is not able to walk, and has to ride about every place he wants to go to in a *chaise*. The great fault I had to find with him was that he never stops drinking,—morning, noon, and night, he is at it; he was the greatest drunkard I ever met: and of all the disgusting, odious, intolerant things in this world is—at least I think so—a drunkard!"

And so speaking, or rather mumbling, Mr. Murfey's head fell upon the table, his hand still grasping a glass, and in an instant afterwards he snored loudly and heavily.

CHAPTER IX.

A DUEL.

PACING up and down the green sward of a retired nook, in the park attached to the mansion of Lady Diana Massey, was a young gentleman, clothed from head to foot in a sombre suit of black. Far different in mood and attire from the gay fop of the preceding day was Lord Arran; for then he desired to make himself attractive in the eyes of a youthful beauty, whereas now he was about to encounter in mortal, and it might be, to him, fatal combat, a person of whose existence he had previously been ignorant, but whose enmity his own indiscretion of language had provoked.

"In a few moments," so mused Lord Arran, "my friend with my adversaries will be here. In a few moments this sword will, for the first time, be unsheathed to defend my own life, and to assail the life of another. Fatal—fatal necessity; but it is unavoidable. My person has been dishonored by a blow, and I must avenge that blow, or—be scouted out of society.

"And why is this? What right had I, upon no better foundation than the vague assertions of a weak woman, to denounce as an impostor a person I had never seen, and of whose pretensions I was wholly ignorant? Had he, without any provocation upon my part, so spoken of me as I presumed to speak of him, I would have done as he did—punished the gratuitous aggressor.

"And for his doing that which I forced him to do, I am now bound to do my utmost to slay him!

"It is an unjust quarrel, and I have aggravated the injustice by challenging him to this combat; and I have so done, not because I think I am right in thus acting, but because I have to choose between his death and my own infamy.

"And then, if I fall in this encounter, as it is probable I may, for I have not a particle of justice on my side, how shall I appear before that just Judge who laid down His life for my salvation? How shall I, covered with my own blood, self-sacrificed, ask for mercy from Him, whose great law, 'thou shalt not kill,' I have died in the attempt to violate in the person of my neighbour?

"A suicide! a murderer! or, an infamous and degraded coward. Such are the alternatives before me; and I can only avoid the one, or become the other, by voluntarily choosing the last.

"Can I do so? Am I in a position to do so? Am I in any respect a free agent in this matter?

"If I were a free agent; if I had any free will at this moment, I would give all I am worth, all my dearest, long-cherished hopes of worldly honors, ay, twenty years of my life, to have unsaid, or unrecorded, or unheard, the few giddy words to which I gave utterance yesterday, and so not have brought this train of calamities upon myself.

"To recall the past is impossible. The words have been spoken; the blow has been received; the challenge has been sent, and—the duel is to be fought. Yes, it must—it must be gone through, be the consequences to myself what they may; for if I should not fight, if now, at the last hour, I were to shrink from the combat, not only should I become infamous, but in my infamy would be involved the innocent. I would bring the grey hairs of my father to the grave with shame, sorrow, and infamy. In that infamy of mine would be involved the name I bear, a name that as yet has never known disgrace. Nay, more, unborn members of my family would inherit with their rank the disgrace I had, by my own act of craven cowardice, attached to them.

"What, then, is to be said?—that in this case I am not a free agent; that in these sad circumstances I have no free will of my own. I am as a man who has incautiously put to sea in a fragile bark, and when the storm is bursting over his head, and the waves are yawning around his sinking ship, sees death to be inevitable but cannot fly from his fate, though he may lament the ignorance, the indiscretion, and the folly which induced him to place himself in such a position. The duel is to be fought—it is inevitable. I can neither avoid it nor prevent it. It is to be done. But there is no use in considering the matter further. Here comes my friend Harvey, and with him my adversary and his second. The time for reflection has gone by; the time for action has arrived. It is a foul and a bad deed. Heaven have mercy on me, as I enter upon this conflict with grief, with pain, and with unwillingness."

"Gentlemen, with your leave," said Major Harvey, the

second of Lord Arran, "I will speak a few words in private with my Lord before the preliminaries of the combat are arranged."

Vincent Fitzpatrick and his companion stopped on their way towards the spot in which Lord Arran was standing, when these few words were addressed to them.

"Well, Harvey, you are a true Englishman, punctual to an appointment to the moment, whether it be to a feast or a fight," said Lord Arran, assuming an air of gaiety, although his heart was heavy with grief.

"I have come, my Lord," said Harvey, gravely, "to apprise you of facts which it is necessary should be known to you, before you risk your own life or put in peril that of another. This unfortunate quarrel between you and the gentleman yonder has arisen out of one unhappy circumstance—your undertaking to brand him, whenever you met him, as an impostor. It was a rash undertaking, my Lord, and could not but lead to a calamitous result; for the gentleman has proved to me that he is undoubtedly Vincent Fitzpatrick, the son of Colonel Fitzpatrick, who won high honor for himself, and I may add for his country, in battling for years against the armies of the Usurper, Oliver Cromwell, and other king-murderers and republicans."

"And who has vouched for these facts, Major Harvey?" asked Lord Arran. "Is it that tall, fine, manly-looking gentleman yonder, in the brown suit? If it be, who is to vouch for the voucher, and who to prove the truth and worth of the dashing compurgator, who frowns at me, this moment, with a most cut-throat countenance?"

"As the second of Mr. Vincent Fitzpatrick," replied Major Harvey, "his name, his real name is known to me, although it is not his convenience it should be publicly disclosed. Sufficient is it for me to say, that I pledge you my honor, as a gentleman, he is a man of good birth, and ennobled by a foreign sovereign."

"Very well, Harvey," replied Lord Arran. "If you, the grandson of an English peer, are satisfied with the rank and respectability of the gentleman with whom you have treated as a second, it is your affair and not mine. All I have to do is with the principal, and the sooner my business with him is disposed of the better. Give us our swords."

"Nay, my lord, before I do so," added Major Harvey. "I think it an imperative duty upon me as a man, a soldier and a Christian gentleman, to say that in this quarrel you are altogether wrong, that the gentleman whose reputation is assailed is not what you called him. I have seen the documents which fully establish his right to what he claims; and amongst those documents is one from his Highness the Duke of York, showing that there exists between your opponent and that illustrious personage terms of cordial and intimate friendship."

"And, good heavens! Harvey," said Lord Arran, impatiently, "what would you have me to do? Is it because the Papist Duke of York addresses the gentleman yonder as 'my dear Tom, Dick, or Harry, or Vincent,' or whatever else his name may be, that I am to allow the gentleman, another Papist, too, most probably, to fling his glove in my face with impunity? Do you, in whose hands I have placed my honor, take upon yourself the responsibility of advising me to withdraw my challenge, and apologize to the gentleman, because he proves to be the son of his father. Come Harvey, speak out, as an officer and a gentleman. You know this is not the time nor the place to descant about Christianity; but do you, I repeat, as an officer and as a gentleman, advise, and will you take upon yourself the consequences of any such proceeding?"

"No, my Lord," replied Harvey, shaking his head, "I grieve to say I can do no such thing."

"Very well, then, Harvey, be assured I will not do anything which you as my second in an affair of honour will not advise me to do. Let us then lose no more time. Give us our swords."

"I grieve that it must be so," added Harvey, "but still I thought it right that you should not enter upon this unhappy combat without being fully cognizant of the fact, that you were the first aggressor. Advance, gentlemen, if you please," he added, as he turned round to the place in which Vincent Fitzpatrick remained still standing.

The combatants stood face to face, and coldly saluted each other, as their respective seconds placed rapiers in their hands.

"We have agreed," said Major Harvey, "that upon the first blood being drawn, or the first accident occurring which may interrupt the combat, it shall cease, for the purpose of seeing if terms of accommodation cannot be arranged, because it is the opinion of the seconds that there has been indiscretion on both sides."

The weapons of the combatants crossed, and it was remarked that Lord Arran turned deadly pale as the thin sword grasped by him touched the steel of his opponent.

A few passes were made, and a few feints followed, and then Lord Arran commenced the assault with vigour and audacity, leaving himself open to his more skilful adversary, had the latter chosen to take advantage of his rashness. It was plain to the practised lookers-on that what Lord Arran was seeking to accomplish was to inflict a

K

flesh wound upon his adversary, and that the object aimed at by Fitzpatrick was to disarm his lordship.

At the same instant each of the duellists attained the end he had been striving for. The point of Lord Arran's rapier slightly grazed the shoulder of Vincent Fitzpatrick, whilst its hilt was caught by his adversary, and his lordship stood disarmed.

Major Harvey and Fitzpatrick's second stepped between the combatants, and the latter addressing his principal said :—

"Mr. Fitzpatrick, at once return to my Lord Arran his sword, for by your act you forced him to draw it in a hostile spirit against you."

"My Lord," said Vincent Fitzpatrick, as he presented the hilt of Lord Arran's sword to him, "I pray you to take back your sword, and in making that request of you, I wish to say, that I regret the act which forced you to draw it, and I feel the less reluctance in making that avowal, because already such reparation as I could afford has been tendered to you by the shedding of my blood."

"Mr. Fitzpatrick," replied Lord Arran, "I take back my sword on one condition, that I may be permitted the honour to grasp, as a friend, the hand that tenders it. Believe me, Sir, I am deeply sorry for the expressions which gave you just offence. I recall them; I regret them; I apologise to you for having spoken them."

"Nobly spoken! Most worthy of yourself, my Lord Arran," said Major Harvey. I never believed you, my Lord, to be free from faults and weaknesses; but I always felt convinced that on a great occasion you would prove worthy of your name, your rank, and your family. You have endeavoured to equal, but you could not surpass, the bravery and generosity of your adversary, who has proved in this conflict that his courage was on a par, and his skill as a swordsman superior to your own."

Lord Arran and Vincent Fitzpatrick were in the act of shaking hands with each other, when a horseman, at full speed, was seen riding towards them.

The horseman wore the gorgeous livery of an attendant upon the Lord Lieutenant; and the moment he reached the spot where Lord Arran was standing, he bounded from his horse, and presenting a letter to his lordship, exclaimed, in an agitated voice:—" Oh! my Lord, I have been seeking for you everywhere. A privy council is summoned at the Castle, at which your lordship's presence is expected in all haste."

"What is the matter, Jermyn?" asked Lord Arran, "for if the matter that brings you here be an affair of state, you seem in such a flurry as to be acquainted with it. Is his Excellency under any apprehension that the British coasts are again to be ravaged by a Dutch fleet? or is he fearful of another great rebellion in Ireland?"

"Oh! my Lord, my Lord," cried Jermyn, "we live in awful times, and we know not but to-morrow morning every Protestant in Ireland may awaken with his throat cut. Dublin is in a frightful state with all sort of rumours. As I was mounting my horse, opposite the eastern gateway tower, one of the wardens assured me that he had just been informed, by the Constable of the Castle, that intelligence had been received of an army of one hundred thousand Frenchmen and Spaniards having been landed in the Bay of Dublin; of fifty thousand men being already landed at Kinsale; and that there were sixty thousand Irish Papists marching from the North, to capture the Castle; and that these Northern Papists were under the command of

Doctor Oliver Plunkett, the titular Archbishop of Armagh, and of that notorious Rapparee, Redmond O'Hanlon."

"It is probable," said Lord Arran, smiling as he opened the letter handed to him, "that the despatch of which you are bearer will contain more authentic and less frightful intelligence than that which you, Jermyn, have picked up from that old alarmist, the Constable of Dublin Castle."

Vincent Fitzpatrick and his second exchanged significant glances when the frightened Jermyn mentioned the name of Redmond O'Hanlon in conjunction with that of the Catholic Primate, and the absurd story of a French and Spanish invasion.

Lord Arran had opened the despatch with a smiling countenance; but as he proceeded in its perusal, the smile changed into a frown, and when he had come to the conclusion of it, he sighed deeply, and said:—

"Major Harvey, we must at once return to the Castle. Jermyn has stated the truth, my presence is required in the Privy Council, for which my father tells me there are prepared several proclamations—scandalous proclamations, in my judgment, but which my father must perforce issue, or he will himself be denounced as a participator in the Popish plot. It is plain, Harvey, that what the plot-mongers in England have long been seeking for, they have, at last, succeeded in obtaining, and they have now shoals of Irish witnesses to depose to a branch of the plot in this country. Not only have these conspirators succeeded to the full extent of their wishes, but, as it appears, they have been too successful, for there is, as I learn from my father's letter, a rivalry of swearers and a competition of perjurers. He gives me the names of some of these witnesses, which I now mention, as you or these gentlemen may know or have heard something of them before. Amongst those worthies there are John Moyer, Paul Gormley, Edmund *alias* Owen Murphy, Murtagh Downing, a Maurice Fitzgerald, and a David Fitzgerald, George Coddan, James Geoghegan, and a fellow named Honagan. Some of 'these miserable wretches' have, it seems, been already ' sent over from Ireland to serve in England as witnesses of a plot, of which they knew nothing till they were instructed by Mr. Hetherington, Lord Shaftesbury's chief agent in managing and providing for them.' My father has seen some of these fellows, and I cannot refrain from reading for you this extract from his letter, in which he gives a description of them.

"'All the business here belongs to the term and the judges, and at Council there is little more to do than to hear witnesses; some come out of England, and some producing themselves here; and *all go there* (I doubt) *forswearing themselves*. Those that went out of Ireland with bad English and worse clothes, are returned well-bred gentlemen, well caronated, periwigged, and clothed. Brogues and leather straps are converted to fashionable shoes and glittering buckles; which, next to the zeal tories, thieves, and friars have for the Protestant religion, is a main ingredient to bring in a shoal of informers. The worst is, they are so miserably poor that we are forced to give them some allowance; and they find it more honourable and safe to be the King's evidence, than a cow stealer, though that be their natural profession. But, seriously, it is vexatious and uneasy to be in awe of such a sort of rogues.'

"But, Mr. Vincent Fitzpatrick," continued Lord Arran, " my new-found and justly honoured friend, I regret to say that there is something in my father's letter which deeply affects you; but the timely knowledge of which may, I hope, be useful to you. It seems that some one, or, for all I can tell, mayhap two or more, of those vile witnesses have deposed before the Privy Council, that you, as well as your father, Colonel Fitzpatrick, are participators in the Popish plot. A general warrant has, therefore been issued authorizing your arrest, as also that of your father, of the Roman Catholic Primate, of Redmond O'Haulon, Lord Carlingford, Colonel Garrett Morre, a Mr. Nugent, and I know not how many more."

"A warrant for my arrest, as a participator in an Irish Popish plot!" exclaimed Fitzpatrick, in surprise, "why, I have not been a fortnight in Ireland, and this day month I was in Paris."

"Your own admission as to your movements would, in the present temper of the times," remarked Lord Arran, "be sufficient to hang you. Against such an accusation there is but one means of safety, a sudden and speedy flight from Ireland, or a place of secure retreat, until this storm blows over. Innocence is no defence now-a-days. So far as my poor opinion goes, I am as sure you are perfectly innocent, as I am positive I could lay my hand on the man who has instigated a band of perjurers to assail you."

"And who can that be?" asked Vincent, "for I am not conscious that I have ever, by any act or word of mine, excited against myself the malignant hatred of a human being living."

"In this world you cannot escape your enemies by always doing good, and never doing evil," replied Lord Arran. "The devil hates virtue because it is opposed to vice, and bad men, instigated by the devil, hate those who are good men, if for no better, or rather if for no worse reason, than because they are not wicked. Remember you the words of Lady Macduff, when she who had by her whole life provoked no enmity against herself or her poor children, yet found murderers in her home prepared to slaughter herself and them:

> "'But I remember now
> I am in this earthly world; where to do harm
> Is often laudable; to do good, sometimes
> Accounted dangerous folly: why then, alas!
> Do I put up that womanly defence,
> To say, I have done no harm ?'"

"In your case, Mr. Fitzpatrick," added Lord Arran, "you cannot say that you have not provoked a foe; or that you have lived unconscious of the persecution of an enemy Your enemy is the man who wishes to obtain possession of the Fitzpatrick property. It is Mr. Edward Ludlow, formerly a captain in Cromwell's dragoons, and now a landed proprietor in Ireland, possessing amongst others, a portion of your father's estates."

"How know you of that base villain, Ludlow?" asked Fitzpatrick, astonished.

"By a letter," answered Lord Arran, "shown to me by your fair cousin, Kathleen, yesterday, in which she was warned against this same Ludlow, and directed to be on her guard against a project contemplated by him, of carrying her off, and by a forced marriage with her becoming entitled to the Fitzpatrick inheritance. The wretch who could be base enough to be guilty of such an act of atrocity would certainly not boggle at a perjury, to remove from his path a rival or an opponent."

"Your lordship judges justly of the man; to deprive me of my inheritance he has plotted against my life since infacy," remarked Vincent; "but how comes he in connexion with Titus Oates and his backers?"

"There are three persons, my father tells me, under whose protection these plot witnesses are to be found. First, that of a man named Hetherington, who is the agent of Lord Shaftesbury; secondly, under that of the Bishop of Meath, a person who had formerly been Scout-master-General to Oliver Cromwell's army; and lastly, under that of Mr. Edward Ludlow, who, I suspect, has taken part in such a plan for no other purpose than to serve his own private interests, by the destruction of you and your father, by making you victims to this plot, and the popular credulity respecting it. I regret to add, that my conviction is, your destruction is inevitable, if you are arrested in Ireland or England; or, if you cannot conceal yourself from pursuit. Not a moment is, on this account, to be lost."

"My Lord," said Fitzpatrick's second, "my young friend and myself have, by accident, become acquainted with the project of Ludlow against the honour and happiness of Miss Kathleen. We know that Ludlow intends, with the aid of a band of armed men, to attack the house in which she lives, if they can gain their ends by no milder means. Now, it occurs to me that the best and surest mode to defeat such a project would be for Mr. Fitzpatrick to remain in the house with his cousin; whilst, by so doing, he will secure for himself a hiding place, in which his enemies will never think of searching for him."

"An admirable plan!" exclaimed Lord Arran; "and reflects great credit, Sir, upon your ingenuity. I highly approve of it, and will, at once, introduce Mr. Fitzpatrick to his aunt and cousin. But stop—not so fast," cried Lord Arran, "let me think a moment. An objection *does* present itself to my mind. Let me think over it."

And thus thought Lord Arran to himself:—

"What am I about to do?

"To introduce the two cousins to each other.

"What will be the consequence of that introduction?

"Both are young, both are handsome, both will be thrown constantly into each other's society.

"They will inevitably fall in love with one another.

"What then?

"Have I a right to complain if the young lady should prove not unwilling to marry her cousin?

"Have I ever asked her in marriage? No. Would my father sanction my marriage with her, if she had not the large fortune he supposes? No.

"She cannot have that fortune; she has no right to it. Those to whom it belongs are here to claim their right.

"Then Kathleen will be without that fortune my father supposes she possesses.

"Then I can never marry Kathleen.

"Then, as I cannot marry Kathleen, I will do what I can to promote her marriage with this fine young fellow here, who acted nobly by me, and who had my life in his hands not an hour ago, and who spared it, although I had offended him.

"Then I will, on the instant, introduce Vincent to Kathleen Fitzpatrick."

Lord Arran's reverie was at an end, and turning to Harvey and his companions, he said:—

"I must hurry off to the Castle; but, before doing so, I wish to introduce you, Gentlemen, to Lady Diana Massey and Miss Kathleen Fitzpatrick."

"I thank you, my Lord, for the proposed honour," said Fitzpatrick's second; "but am reluctantly compelled to decline it. Urgent affairs compel me to quit my friend here, to fly to the succour of other friends elsewhere, whose safety is, like his own, in peril by this incomprehensible plot, which involves almost as many conflicting interests as individuals. Farewell, Fitzpatrick. I shall know where to communicate with you. Farewell, my Lord; farewell, Major Harvey, I am happy to meet in you a man who is an honour to his country, superior to its prejudices, and vindicating, in every action, its ancient fame for manliness, candour, generosity, and fair play."

"Come Major, my old friend, and come Mr. Fitzpatrick, my new friend," said Lord Arran, as he linked the arms of both gentlemen in his own. "Come, until I introduce you to two ladies, each remarkable in her own peculiar style for her feminine charms. I warn you, Mr. Fitzpatrick, to be on your guard against the unpractised wiles of your young cousin, Kathleen, for a fairer, brighter, lovelier maiden never shed the light of her eyes around the ball-room of the Castle. Happy the man who woos her, and thrice happy the man who wins her. As to you, Harvey, you are a veteran in war as in love; and who can tell for how many years your watchword in battle has been that of the old campaigner Julius Cæsar, 'Venus the victorious;' but still, I warn the veteran, as I would the recruit, take care *you too* do not succumb. I am not afraid of you, Major, with Kathleen, but I dread your downfall, should the aunt resolve upon entrapping you. Lady Diana Massey is the daughter of the Duke of Aylesbury, she bestowed her hand at an early period of life, a very early period indeed, upon the uncle of Kathleen; and she was not fully of age when she was once a widow and a second time a wife, married to Mr. Massey; and then before she was thirty, she was a second time a widow, and, I strongly suspect, has resolved to be, a third time, a wife. She is still a dangerously splendid woman. Be on your guard, then, Harvey. I have acted the part of a friend to you, if you are resolved not to marry; 'fore-warned is fore-armed.'"

"I thank your lordship for your kind advice," replied Harvey, smiling. "In entering the mansion of Lady Diana Massey, with your warning words in my ear, I shall strengthen myself with a proverb I picked up in the Spanish wars: '*Hombre apercido medio combatido;*'— 'the man who is upon his guard is the least hurt.'"

CHAPTER X.

MUTUAL PREJUDICES.

THREE days' imprisonment had produced a fearful change in the appearance of Judith Lawson. All life, all motion, all vigour, and nearly all vitality seemed to have departed from her frame. She ate mechanically whatever was set before her. She sat during the whole day in the same seat, and nearly in the same position. Like an automaton, she opened the door whenever she heard a knocking, and then, when the person who had called upon her departed, she again bolted the door regularly on the inside. It was the same at night as in the morning. A mechanical, habitual undoing of the bolts, and a sedulous shutting to of them again. But all this while Judith spoke not a word, asked for nothing, and if spoken to remained obdurately silent.

Her attendant for these three days was the wicked old jailer, Gerald Geraghty. The silence of Judith puzzled the old man at first, then annoyed him, and then disappointed him, for his rage was not yet sated, nor his animosity against the hated name and blood of Lawson fully gratified. He had hoped to find Judith again tempting him with gold, again entreating him to aid in her escape, in order that he might again have the opportunity of refusing her, and of again taunting her with the misdeeds of her father.

Judith either did not seem to be conscious of his presence, or if her eyes ever by accident met his, it was but to turn them away from him, as if they had fallen upon some inanimate piece of furniture in the room; for there was, in those large, black, fierce, lustrous eyes, not one spark of recognition, nor one gleam of resentment.

"I have struck," said the old man to himself, "this proud, haughty young dame too strong a blow at first. I should have managed her more delicately; she should have been made, like the worm, to feel the barb thrilling in every vital; not treated like the fish, which is dragged, at one pull, out of the element in which it had hitherto lived, and in that moment expires. The native element of Judith, wicked Lawson's daughter, was pride, conceit, ambition; the notion that she, because she was richer, was better than others. I have, like a bungler, struck a mortal blow on her pride, and in that blow I have shattered her intellect. Her brain is fast going. I see it in her eye. A week more of such a listless life as she is now leading, and she will become a moping idiot, and the instrument whereby I hope to break Ebenezer's heart will be shattered in my hand, and the massacre of wife and children unavenged; because the child of the murderer will have passed out of my reach.

"What, then, is to be done? or how is she to be aroused from her stupor? or in what way can she be brought back again to think of life—of its vain hopes, and its barren pleasures? She is young—still very young—and life must still be an enjoyment to her. How force her again to think of it?

"Of myself I cannot do anything with her. My grandson has been in and out of her room also, and she has taken no more notice of him than if he had been a dog; and yet he did his best to attract her attention, by pretending for her a sympathy he did not feel. All in vain—quite vain. His voice did not quicken the motion of her eye-lid, no more than if his words were the twittering of sparrows in her ears.

"Ah!" said the old man, clapping his withered hands together with delight, as the idea occurred to him, "there is one mode of arousing her faculties I have not yet tried, and that must be resorted to at once. I remember the drunkard, Murfey, mentioning that she wished to have a woman to wait on her. That wish must now be complied with. At once, that vile old, foul-tongued Puritan, Psalm-singing harridan, the widow of old Jack Gregg, one of Cromwell's hanging provost-marshals, must be sent for. That shrew's shrill voice and loud tongue would rouse the dead. Yes, she must be with this miserable girl to-day, for there is not an hour to be lost, if one would save her from insanity. Never had a handsome maiden so ugly a tire-woman as Judith Lawson will be provided with in the course of a few hours."

It was whilst sitting on a chair on the opposite side of the table at which Judith sat, that the old man had indulged in this soliloquy. But neither whilst he sat there, nor when he rose to go away, did Judith testify by word or look that she was conscious of his presence or his absence. It was only when he closed the door after him, and bolted it on the outside, that she arose, and shot the inside bolts.

She then returned to her chair, and sat in the same listless attitude, her eyes moveless, her hands hanging—drooping by her side, and her frequent deep sighs only testifying that there was life and pain beating at her heart.

The old man, Geraghty, had judged rightly ; he had " struck too strong a blow at first." He had inflicted by a single stab a wound calculated to be mortal in a vital part —Judith's pride—her pride in her father, and her pride in herself as the daughter of that father. There was but one mode of preventing that deep and bleeding wound from becoming instantly mortal, and that was by leading Judith to believe that the old man was a slanderer, and that he wilfully—artfully exaggerated some military excess in which it was her father's duty, in obedience to the orders of his superiors, to participate.

For three days, the first three days of her unjust and cruel captivity, Judith believed the tale of horror as the old man had narrated it. She had the corroborative proof of its truth in a living witness, whose voice, whose manner, whose conduct, and whose rejection of her offer of a thousand pounds to aid in her escape, testified to his sincerity, and demonstrated the accuracy of his narrative. And from the time she had heard that awful accusation against her father—the beloved, and the ever-loving father —Judith thought no more of escape ; in fact, thought no more of herself, but in connexion with her father and her father's crimes. One time she was picturing him to herself, as he had been to her when she was a little child— his hand in hers as they walked together, his playing and rolling with her on the green grass, pulling primroses and violets with her, weaving garlands for her hair, then bearing her in his arms, then carrying her on his back, and then joining in her sports with hoop, with ball, and even with dolls; and then she saw him, as from a child she became a woman, exulting in her beauty, boasting of her as *his* daughter, and, amongst a crowd of admirers, her greatest flatterer, and still the only one that spoke with sincerity and from the bottom of his heart; and then she thought of his gifts in gold and diamonds, and then of his giving over to her an absolute command of all his wealth; and then came, in the midst of all these thoughts, that *same father* hacking the throats of children that had been like herself at one time, and then of his blood-stained hands laid on the hearts of women of her own age; and then, as these two contrasting scenes and figures jumbled and mixed together, the loved object in one being, a human demon in the other, and yet both the same, and that same person her own father! Then came a sense of confusion and distraction, and with it a notion growing hourly stronger the more perceptible it was, that she, Judith, was going mad; or that, by a sudden stoppage of the blood at her heart, where she fancied she found it sometimes cease from beating, that in an instant she would be dead. And at the moment these horrid notions obtained a resting-place in her brain, Judith felt a wish that she either could not or would not restrain, that madness or death might come upon her—an incurable madness, or an instantaneous death!

And thus remained Judith Lawson for three days, but on the fourth day there was a change.

On the morning of the fourth day, when Judith, in response to the knocking at and unchaining the bolts on the door, withdrew the bars that protected it inside, there presented itself to her view, not the accustomed and loathsome form of Gerald Geraghty, but that of an old woman, whose snow-white hairs were confined by a close-fitting black cloth cap, and whose small, thin, wasted figure was fastened in, as it appeared, tightly into a black cloth gown. The head, face, feet, and hands of this old woman, the widow Gregg, were so large, as compared with her body, legs, and arms, that she looked as if nature, in fashioning her, had, in a freak, united the head, face, and hands of a giant to the person of a pigmy. The astonishment, if not terror, which her first appearance was calculated to produce, was likely to be aggravated the moment she opened her mouth, for then she displayed a range of broad, thickset, white teeth, that looked, in their shocking brightness, and terrific strength, as if they were destined to be everlasting, and that she who owned them was, for the misfortune of her fellow-creatures, never doomed to decay.

Shocking as would have been the apparition of this wretched old widow at any other time to Judith, it was far otherwise now. The new face and form at once produced a change in her; for in her abandonment and loneliness, the unhappy young woman felt and recognised she was in the presence of one of her own sex, and the moment she did so, the light of intelligence returned to her eyes, and the flush of surprise mantled upon her cheek.

Judith spoke, however, not one word, in reply to the greeting of the widow Gregg, but having opened the door for her, at once returned to her accustomed seat, and again appeared to abandon herself to that impassible lassitude which had overwhelmed her for the preceding three days.

This state of impassibility was not, however, of long continuance, for Judith felt the change of a woman's hand— even though that was the hand of a forbidden-looking old woman, upon her and about her. Her face and hands were bathed with cold, refreshing, life-giving water; her hair was unplaitted, combed, and re-arranged for her; the room was swept; the table had a clean, snow-white cloth put upon it; the simple breakfast of bread and milk was placed before her, and she was urged—it was by a woman's voice—to take some refreshment, and she mechanically complied with the request so made.

The widow Gregg's general character had been already given by Murfey, who considered her a "shrew," and by Geraghty, who designated her "a harridan," and the truth must be told, that, with the exception of the deceased Provost-marshall in the Cromwellian army, the redoubtable Jack Gregg, there never yet was a man who saw or spoke with this formidable old female, who did not look upon her with repugnance. Whether it was her unsightly form, or her copiousness of hard words, to which her strong teeth gave a perfect distinctness of articulation, it would be difficult to tell. But such was the fact. She was universally hated by men, and she repaid their hatred with interest. But such was not the case with women—for with many, and especially with neglected widows and hopeless old maids, she was regarded as a champion of her sex, and such were disposed to pardon her faults of temper, her irritability, and her vehement rages, because the effects of both were poured forth with an energy that seemed to be inexhaustible on "the ruder sex."

"You have pressed me to eat," said Judith, at last looking up at this terrible old woman; "you have kindly waited upon me. Will you not sit down now and take something yourself?"

"I will do anything that is asked me so civilly," replied the woman, seating herself, and cutting a huge slice of bread, and pouring out a full pitcher of milk; "and I will do it the more readily, when I am asked to do so by one like you, who speaks to me with an English accent. Are you an Englishwoman?"

"I am," replied Judith. "Though I have now lived many years in Ireland, I was born and educated in England. My mother was a Welchwoman, and my father—— oh! Heavens!"

And on the recollection of what she had been told of that father, to whom, as in the time gone by, it was her habit to refer with pride and pleasure, the unhappy young girl burst into a flood of tears, which the old woman, well practised in the ways of her sex, did not by a single word attempt to check or control; but steadfastly went on with her own breakfast, waiting patiently until the storm of passion should subside.

"You have told me," said the widow Gregg, "that you are by birth an Englishwoman—that you have been educated in England; I hope also that you have been instructed in the religion of England—that you are not a Papist."

"I was taught to abominate Popery," replied Judith,— "for I have been directed to believe that it is a profesion of faith that is 'religiously corrupt, and politically dangerous,' and also, that it 'degrades the intellect and enslaves the soul.'"

"Your education reflects great credit on your teachers," observed the old woman, with a distortion of the face intended to be a smile, but which was as hideous as the grin of a hyæna. I have asked you these questions, because the answers you have given me are such as I expected to receive. The moment I looked at you, I at once perceived that the old villain, Gerald Geraghty, was trying to deceive me; for he told me, that in sending me to wait on you, I was to regard you as a person sent here on a charge of being concerned in the Popish plot."

"Did Gerald Geraghty tell you so monstrous an untruth about me?" asked Judith, anxiously.

"As sure as I am an honest woman, he did," replied the widow Gregg.

"How long is the old man Gerald Geraghty known to you?" inquired Judith.

"Gerald Geraghty is known to me—how long, let me see," replied the women, as she rubbed her gigantic chin with a more gigantic hand—"Gerald Geraghty is known to me—ah! I ought to recollect the year well—it was the same year in which that brave patriot, Sir Hardress Waller, seized the Castle of Dublin, and endeavoured to hold it for Parliament against the King's friends, but was obliged to yield it after a siege of five days. In that siege my late blessed husband was blown clean off the top of the Arms Tower of Dublin Castle by a cannon ball, and no part of him was ever afterwards discovered but the butt-end of his matchlock. Yes, it was that same year, the year of grace 1660, that I first saw the ill-looking countenance of that unhanged thief, Gerald Geraghty; that is, I may say, I now know Gerald Geraghty for full twenty years. And all the good of him I have to tell is, that it would be hard, very hard, if not impossible, to determine, whether he is a greater rogue, or a greater liar."

"A liar! a liar!" repeated Judith, as if there was a ray of hope shining in upon her darkened spirit. "Are you quite sure, that the terrible old man has acquired by his own misconduct that worst of all characters, a notorious liar?"

"He is so great a liar," replied Mrs. Gregg, that he could not tell the truth even by accident. Remember what he told me about yourself—that you were a Papist. I knew that it was a lie—must be a lie—could not be the truth, because he said it."

"Then, if he told me a long and dreadful story about my——" Judith's tongue stammered, and she could not pronounce the word,—" about a person in whose honour I am deeply interested, you think that I ought not, because of his notorious character, attach much weight to it?"

"I would not kill a fly upon the oath of Gerald Geraghty," observed Mrs. Gregg. "Why, he is such a liar, and his mind is so crooked, that the straightest road that ever was made, when it is looked at by him, appears to have a bend in it."

"He belied *me* most undoubtedly to you," observed Judith ; " that I am quite sure of ; why then should I not believe—as certainly it is my duty to believe—that he belied him to whom my love and honour are due, by the invention of the most horrible story that ever was told ?"

" And what, may I ask, was the horrible story that wicked old Geraghty invented for the purpose of frightening you ? For to frighten honest people, and good young women like you, who hate Papists, is all that the old scoundrel is now good for," charitably observed the widow Gregg.

"Oh! the most terrible story," replied Judith, "that ever was heard ; it was about soldiers in the Cromwellian army acting most cruelly——"

" A lie !" said Mrs. Gregg.

" And of their pursuing some fugitives, men, women, and children, to a cave, for the purpose of destroying them——"

" A wicked lie !" added Mrs. Gregg.

" And of their stopping up the outlets of the cave, and

burning combustibles around it, for the purpose of smothering the inmates——"

"An atrocious lie," chimed in Mrs. Gregg.

"And then of opening the cave, and killing the survivors——"

"An abominable lie!" remarked Mrs. Gregg.

"And then the throats of wives, daughters, and infants being cut——."

"A most diabolical lie!" roared out Mrs. Gregg, as she jumped up and stamped with her ponderous feet upon the floor. "I have no patience to listen further to such nefarious falsehoods. "But, who, my good woman, was said by this vile miscreant to be a chief actor in these iniquities? I should not be surprised if he fathered them on my late blessed husband, of whose precious remains there is no relic left, but the butt-end of a matchlock."

"No, replied Judith, "the person to whom he assigned the perpetration of all these misdeeds is, I tremble with horror whilst I mention it, my father!"

"*Your* father!!!" cried Mrs. Gregg, almost losing her breath with astonishment, and again seating herself, and repeating "your father!" as if she was astounded at the particularity brought into the narrative of his falsehood, in this instance, by Gerald Geraghty,—"your father! and *who* is your father?"

"My father," answered Judith, hesitating, and as if her whole fate depended upon the manner in which her explanation would be received by the widow Gregg. "My father is Ebenezer Lawson, now a man of large wealth, but formerly such as Gerald Geraghty described him, a soldier in the army of Cromwell, in Ireland, and serving for a time under Lieutenant-General Ludlow."

"Do you mean by your father, Ebenezer Lawson, the

same man who was in the troop of Captain Edward Ludlow?" asked the old woman.

"I do, I do," answered Judith, pale with fear and agitation.

"Ebenezer Lawson," observed the widow Gregg, "I remember him well, and knew his reputation thoroughly. There was not a more active man, nor a more zealous soldier, in the Cromwellian army. A braver or a better man never handled a matchlock, nor quoted a text from Scripture. Ah! if all the army had been like him in spirit, we should be little troubled now with Papists or a Popish plot."

Judith was not sufficiently instructed in the history of the thirty preceding years to be aware how dubious was the compliment conveyed in the last few words of the zealous Mrs. Gregg, to the prowess of her father. That which came home to her heart was the declaration from one who knew him, that there could be no "braver or better man; and as she heard these words her heart thrilled with delight, and bursting into tears, and then casting herself on her knees, she kissed with her rich rosy lips the thick clumsy fingers of the Puritan widow, whilst she exclaimed with trembling voice, and streaming eyes:—

"Thanks! thanks! a thousand, and ten thousand thanks, for the words you have spoken in praise of my most dear and justly loved father. Oh! my good, dear, kind creature, I never, never can repay you for all the happiness your words have given me. You have brought light to the dark, strength to the weak, hope to the despairing. Oh! dear, dear, good woman, tell me your name, that I may ever remember it in my prayers, and that my whole future life may prove to you the depth of my gratitude."

"The name I bear," replied the old widow, "is Abigail

Gregg, at your service; but rise, my dear, good young woman, in order that we may converse at our ease."

"Oh! command me as you please," replied the delighted Judith, "you will find me as obedient as a child."

"You have been religiously educated: you have proper notions about the Papists," observed Mrs. Gregg, "and your principles, therefore, must be good. And so that vile old thief, liar, and miscreant, Gerald Geraghty, went and frightened you with so montrous a lie about that good and godly man your father?"

"Indeed he did," replied Judith.

"And what reason did he give you, or pretend to give you, for your saint-like parent smothering fugitives in a cave, and slaughtering girls and children?"

"What reason!" said Judith, somewhat puzzled by the question. "Well, I am not quite sure, my mind has been in such a state of confusion ever since; but, if I recollect aright, I think, he said it was because they were Irish Papists."

"Ah! ha! I will engage for it, that was the very thing he said," sagaciously remarked the widow Gregg. "You are not aware, perhaps, that Gerald Geraghty is himself an Irish Papist, and that for the purpose of carrying out the nefarious designs of his faction, he has pretended to conform to our religion, so that, whilst he professes Protestantism, he is at heart a Papist; and the sure proof that he is a hypocrite as well as a liar and a thief is, his inventing this horrid story against your father. That is the way those Papists have been going on from the beginning. All liars and all thieves, from the first Papist, the serpent who deluded our mother Eve with a falsehood about an apple tree, down to that most flagrant, money-seeking Papist, Judas Iscariot. He talks of your father murdering women and children. The dear, good, holy man never did any such thing; but what put the lie about him into wicked Gerald Geraghty's head is, that he well knows that such deeds as he attributes to good Ebenezer Lawson were done by the Irish Papists; that these same Irish Papists, in the year 1641, massacred in one morning one hundred and ten thousand two hundred and fifty-one English Protestants; killing seventy-five thousand three hundred and four persons, whilst they were fast asleep in their beds; knocking the brains out of ten thousand one hundred and one persons whilst in the peaceable and harmless occupation of eating their own breakfasts; drowning six thousand eight hundred and nine persons in ponds, rivers, and lakes; burning alive one thousand eight hundred and one persons; cutting the throats of one thousand eight hundred and fifty-seven persons, mostly children under the age of two years, and orthodox Protestants; whilst the remainder were put to death in various ways, and such only as the diabolical ingenuity of a Papist could suggest."

Judith paused at this extraordinary statement. Gerald Geraghty, it appeared to her, was not more minute nor as particular in detailing the deeds of blood he attributed to her father than was the widow Gregg in her specification of other greater and more horrible acts of cruelty, which she imputed, not to the extraordinary wickedness of one individual, but to a whole race of people professing a certain form of the Christian religion.

"Is it not possible, at least I hope so, that there is exaggeration in the account you give of the massacres of 1641?" asked Judith.

"Exaggeration!" cried the widow Gregg, surprised. "On the contrary, there is, if anything, an under statement. Did not that marvellous saint and most wonderful convert from Popery, the Rev. Malachy Marprelate, travel from parish to parish through Ireland, counting the graves of the victims, and authenticating, in the most satisfactory and edifying manner, every single case of monstrous, merciless, and inhuman massacre perpetrated by the Papists? Besides, were not the bodies of thousands of those who had been drowned seen floating on the rivers for months after the massacre? Nay, is not this fact as notorious as that there is sunshine in June, that in one particular place, I think it was in Athlone, some of the dead, murdered Protestants, were to be seen every Saturday-night standing bold upright in the water, and crying out in stentorian voices—'We want to be revenged on the bloody Irish Papists? and are there not cases cited by that lamb of grace, the Rev. Jacob Roundhead, in which it is shewn by a multitude of affidavits, that dead little Protestant children, who had been killed by the Papists and eaten, were heard at night crying around the doors of their carnivorous murderers—' *Give us our heads, or the bones itself ?*' The least and smallest of all crimes that a Papist can commit is to tell lies; and be assured that the old rapscallion, Gerald Geraghty, was, only doing what he thought was a laudable action, when he invented a falsehood, and attributed to your father those deeds of cruelty, which, probably, his own hand had perpetrated, and which, Protestants being the victims, his own cruel hand had readily inflicted."

With these words the widow Gregg resumed her occupation.

Judith remained for some time in deep thought; and the result of her reflections she thus briefly expressed, as she rose from her chair with renewed life and vigour in her limbs :—

"I have permitted myself to be deceived by the cunning and wickedness of a heartless old man. Alas! for this poor country; it seems to me to be divided between two classes of persons, each hating the other with such remorseless animosity, they are willing each to believe the worst things that can be said against the other, and when they can find no facts on which to justify their hatreds, then they have recourse to a fertile fancy, and concoct against one another accusations that are incredible; and things, that their own hearts must tell them they could not and would not themselves do, they are willing to suppose could and would be done by those they detest."

CHAPTER XI.

FACTS AND FICTIONS.

To the whole of the conversation between Judith Lawson and Abigail Gregg there had been an attentive listener; and there was not one word, and not one single abusive phrase applied by the latter to himself, or to the religion to which he formerly belonged, and had publicly abjured, that came to the ears of the listener, Gerald Geraghty, as a novelty.

It was as a last and desperate experiment, (the only one by which he could revive the faculties of Judith, and make her again capable of suffering,) that he had introduced the widow Gregg to her. In his craving, and truly diabolical desire for revenge, he sought to afflict Judith because she *was* the daughter of Lawson; and through her he hoped to bring agony and despair, such as he himself had once felt, to the heart and affections of Ebenezer. What cared he, then, with all his faculties fixed upon the attainment of his revenge, (and he had resolved upon something that would be as awful as the injuries that had been done to himself,) if in the progress necessary to be made before that great purpose was reached, an old and hated woman should mention his name with scorn, or abuse the faith to which he had formerly been an avowed adherent? If abuse and vituperation of himself helped him on his path, he welcomed them as an ally, and would, if such could be serviceable have provoked their further display, and still more intense expression.

"This venomous old harridan," said Gerald to himself, when silence had succeeded to the animated conversation carried on between the old and young woman, "will now, doubtless, conceive it to be a duty to make herself the medium of communication between this miserable girl and that bloodthirsty miscreant, her father; and so take that very step which will hasten the downfall both of father and daughter. I hope so, for I long for the hour when I shall see both stretched as lifeless corpses before me; but still more do I pine for the moment when I shall bid Lawson despair and die, as he thinks over his innocent and unprovoked victims in the cave of Dundalk. And now to concert with that good boy, my grandson, upon the means of ensnaring the young woman, and of baffling the plots of that detestable old hag. The boy or I must ever be on the watch, our eyes know no sleep, and our bodies no rest, until that purpose is secured for which, I believe, my life has been prolonged."

Unrelenting, untiring, insatiable in his fell designs, the

wicked old man devoted himself to the murderous task on which he had now concentrated all his energies.

The conversation with the widow Gregg had given to Judith Lawson not only refreshed strength of body, but also renewed power of mind. The horrid tale told to her about her father had weighed down upon her heart and head as if it were a mountain of lead oppressing her to the very earth, and rendering her alike incapable of thought, feeling, and motion. That awful crushing weight had now been removed, and with revived strength and spirits came back her natural courage and her indomitable resolution.

For three long days she had ceased to think of her incarceration, of its injustice, of the cruel and unprovoked wrong that had been done to her; but now all these sentiments returned to her, and she felt herself to be the same dauntless Judith Lawson who had discharged a musket at the heart of her captor with the intention of slaying him; and again, as on the first night she had entered that abode, which was called a prison, she resolved that if courage and determination could burst her bonds, her captivity must speedily be at an end.

With this view, Judith, for the first time, commenced an examination of the prison in which she had been confined. She wished to ascertain whether it presented any or no facilities for escape. She at once perceived that the chamber and sleeping-room allocated to her use, with the passage leading to them, must occupy the entire floor of what was a circular tower. To that tower light and air were admitted to the sitting-room by a large square window, and to the bed-room by a long narrow slit in the wall, eight inches in length and not more than one inch in breadth.

The only outlets for escape from her prison were, as she at first conjectured, either by the window of the sitting-room or by the door—the latter, however, leading to the lower apartments, where her jailers were to be expected to be always on the watch.

As she looked through the latticed window of the sitting-room, she perceived that it fronted another window like itself, in a tower about thirty paces distant, and that the two towers were on both sides flanked by connecting walls; and in each of these walls were square windows of the same size, and on a level with the room in which she stood. Beyond this close and narrow space there was no view from the window; and, being desirous to ascertain how the intermediate space below was occupied—by a moat or earth—or to what purposes it was applied, she pushed open the lattice, and looked down into what she at once recognised as a flagged court-yard beneath. This she perceived by a momentary glance, for she was not allowed to take more than a moment in looking beneath her, as the instant her face and person were seen looking out, her ears were saluted by the loud, ferocious, rabid barking of four monstrous bulldogs, that with glaring eyes, and glistening teeth, and open mouths, yelled out in furious rage against her; whilst in the midst of them stood, with malignity in his eye, and a diabolical smile on his lips, the hated old warder of the prison—Gerald Geraghty!

What was it made the brave-hearted Judith shrink back with terror, as she thus gazed upon the old man and the enraged brutes around him—looking like a demon with a band of imps under his control? She could not account for the sickening, fainting sensations that came over her, and that impelled her, with hurried and trembling hands, to close the casement, and so, if she could, to shut out the noise of the growling beasts beneath, and in so doing to put an end to the fear, the horror, and the affright that had so unexpectedly come upon her.

Judith covered her eyes, and endeavoured to close her ears against the noise which was still raging and roaring beneath, when the old woman approached her and said:—

"What is the matter with you, child of honest Ebenezer Lawson? You look pale and ill."

"I feel ill, very ill," said Judith in a trembling voice, as she endeavoured to answer the old woman. "I have, by accident, again seen that terrible old man, who frightened me with the horrid story about my dear father. In looking from that window on the court-yard beneath, I beheld him with four dogs, and it seemed to me—it was a foolish fancy, I know—that he was inciting them to tear me to pieces, and marking me out to them as their destined prey."

"And, no doubt, the wicked old villain would do so, if he had the power and the opportunity," replied Mrs. Gregg. "It is the way with him, and all his sort and creed, to us poor Englishwomen. They would slaughter us all if they could."

"But what have I done to this old man that I should be so hated by him?" asked Judith. "I never did to him or his the slightest harm: on the contrary, I never yet met a poor Irish person I did not aid to the best of my power, and I did this without ever considering what particular form of faith any one of them professed."

"Ah! Lord help your innocent heart," piously exclaimed the widow Gregg, "there is no taming these Irish; the only way to deal with them is to cut them off, root and branch—the old, because they are wicked, and the young, because if they live, they are sure to grow up to be wicked. Ah! my poor, dear, blessed husband, of whom the only relic now left to me is, as I told you, the butt-end of his matchlock, he was the man, in his own charitable way, knew how to manage them. He did not consider them to be fellow-creatures at all, and therefore, wherever he fairly could, he knocked them on the head, or hung them up, as if they were so many wild wolves———"

Loud shrieks and cries, mingled with a noise as of heavy blows, interrupted the widow Gregg in a discourse, which she regarded as alike instructive and edyfying.

"What's this? what's this?" exclaimed the old woman; "what new piece of deviltry is that old miscreant, Gerald Geraghty, now performing? What new piece of mischief is now afoot?"

As the woman thus spoke, she pushed open the casement which Judith had so carefully closed, and looked down into the court-yard, from which the shrieks appeared to be ascending.

So long as blows appeared to be given, and shrieks were heard, the woman continued to gaze into the court-yard. .

Both blows and shrieks ceased at the same instant, and as they did so, the widow withdrew her head, closed the window, and stumping over, with a grin of delight upon her terrific countenance, to the side of Judith, she cried out, as if highly delighted:—

"Wonders will never cease! I never thought that old villain, Gerald Geraghty, would or could do anything that would afford me any satisfaction, and yet he has done so. I have had the infinite pleasure of seeing him beating that imp of the devil, his grandson; a youthful miscreant who has the wit of Belzebub, with the strength and agility of a monkey, to perform any prank or misdeed that his own bad disposition, or the malice of others, may suggest to him. Ho! ho! it did my heart good to see old Gerald flailing him; I did not think the vile old scoundrel had so much strength left; but he knocked the young vagabond clean down five times, with as many blows of his staff. The imp of the devil has at last escaped from his hands, but covered with blood and bruises. What a pity old Gerald did not knock the brains out of the young miscreant; or that the young miscreant had not the spirit to turn against his grandfather, and slay him! Oh! it is a fine thing to see these Irish wretches quarrelling with each other."

Judith did not interrupt the discourse of Mrs. Gregg by a single observation, for so absorbed was she in the contemplation of her own strange position, and with vague dreams of effecting her escape from it, that she scarcely comprehended the purport of Mrs. Gregg's observations. All she gleaned from it was the fact, that there existed, in connexion with her prison, another person, of whom she had never heard before, and that the person so referred to was the grandson of Geraghty."

"So! said Judith, "the wicked old man has a grandson; I did not know that until now. Do you know the grandson? what age is he?"

"The grandson," replied Mrs. Gregg, "is, I should think, above seventeen, but does not look, so stunted is his growth, to be more than ten or twelve years of age. I think it is seven years since I first saw him, and he is, in appearance, the same to-day that he was then. I never knew and I never heard any good of him. On the contrary, he was always doing mischief, and, therefore, always a prime favourite with his grandfather. I do not think it is in the nature of the boy to perform one act of virtue;

and I do not believe that his grandfather would beat him unless he had discovered the lad doing good. I am quite puzzled to know what can be the cause of quarrel, and will, therefore, at once leave you, and try and unravel this, to me, most marvellous and unlooked for event; for I repeat to you, such a detestable set are these Irish Papists, that a young person amongst them would never, of his own accord, so much as think of doing good, and that an old person amongst them would never chastise one of his young people but for being unlike himself, in actually doing or thinking of doing, something which a truly pious English person would either laud or approve of."

And with this observation Abigail Gregg, who always regarded herself as "a model of charity," left the apartment with the intention of descending to the hall of Brass Castle.

Mrs. Gregg quitted the room in which Judith sat, and carefully closed the door of the apartment behind her; but in the passage leading from the chamber to the outward door, from which the stairs descended, she met full front the watchful janitor, Gerald Geraghty, who, with a broad grin on his face, and a bunch of keys in his hand, thus saluted the widow:—

"The top of the morning to you, widow! Might I take the liberty of asking you where are you off to in such a hurry; or has the Doctor told you that a promenade would be good for your precious health?"

The widow Gregg's gigantic eyes, in her large unsightly head, flashed with indignation as these questions were put, in a bantering tone, to her by old Geraghty.

It would have been a curious study for the physiognomist to have contemplated the faces and figures of these two old malevolent individuals, as they gazed with intense hatred and contempt for each other, and neither caring to conceal the abomination they entertained. Mutually inimical, yet there was a common resemblance between the two, for each nurtured in the heart an enmity against unoffending individuals, races, or religions, and each sought to disguise from himself and herself an innate wickedness of disposition, by pretending that its indulgence was but resentment or disgust, felt on account of the offensiveness of others. It was English bigotry face to face with, and frowning at Irish prejudice; and never, perhaps, were unjust national prejudices more appropriately represented than when they were thus personified in senility without love, or honour, or respect; fanaticism, and uncharitableness, and spite, on the one side; passion, vindictiveness, suspicion, and insatiable hate, with unforgiving revenge, upon the other.

"I'm sorry to find we're not on speaking terms, widow Gregg," said Geraghty. "Is this your gratitude to me for making interest with the Government to get you to wait on that beautiful young lady, who has pockets full of gold to give away to anybody she takes a fancy to?"

"What I want to know, Mr. Geraghty, from you is—how come you in this passage? what business have you here?" asked Mrs. Gregg.

"Indeed, very little business of my own," replied Geraghty; "but that I'm greatly afraid politeness will be the death of me. I just came into this passage to save your precious old knuckles being tattered to pieces beating at that door, if you wanted to go down stairs; first, because nobody will mind your knocking, and next, because there are positive orders that so long as the young lady in that room remains there, you will have to stay along with her."

"What do you mean?" exclaimed Mrs. Gregg, bursting

out into a fit of rage—" what do you mean, you old thief of the world?"

"Manners, widow, if you please," replied Geraghty. "Old thief of the world. Why, if you are going out, ma'am, you need not be in such a hurry as to leave your name and title behind you."

"Why, you old thief of the world," repeated Mrs. Gregg, "do you mean to say I am not to come in and go out of this place as I please?"

"As to coming in here, it was your own act, widow," replied Geraghty,—" your own act, of your own free will; but as to going out again, that depends upon those who hold the keys; and may the worst of bad luck overtake me—that is, may I be married to you before I die, but out of this prison you don't stir a single inch as long as I'm warder." And as he said this, he clinked the keys merrily in his withered hands. "Or rather, I should say," he added—"for the Lord forbid you were to stay here for ever—as long as the lady in that room is detained a prisoner."

"Oh, you horrid, vile, wicked wretch," said Mrs. Gregg, "how can you look an honest, truthful, pious, holy Englishwoman in the face, and yet allude to that dear, good young English lady, that you have been driving mad with your shocking, frightful, Irish, Popish lies?"

"What do you mean?" asked Geraghty, with a stare of affected surprise in his red-lidded, inflamed-looking grey eyes. "Did that young English lady—lady, *enagh!*—did she say, or rather, did she dare to say that I had been telling her shocking lies?"

"And so you have, you heartless villain," observed Mrs. Gregg.

"Look there, now! I do my best to help a poor dear little girl to pass away her time agreeably, and what is my reward? I am accused of telling lies! Pray, what lies did she say *I* had been telling? Did she say that I told her *you* were a beauty? because a bigger lie than that the wit of man never invented."

"No, no; I see by your affected mirth that you are trying to conceal from me the shame you cannot but feel at your lies being discovered," sagaciously remarked Mrs. Gregg.

"It is very good in you to say so, widow," said Geraghty, grinning; "but come now, tell us what were the lies she laid at my door? Did she say I was making love to her, or proposing marriage, or any of that sort of thing?"

"Ah, you have asked me a question, and I will strike you dumb with shame and confusion by the plain answer I will give it. She has told me *all!*—mark that—*all*—I said *all*—do you hear that? for I said *all*—aye, every word you said to her."

"Indeed!—well, what is it? out with it. Don't be as stingy with your news as you are with your alms."

"Well, then, here it is," said Mrs. Gregg, triumphantly and solemnly; "she said that you had been telling her a shocking story about her father, and his murdering your wife and children, and——"

"Myself," added Geraghty, with a bantering laugh; "did she not tell you that I told her of my own self being murdered along with my wife and children?"

"No, no, you treacherous, false-hearted miscreant, I know you well," said the infuriated Mrs. Gregg; "you told her an artful, truthful, consistent tale—a tale that froze her very blood with fear, and that was near driving her distracted—that's what you did, and I dare you now to deny it."

"Well, well, widow, it is quite true; I did tell her such

a story," said Geraghty, assuming a half repentant air. "But now, as I have admitted the fact, just answer me one question fairly and truly."

"What is it?" grunted Mrs. Gregg.

"Did she believe it?"

"Did she believe it?" repeated Mrs. Gregg, in surprise. "Did she believe it? To be sure she did."

"What! every word of it?"

"Yes, every word of it."

"From the beginning to the end?"

"Yes, from the beginning to the end."

"Well," exclaimed Geraghty, as if delighted with himself, "that bangs Banagher, and Banagher, it is said, bangs the——but no matter—an old gentleman with a cloven foot, and, according to all accounts, an Englishman by birth. And so she believed all I said, as if it was truth from the beginning to the end. I'd like to see the Saxon could on the instant invent a story that would drive the hearer of it almost mad. Well, after all that you must admit, widow, that I am a clever old chap, when my tongue has had such an effect on the night's rest of a rattling young girl like her yonder."

"I'll admit whatever you wish that you think will please an old scoundrel that is such a coxcomb as to take a pride in what he ought to be ashamed of, and is vain of being considered a clever liar. That I will do for you," said Mrs. Gregg, "if you will admit that the horrid tale you told her was a falsehood, from the first word to the last."

"Did you not tell her so already?" asked Geraghty.

"I did," innocently answered Mrs. Gregg.

"And would you tell lies?" asked Geraghty.

"Not to save my life," replied Mrs. Gregg.

M

"Very well, as you always tell the truth," observed Geraghty, "and as you, being a truth-teller, have assured her that my tale of horrors, as you call it, was nothing but a pure invention, then that assurance of yours must be sufficient for her. If I was to say anything more on the subject it would only puzzle her, and perhaps make the little darling uneasy : it would, as you will see, widow, put her into a complete quandary, because she would say : 'Here is Mr. Geraghty told me a tale about my father; Mr. Geraghty said that tale about my father was the truth ; and then Mr. Geraghty comes and tells me that the tale about my father is a lie ; and he now tells me the truth, when he says that he told that which was a lie—but if he now tells me a lie, when he says he is telling the truth, how am I to know that what he calls a lie is the truth, and that what he calls the truth is a lie ; and then, which is the lie and which is the truth ? is the truth a lie or is the lie a truth ?' There is a riddle for you, widow. See if *you* can make sense out of it, for *I* can't. In fact, I'm so puzzled for the moment, so bewildered, that I am actually inclined to think that it is you, the truth-telling Englishwoman, who have been telling lies to the young woman, whilst all the harm the poor, lying Irishman has been doing to her is telling to her the truth, and, as they say to witnesses about to be sworn, ' the truth, the whole truth, and nothing but the truth.' "

"You are an old villain," cried Mrs. Gregg, in amazement at the volubility of the old man.

"Call me what you like," replied Geraghty, "only don't hurt my feelings by saying I am an old woman, and my name—Abigail Gregg."

"You are an incorrigible old villain," added Mrs. Gregg.

" Not so," answered Geraghty, " for I have renounced the errors of Rome to embrace those of Geneva; and even your favourite preacher, that lamb of grace, the Rev. Jacob Roundhead, once compared me to a brand snatched from the burning. Poor man, he little knew how near I should be placed to *a spit-fire*, who was once the wife of a Cromwellian Provost-Marshal. And now, widow, compliments being passed between us, I must leave you to take care of the young lady. I dare not let you out, lest you should be placed in a condition like her's, and—*somebody run away with you !*"

CHAPTER XII.

THE IMP.

It was with feelings greatly agitated, and her senses in no slight degree confused, that the widow Gregg returned to the apartment of Judith, who, instead of sitting in the chair, in which the old woman had left her, was now standing at the window, and her attention occupied by something that was occurring in the room of the opposite tower.

" Come here, Mrs. Gregg, come here directly," said Judith, the moment she heard the heavy footsteps of the widow in her room. " Come here, and tell me if you can recognise the young person opposite; who he is, or what it is he means by the attitudes into which he is throwing himself."

" As sure as I am an honest holy, pious Englishwoman," said Mrs, Gregg, with characteristic energy and meekness, " that young person opposite is an imp of the devil, and grandson to old Beelzebub, Gerald Geraghty. The young miscreant was at all times diabolically ugly; but now the two black eyes the grandfather has given him, with the cut on his cocked nose, have made him such a fright that the unhappy mother who bore him would not know him. What a terrible mangling he has had! But what does the imp mean, or what is he in such a passion about? Oh! I see he is pointing to us to open the window. Shall I do as he wishes? There can be no harm in it."

"Do," said Judith, "what you think right. Nothing can occur but what may serve us. At present, and without help from outside, I see no chance of escape; and in an attempt to effect that, I am sure you will aid me as far as lies in your power."

"I will do anything that I by any means possibly can to vex and thwart Gerald Geraghty," answered Mrs. Gregg, "who is, I see, determined upon keeping you and me here for the rest of our lives, if he can. There now, the window is open; what can the imp mean? What does he want? If he has anything to say to us, instead of going on with his antics, why does he not bawl it out, as he must know right well we could hear him at the short distance he is from us?".

"Perhaps," remarked Judith, "he is afraid of being overheard by his grandfather."

"Afraid of being overheard by his grandfather!" repeated Mrs. Gregg. "And why so? Ah!" she exclaimed, delighted, as the idea occurred to her, "I see and understand it all now. The imp is vexed with his grandfather, and, whilst his bones are sore and his wounds smarting, he wishes to have revenge upon the old man—and the surest and best revenge is to spite the old grandfather by helping you to escape."

"I hope in heaven such may be be the case," replied Judith; "but how are we to place ourselves in communication with him?"

"He is telling us the way, if we could understand him," replied Mrs. Gregg. "What does he intend by pointing down to the bottom of the window, and placing his hand inside, and low down, near to the spot at which he is standing, and then showing a rope with a nooze at the end: Is it that his grandfather is going to hang us out of the window?"

"No—no," replied Judith; "I comprehend now perfectly what he proposes. See, there is a strong iron hook in here, corresponding with, I suppose, a hook on the opposite side—and what he means is, that he will cast over the rope here, which we can at once fasten on with the noose to this hook. I will stoop down and show him I do understand him. See, he jumps at if with joy he is so understood; and now he waves to us to go back. It is to cast his rope. Stand by, good Mrs. Gregg; depend upon it, I shall be sure to catch the rope."

As Judith had supposed his intentions, from the boy's actions, the result proved she was correct. The rope was flung with an unerring, and, as it would appear, a long practised hand into the room, where it was instantly caught by Judith, the noose fastened on, then pulled tightly by the boy, until it seemed as rigidly fixed as if it had been arranged for a tight-rope dancer; and the moment it was so fastened the boy appeared outside, caught it with hands and knees, and then, flinging himself round as if falling on his back, he, with the rapidity of a squirrel, sped across by it, and stood in the same apartment with Judith and Mrs. Gregg.

Judith could not refrain from starting when she saw

standing opposite to, and gazing up at her with black, brilliant, small, ferret-like eyes, that strange little being that Mrs. Gregg had denominated "the imp."

There were few epithets of Abigail Gregg, the venerable relict of the Cromwellian Provost-Marshal, applied by her, with an unction peculiarly her own, to any one of her fellow-creatures, that did not smack of an exaggeration closely bordering upon uncharitableness. And yet, her designation of the grandson of Gerald Geraghty as "the imp," might be fairly alleged as an exception to that general objection to which her language was liable.

"The imp" was fully as old as Mrs. Gregg had declared him to be, while his appearance was that of a stunted boy. His small, round, bullet-shaped head was covered by bristly blood-red hair, close cut, or, as it appeared to be, almost close shaven, as if it were for the purpose of exhibiting, in their full deformity, two enormously large ears, that stuck stiffly out on both sides, as if they were horns. There was not a quarter of an inch of forehead, and even that little ran in a sharp line backwards, from the projecting eye-brows and short cocked nose, which seemed to turn away from the pursed-out thick lips, and projecting pig-like teeth. The long chin was turned up as if it wished to follow the example of the nose; the eyes we have already described; they were so small and black, that they seemed to be without any white or yellow colour beneath the eyelids. The body was small and starved-looking, the hands and legs had unnaturally long fingers and toes, and the dress of "the imp" was wretched in the extreme, the coat being not only patched but ragged, and the small old leather breeches scarcely reaching to the bare-legged knees, whilst the feet were as uncovered as the hands.

The widow Gregg had compared "the imp" to a monkey, and there was some aptitude in the simile, not merely on account of his marvellous activity; but also, because when his body was not in movement he exactly resembled one of that tribe of animals, standing on its hind legs; the arms with the long fingers, hanging down, and the round head and cunning face, and black malevolent eyes, constantly oscillating from one side to the other, or wagging up and down, or turning suddenly round.

Thus stood the imp the moment he reached the room in which Judith was confined. He stopped looking up in her face, as if waiting for her to address him, but as he did so, he was like a wild beast, watching with his stretched-out ears, for any sound that might warn him against a surprise; as if his sight alone was given to that which was present, and his hearing reserved for all that was beyond the scope of his vision.

"Why have you desired to come here?" asked Judith, so soon as she was able to recover from the surprise occasioned by this almost unearthly apparition.

"For revenge!" responded the boy, in a voice as hoarse, as abrupt, and as quick as that of a parrot: as if the use of words was not a faculty that belonged to him, as a man, but was a trick of language, taught to him by beings superior to himself.

"Revenge!" cried Judith; "revenge! who could have wronged a creature such as you? Upon whom or against whom do you seek revenge?'

"Grand-daddy," replied the boy.

"What has he done to you?" asked Judith.

"Look," said the boy, as he pointed with lightning-like nimbleness to his eyes, nose, arms, and legs, on the two latter of which there were blue swollen marks, as if the memorials of heavy blows.

"Oh!" the horrid old villain," exclaimed Mrs. Gregg, manifesting a sympathy for the boy, by abusing a person she had previously detested. "I always knew he was a cruel, heartless wretch. So you want to revenge yourself upon that dried up remnant of an ill-spent life. But how have revenge?"

The imp pointed to Judith.

"What!" said Judith, delighted, "by helping me to escape?"

The imp nodded his head.

"You wish to vex your grandfather: and to revenge the injuries he has done to you, by coming here to tell me you will help me to escape from this place?"

The imp nodded his head.

"Good boy! good, dear boy," exclaimed the delighted Judith. "Help me to escape, and I will clothe you in satin and diamonds like one of the Queen's pages. You shall have bright shoes of Spanish leather, and gold-embroidered stockings."

"Bah!" snorted out contemptuously the imp.

"Help me to escape, and I will give you as a reward for yourself, gold that would be equal to a king's ransom."

"Bah!" again impatiently and contemptuously snorted out the imp.

"Oh!" say, dear boy," said Judith, terrified at finding that she was by her offers irritating, when she intended to soothe the little savage before her. "Oh! say, in what way I can be most serviceable to you. What I can do to afford you pleasure, by my escaping from this den? What can I give you?"

"Revenge," shrieked out the imp.

"I see, I see plainly what the im—, the youth means," said Mrs. Gregg. "He wants not from you, and will not take from you, silver or gold, or rich clothes, for helping you to escape, because your escape will give him that revenge he wishes for. Thus he has come to you to aid him in having that revenge."

"Right," said the imp, nodding his wicked little head approvingly at Mrs. Gregg.

"I care not what his motives may be, so that he does a good action," remarked Judith, "by aiding me in the object of my wishes, and releasing me from the hands of wicked men. He intimated, as I understood him, that he comes here to punish his grandfather, by assisting me. But how can he do so? Knows he any secret passage from this chamber by which I may pass into the open air?"

The imp shook his head,

"Then can you get hold of the keys which your grandfather has?" asked Judith, directly appealing to the boy.

The imp again shook his head.

"Or is there any one in the prison that you know who would, for the sake of a large reward, aid me in my flight?" asked Judith.

The imp again shook his head.

"Then how, in God's name, am I to escape from this prison, or how can you render me the slightest assistance?"

The imp opened the palm of his left hand, and, then with the forefinger of the right hand, appeared to be writing on it with the speed of a stenographer.

"By writing a letter?" said Judith, surprised.

The imp nodded approvingly.

"Writing a letter!" exclaimed Judith, "alas! I perceive I have neither pen, ink, nor paper."

The imp looked around the room, jumping up and down, on and off tables and chairs with the lightness of a bird, and the agility of a cat; and then, not discovering the objects of his search, he, without uttering a word, jumped out of the window, ran along the rope, and disappeared.

"Is the creature mad?" asked Judith, equally confounded by the sudden appearance and unexpected disappearance of the imp. "Or rather, are we not wasting our time by holding communication with a half-witted being, who seems destitute of the faculties and sense commonly given to the great bulk of mankind?"

"He is Irish," remarked the widow Gregg—"purely Irish—of Irish birth and Irish race—and I never yet knew one of the breed, no matter how naturally dull, stupid, or destitute of sense he might be, who had not wit enough to do mischief. Never you mind the imp. He fancies he is breaking one of the ten Commandments, 'Honour thy father and thy mother,' in helping you, and with this temptation for him to commit what he fancies is a sin, be sure of him: he will not rest easy until he has carried into action what he believes and nourishes as an evil intention. Behold him now!—did I not judge rightly of the imp?"

As the widow Gregg spoke, the imp was seen crossing he rope, with a pen and a single sheet of paper in his mouth, and an ink-bottle in his left hand, whilst, with the right alone he pulled himself from one window to the other. The moment he reached the room, he bounded over to the table, placed the writing materials upon it, and then pointed to Judith to sit down.

"He wishes me to write," remarked Judith, unable to bring herself into direct communication with him, or rather feeling as if the boy spoke a different language from her own, and that he as well as herself, stood in need of an interpreter. "Write!" she exclaimed, "to whom does he want me to write?"

"Daddy," croaked out the imp.

"He means your father," said Mrs. Gregg, "these brutal Irish always call their fathers '*daddies.*'"

Oh! now I guess what he means," said Judith; "he suggests to me to write to my father telling him to come to me, and so obtain my release."

The imp nodded his head.

"I will do so," observed Judith, "I will write to my dear father. But what shall I say to him; at once expressing to him the desire, he should come directly to my aid, and yet relieve his mind, so far as I can, with truth, from that pain and grief he must have endured on my account? Let me think."

Judith leant her head upon her hand in reflection for some minutes, and then, with a firm nerve, wrote the following lines:

"MY DEAREST FATHER,—This letter will be placed in your hands by one who wishes to release me from my present place of confinement. He will be your guide.

"The person who seized upon me, and carried me off by violence, I have never seen since he effected that object. His purpose, I believe, was to force me to marry him; but he has never, since he put me into a place of confinement ventured to appear before me. I therefore cannot tell you his name, nor give you a description of his person.

"He who takes to you this letter can tell you what force, if any, you should bring with you to ensure my freedom—my restoration to home, and to you, my beloved father. Ever your true and loving child,

"JUDITH.

"P.S.—I have met in my prison with a very good woman, whose late husband served in the army with you. The grief of my captivity has been relieved by her praises of you, and of your good and glorious achievements, when you were a soldier. One of my first acts, on being restored to home, will, with your permission, be to make such a provision for this good and pious woman, a native of our own dear country, as will secure her a comfortable maintenance for the remainder of her days."

All the time that Judith had been thinking over and writing her letter, the imp had been employing his natural gifts and accomplishments as a posture-master, an acrobat, and a tight-rope dancer, for the edification of Mrs. Gregg, exciting that good waman's astonishment, and her disposition to piety, by repeated prayers that he might break his back, or crack his neck, or give himself such a fall as would disable him for life, if not bring his existence then and there to a natural conclusion at once.

As soon as Judith had written the letter, and addressed it to her father, she read the contents aloud; and it would be difficult to tell which of the two, the widow or the imp, manifested the greater satisfaction at its perusal. The widow being unaccustomed to employ words of approval or admiration of anything, said nothing, but wiped her great goggle eyes, from which the tears were flowing abundantly; whilst the imp, who never spoke a word of any kind he could avoid, grinned like a baboon, whilst he performed six somersaults in succession.

"Here," said Judith, folding up the letter in a small silk, black neckband, or kerchief, which she removed from her throat, "here, boy, take this letter. Be you the bearer of it to my father, and then ask of him what you most desire, and he will give it, if it's his own, or obtain it for you from another. In my own name he will, I promise it, give you that which you most desire."

"Revenge! revenge! revenge!" exclaimed the imp, as he danced about with hellish glee.

In the midst of the imp's glee there was a sudden pause. Although no sound was perceptible to the ears of Judith or Mrs. Gregg, he stopped as if he had heard something. Then, placing one of his long, bony fingers to his puckered-up lips, he nodded to them to be silent; and darting suddenly out of the window, he ran over the outstretched rope to the room opposite, then pointed, as if in alarm, to them to let loose the rope, having previously relaxed it himself for that purpose. His wish was at once complied with; the rope at the same moment withdrawn, and the casement of the window at which he had first appeared suddenly closed, and as it did so he disappeared from view.

All this was so hurriedly and precipitately done—not one minute elapsing between Judith's placing the letter to her father in the imp's hand, and every vestige of his having been in the room effaced—that Judith felt a sudden shock, as if the presentiment of future evil to herself for having written the letter, and to her father, to whom it had been addressed.

"Alas!" exclaimed Judith, endeavouring to account to herself for the sad and mournful feelings which were overcoming her. "Alas! I know not when I may expect that letter to reach my father, nor how much longer I am therefore to remain here. I hope we may soon see that strange boy again."

"If he can do any more mischief, you may be sure of seeing him again," replied Mrs. Gregg; "but if there is nothing else to be gained from an interview than doing you good, or rendering you a service, there is the certainty you will never again look upon the ugly, inhuman visage of the imp."

Even whilst Judith was lamenting the precipitation with

which the imp had left her, and the old woman was speculating on the probabilities of the imp re-appearing, that strange being was with his grandsire, and delivering into the hands of the old man the letter that had been addressed by the captive to her father, Ebenezer Lawson.

It was with an eager, trembling, but still careful hand, that Gerald Geraghty unrolled the black silk kerchief of Judith, coolly turning it out, fold by fold, as if it was his intention thus to refold it again; and it was with a scrupulous, tender touch he laid his hand on the enclosed letter, opening it as timidly as if he was apprehensive that the smallest crease or most minute soil might serve to detect its having been surreptitiously read.

At last the letter lay unfolded before the old man. With hawk-like eye he ran, in an instant, over its contents. Then perused it slowly and deliberately; then re-perused it a second time, stopping at every line, and every portion of a sentence, and then taking in the whole sentence again, as if he were weighing the words, and balancing in his mind whether each and all could be subservient to the fell purposes he had in view. At last he had the letter off by heart; could repeat it without difficulty; and, as he rehearsed it over to himself, there was the red flush of malignant joy diffused over every feature, whilst a bright fire, as of hell, shone out of his eyes.

"Dear, good, precious child!" said Gerald, as he stooped down and patted, with his withered, trembling hand, the fiery bullet-head of the imp, who sat, resting on his hams, looking up at him, and as he did so, grinning with all the mischief-loving cunning of an ape, "Dear, good, precious child," said the old man, "you have done my bidding beautifully; and you shall have your reward."

"Oh, ho!" croaked with triumph the imp, as he

tumbled heels over head, coming round to the same position, and back to the same spot on which he had bounded as if he were a tennis ball.

"Yes, child," added Gerald Geraghty, "I, and I alone, know how to reward you. Do I not, my precious gossoon?"

The imp grinned from ear to ear, and nodded.

"They wished to bribe you?"

The imp nodded.

"They wished to tempt you to betray your poor, dear, good, loving grand-daddy?"

The imp again nodded.

"They offered you gold, I warrant?"

Again the imp nodded.

"They offered you, too, I suppose, rich clothes, fine stockings, new shoes, silks and satins to your heart's content?"

The imp nodded.

"Ah! the fools, the fools, the born fools! they never heard or read, I suppose, of the old fable of the cock and the jewel, and the sensible remark of chanticleer, that he would sooner have one good grain of corn to fill his craw, than all the diamonds and jewels in an Emperor's crown. They offered to my brave gossoon things that would tempt themselves, and for the sake of which they and their betters sell themselves—bodies, souls, honour, friends, wives, and children. They never thought—and it is well they did not—of that which, if offered to you, might have tempted you to sell your poor grand-daddy to them. They would never offer you what I, my darling, will give you. They have no such stuff as this for you, my precious baby."

As the old man so spoke he opened a cupboard, and took from it a large black bottle.

The eyes of the imp glistened with delight as he beheld the bottle, and he went jumping about the room, and clapping his hands with delight.

"Yes, there is the reward, and *that* would have been the temptation *for you*," said the old man, laughing, as he filled out from the bottle a full glass of the strong, ardent liquor.

The imp bounded to his side.

"Open your blessed lips," said the old man, "open your darling mouth wide—wider—wider. Shut your dear, good-looking eyes, and see what the Lord will send you."

The imp did as he was directed, and the full glass was slowly emptied into his open mouth, and no sooner was the last drop imbibed, then the imp jumped upon his feet, and threw his arms around the neck of the old man, and kissed him on both cheeks.

"Ah! the dear, good, sweet little precious baby," cried the old man, chuckling with delight. "But I have only given you a taste. There, my dearest, there is the whole bottle for you. I owe you a deal—first, for the beating I gave you, and then for doing what I bid you so exactly, and so cleverly. Oh! this invaluable letter—this thrice priceless, invaluable letter—that I would not part with until it has done its work, for all the wealth and grandeur of the world."

"There, good boy;" said the old man, addressing the imp, who had now clutched the bottle between both his long-fingered hands. "Away with your treasure, away with what is dearer and more precious in your eyes than diamonds, silk, satins, and gold. Away! drink your fill, drink till you can drink no more; drink till your eyes wink, and all the world seems on the whirligig with your brain. Go, my darling, drink till you can drink no more. Drink till you are dead drunk. Old grand-daddy, you see, is the only one who knows what can cure sore bones, and plaster bruised limbs. Grand-daddy is the only one in the universe who has good things in store for his precious baby. Is it not so, my darling?"

"Yes, yes, yes," shrieked the imp, as he grinned with delight, and slinking into a hole beneath the stairs, commenced sipping slowly and deliberately, the fragrant liquid, as if he had resolved that the process of becoming intoxicated should be a prolonged pleasure.

The old man watched him to his retreat, and then returned to the table on which Judith's letter lay still open; he re-arranged it, and then enrolled it in the silken kerchief, fold by fold, as it had reached his hand; and then placing it in a small casket, and shutting it with a secret bolt, he locked the casket up in the cupboard from which he had taken the huge black bottle of usquebaugh.

"At last," said Gerald Geraghty, "I have Ebenezer Lawson in my power. With that little letter to make use of, I can lure to destruction the slayer of my wife, and the murderer of my children. To attain this end I have struggled hard, laboured hard—very hard, making use of other men's passions as my instruments; first, inciting a broken down spendthrift to run away with this unhappy girl, playing upon his passion for wealth and pleasure, and so making an instrument of him. Then playing upon the passion for scandal, and the spiteful disposition, combined with the fanaticism of the vicious old woman, to repair the mischief that my own tongue had unintentionally done with the girl; and, lastly, making use of this boy's incessant craving for strong drinks, to obtain for me the means whereby I may take full and ample revenge upon the wretch who, as he showed no mercy for me or mine, shall, himself and his child, find no mercy, no compassion, no tenderness, no forgiveness.

"But intending to destroy Lawson and Lawson's daughter, should I not seek to include another survivor of the massacre? It is true, Edward Ludlow never laid hand to sword against me, my family, or any one who was with us; but still, it was to kill Fitzpatrick's child he had us hunted out in our cave—our last, sole home and refuge. Without him there would have been no such massacre. He was the instigator—he the person that stirred up in Lawson's fierce heart the thirst for blood; and though he did not bid Lawson to do those murders, yet the murders would be unthought of but for him. And though he did not kill, he did not stir hand nor foot to save us. Not so John Elliott, to whom I owe my life, when Lawson's red hand was raised to strike us dead. If I can, as I will, find the opportunity to destroy Lawson, why not destroy with the same blow Ludlow? This letter, which will entrap the father, may be used as a bait to the same pitfall for the father's friend; for Lawson and Ludlow continue fast friends. Their friendship was first cemented in our blood—in *my* blood! Why should not the fitting termination to the friendship of murderers be the revenge taken upon them by one of their intended victims?

"Let me think—let me think.

"Why am I what I *am?* Why, instead of being what I *was,* when those two pitiless villains, Lawson and Ludlow, came in conflict with me, am I now so fallen, so degraded, and so wicked, that I dare not reflect on the condition to which I have been reduced? I dare not, even to myself, describe myself to be what I know I am, professing principles that in my heart I abjure, acting the spy for those I hate, and sustaining a faction in my native land that have never had power but they used it for the oppression of me and mine, and the class I belong to? Detesting myself—detesting those I serve, and, in my innermost heart, feeling all the love that is yet left to me for the very persons I do my utmost to injure. This *is* what I *am*.

"And wherefore am I now, and have I been for years, sustaining this most base, most vile, and most detestable of all parts—the spy and the informer? Solely that I might ingratiate myself with those in power, and that the influence they had might be yet employed by me to do mischief—some mischief at all events—and, if possible, deadly mischief to this Lawson, his family, his connexions, his adherents, and friends.

"And now the means to do so are at last placed within my reach.

"Let me see—let me see that I do not let one particle of those means run to waste—that the mischief to the wrong-doers may be as wide-spread as the original wrong.

"And now let me trace back that original wrong to its primary cause. Neither Lawson nor Ludlow were moved by a spirit of personal hatred against me. I and my poor family only lay in their way to reach the Fitzpatricks, and to destroy them they waded through our blood.

"The hearts—the loving hearts—that were once mine, that ever beat with deep affection for me as husband, or father, or protector, or friend, all—all those dear loving hearts were but as so many stepping-stones for the sanguinary Ludlow and the remorseless Lawson to trample upon and destroy in their path to the Fitzpatrick land, and to murder the rightful heir.

"We were destroyed—*I* was destroyed; I, who might now be an honoured old man, with wife, and children, and grandchildren, at my knee, looking up to me with reverence, and begging my blessing. I have been cast down; and the Fitzpatricks, I am told—at least it is so rumoured—father and son are both living; and Ludlow's crimes, and Lawson's cruelties, and 'my sufferings, have been all gone through, and yet the end aimed at not attained!

"Why not, whilst preparing for the last grand final act of the bloody tragedy I contemplate—why not, as a means to render the enactment of that tragedy more complete—why not make use of the name, at least, of the Fitzpatricks, to gall and worry into a pitfall those two avaricious miscreants, Lawson and Ludlow?

"Let me think—let me think how all these things are to be done; and, in the meanwhile, how I may make use, or get rid of the poor stupid dupe, who in seeking an heiress for a bride, has placed Judith Lawson within the grasp of him from whom she never shall escape with life."

And so for many hours that same day the old man, Gerald Geraghty, sat pondering upon a plan of vengeance, which should be so well laid, and so carefully contrived, that its success should be certain—its failure, in any one particular, an impossibility.

It was a late hour in the evening of the same day that the attention of Judith and Mrs. Gregg was attracted to the window of the room opposite their own by loud, yelling shrieks of laughter. And when they looked to see what was the matter, they beheld the imp, with a face as red as his hair, dancing and capering about the room as if he was mad, and then opening the window and letting the rope hang down into the court-yard beneath, swinging himself at the end of it, and provoking and inciting the fierce bulldogs beneath to bark and bound up in the air after him, in the hope of fastening their glistening teeth in his naked feet. And whilst this wild scene excited their apprehension that the mad, rash boy might be caught, and dragged down, and devoured by the infuriated animals, they perceived the old man with difficulty pulling up rope and boy into the room, and then binding the limbs of the imp, and when the poor wretch lay helpless before him, beating him mercilessly with a stick; and as both women turned away their eyes with horror from the scene, the last sound that reached their ears, as the casement closed, was the loud yelling, but still mirthful-sounding laughter of the imp!

CHAPTER XIII.
THE WRONGED AND THE WRONG-DOER.

For two days had Judith endured the most painful and most afflicting of all conditions, for she was a prisoner, and hoping in vain for a deliverer. She was suffering a great and unexpected calamity, and yet, at the same time, untiringly but vainly hoping that each moment, as it came, would release her from her sufferings. To the evil that others have done to such a victim another is added, another and a worse; the heart-sickening hope of the sufferer, who, tormented by enemies, becomes their ally in being a self-tormentor.

In vain, in vain, had hour after hour been watched by her: in vain had she listened for a sound that might indicate a change in the wardship of her prison, and gave to her the smallest reason for supposing that her father was coming to her. In vain had she listened at the door, and watched at the window, on the chance that the imp would re-appear, or find the means of intimating to her that he had succeeded in delivering her letter.

Nothing was seen, nothing was known of the imp, and the only conclusion that Judith could draw from his absence and his silence was, that he had been so maimed by the last beating she saw inflicted upon him by his grandfather that he was unable to move, and so could neither perform the commission she had confided to him, nor even rise from his bed to tell her of what had happened.

As to her father, Judith was perfectly certain, that if living, he would have broken through all obstacles, and overcome every species of danger to reach her; and, therefore, not seeing him was the proof, from whatever cause it had arisen, that the imp had not been able to deliver her message to him.

Two days had thus passed away since she had seen the imp, and each hour, as it passed, served to increase her perplexities, to aggravate her doubts, and to magnify her apprehensions, and to break her spirit. It did so, because, as each hour passed away, it brought with itself diminished hopes. Such was her condition when the hateful face of the old man, Geraghty, appeared in her room, and his raven-like voice was heard croaking in her ears.

"A gentleman, who says he is an acquaintance, wishes to see you."

Judith's heart thrilled with joy as she heard these words, and, without a moment's hesitation, she replied:

"Thank you, thank you! Admit him instantly."

"I do not know that you will be so very grateful to me when you see him," replied the old man, with a malignant grin. "But as you wish to see him, you shall see him. Wait a minute: I will send him up to you."

And so saying, old Geraghty left the room; but before doing so, he stopped an instant before Mrs. Gregg, and bowing down so very low before her, that his head appeared almost to touch his knees, he exclaimed with mock humility: "The top of the morning to you, widow: I am happy to see you look so blooming. Delicate plants like you thrive best when kept from the open air."

"There is some wicked piece of mischief on foot, or that old villain would not be in such good spirits," observed Mrs. Gregg. "Be sure this is one of his myrmidons coming to you."

Poor Judith turned deadly pale at this suggestion, and she replied in a hurried voice: "Oh! no, no, no—impossible. I know none of his associates; and you heard what he said—and how he mentioned this visiter as an acquaintance. It is my father—my dear father—who is coming to me, and who wished to break the surprise of his appearance suddenly before me by describing himself as 'an acquaintance.' It is—it is, my good Mrs. Gregg—it is—it must be my dear father."

"Ah! God help your poor innocent heart. You do not know these wicked Irish as well as I do. Do you think," said Mrs. Gregg, "that old Geraghty would bring your father here to you? Not he—the old infidel; he would as soon think of cheering you up by letting you out of this place to be comforted by hearing a two hours' discourse on some damnable and hellish doctrine of Popery, from the blessed lips of that lamb of grace, the Rev. Isaac Poundtext."

"Oh! do not say—do not think, dear Mrs. Gregg, that it is, or can be any one else than my own, my beloved father. Hist! there is the lower door opening. I hear steps on the stone stairs outside. Ah!" cried Judith, falling back into her chair. "Ah! that is not my father's step. Oh! Heaven have mercy on me!"

The door opened, and a tall man of middle age entered. He was of full figure, with light yellow hair, and his face, whether from habitual indulgence at the table, or from constant exposure to the air, or from the excitement of the moment, was all one unvarying colour, and that a deep scarlet.

In her indignation at beholding this man, all Judith's fears, doubts, and hopes, so vividly entertained, and so rudely broken, were alike forgotten, and starting to her feet, she exclaimed:—

"I have seen you, Sir, before; I am sure I know you. If I am not mistaken, you were introduced to me on the race-course by Lord Arran."

The stranger bowed.

"If I recollect aright, Sir, you were introduced to me as Mr. David Fitzgerald, of the County Limerick."

The stranger again bowed.

"Emboldened by an introduction to me by Lord Arran, you kept by my bridle rein during the entire day, and though I did not offer, by word, or look, or gesture, the slightest encouragement to you, still you professed sentiments with respect to me, which no unmarried woman should hear without the approval of her parents."

Again the stranger bowed.

"Is it because you have been informed of my helpless condition here—without the protection of my father—with no companion but this poor, good woman by my side, that you have come here to renew those proposals which did not find a willing listener on the race-course?"

"I come here, Miss Lawson, with no unkind intentions towards ou; but in order that there may be a proper understanding between us, it will be indispensable that no one be a witness to the interview. The old lady by your side can retire to that room," said Fitzgerald, as he pointed to Judith's sleeping chamber; "she will then be within call, if you require her presence; but what I have to say to you, if said at all, must be said with no one to listen to us."

Judith started as she noted the words which Fitzgerald used; but, whatever the cause of her emotion, she confined it to her own breast for the moment.

"We are captives, and must do as our jailers command. Leave us, Mrs. Gregg, for a few moments."

Mrs. Gregg at once quitted the room, drawing the door close after her, so that the visiter might perceive she was determined upon not being an eaves-dropper.

No sooner had the widow departed on one side than Fitzgerald proceeded to the outer door of the passage, and, bolting it on the inside, he left the inner chamber door open, so as to be sure no one could approach it unperceived by him, nor gain a position in which the conversation between him and Judith could be overheard.

Having done this, he returned to take a chair, which he placed in such a position as to have a full command of the door and outward passage.

Judith made no remark whilst Fitzgerald was thus acting. She remained perfectly quiescent until he had seated himself, when she at once thus bluntly addressed him:—

"Mr. David Fitzgerald, it may be a saving of much time, and of vain discussion between both of us, if, instead of my listening to you, you should, on the contrary, at once listen to me, and what I have to say *to* you and *of* you. I will frankly own to you that the great, unlooked for, and unwished for attention paid to me by you, on the race-

N

course, induced me to inquire who and what you were. I was informed that you were a gentleman of good family in the County Limerick; that you had inherited a considerable estate; and that estate had been wasted by you in pursuits that reflected no credit either on your head or heart. I was also informed that, in the hope of repairing your broken fortunes, you had in some way or other, which no one could explain to me, connected yourself, as a witness, with what is called 'the Popish plot;' and I was also informed that you were seeking for the means to waste on your own pleasures another fortune, by obtaining some rich heiress as a wife. Such was the information which made me put what I conceived to be a proper interpretation upon your attentions to me. Suffice it to say, that a thought of you, as a husband, never entered into my contemplation; and what has since happened, the seizure of my person, with brutal violence, by common thieves and highwaymen, on the public roads, had driven all recollection of the incidents on the race-course from my mind. I had absolutely forgotten that such a person as Mr. David Fitzgerald had ever existed, when you again appeared before me; and now the sound of your voice—I recognise it, Sir—proves to me that the suitor on the race-course was the robber on the high-road; the brave gentleman who threatened me with his vengeance; who declared I should live to be his slave; who even vowed he would make me the boon companion of so vile and abandoned a wretch as the excommunicated Murfey; even he, this assailant of women, this braggadocio bandit, has come into the cage which he had assigned to his victim, and—*there he sits!*"

"Listen to me, madam," said Fitzgerald, now pale and trembling visibly.

"First listen to me, Sir. You have chosen to come to

me. Now, hear what I have to say to you. You call yourself a gentleman, and no doubt you are so—by birth. I, on the contrary, am the daughter of an humble, a very humble man; I am nothing more, and nothing better than the child of him, who, when I was born, was a common soldier in the British army. My father had inherited neither fortune, name, nor rank, and he could not, if he would, have wasted the wealth he had not received, nor brought dishonour upon the name of illustrious ancestors, nor descended from the ranks of the gentry to be a companion for the dregs of society, the outcasts of a prison, or fugitives from the gallows. I was the daughter of a soldier, that soldier had become rich, and I was his declared heiress. Well, Sir, in what way was all this a matter of any concern to you? I was not of your sphere: I was outside of it. I could not come in contact with you, be seen by you, known by you, except casually meeting you on one of those festive occasions, which are alike the common sources of enjoyment to the lord and the citizen, the squire and the farmer, the king and the beggar. Base, cruel, unmanly Irishman, what cause of offence had I given to you, that you would not let me be at peace in that obscurity which I preferred, and with which I was fully content? Base and cruel man, until you cast eyes upon me, I had never dwelt, even for a single night, beneath any other roof than that which was a parent's home, and never fixed my heart upon any love except that pure, holy, and undying love which a fond father can bestow upon an affectionate and an obedient child. For full six and twenty years I had thus lived; and then I was looked upon by a man who had reduced himself to penury by his own vices, and who had, with all the world in his favour, contrived to strip himself of what is the best gift the world has to bestow—a respect for unblemished honour? And what is the consequence to me of that wicked man's observation? Oh! for shame! for shame! base, cruel, and heartless man, who, not content with the mischief you have done, now come to gloat your eyes with gazing upon the agonies of your victim. Aye, look upon me, behold what you have done. Hear me, whilst I tell you, that, within one week of my life, you have had the power to crowd a century of suffering. Remember that the woman you have so afflicted never did you wrong. Know, that until you and your gang of hired ruffians laid hands upon that same woman, her whole previous life had been one of peace, of contentment, and of happiness. Know, that you have done a mischief that never can be repaired, for, supposing you were at this moment to open the prison doors for me, still, you must be aware, that Judith Lawson, going forth from this prison, and returning to her father's home, would not, and could not ever be the same Judith Lawson, who left her father's home to enjoy, as she supposed, a few hours of innocent, unoffending recreation on the race-course. *That* Judith Lawson was stainless in her honour, as she had been pure in her life; but *this* Judith Lawson, the Judith Lawson that your foul robber hand has once touched, is, by having come in contact with you and your myrmidons, contaminated, and an evil thinking world will point to a week's unaccounted absence from home as an incident in my career on which slander will ever be, for the future, free to put an interpretation of its own, and calumny can convert to its most malignant purposes. Oh! base, thrice base and most cruel man, and cowardly as you are base, who, not content with all the other crimes you have committed; who, not ashamed of countenancing the robbery of poor servants of their purses, have, in your craven fears of me—of a woman!—deprived me of the weapons wherewith I might defend my life, my honour."

"What mean you?" exclaimed the abashed and conscience-stricken Fitzgerald. "Is it that your hunting-knife has been taken from you? Why, I gave express directions that your riding-whip, hunting-knife, and everything that belonged to you should be treated as sacred property."

"Oh! generous captor!" cried the excited Judith. "He ordered that I myself should be regarded as a criminal, and bound as a captive, but the inanimate things that belonged to me should be respected as sacred. But it was not so. Your menials did all the mischief that you commanded, but when you desired them to desist from evil they disobeyed you; and what is the consequence? that I am, at this moment, in a strange place, in the midst not only of strangers but of enemies, and that if any one of these—the old villain who introduced you, for instance, and who looks at me, as if he wished to murder me, and his evil passions should dispose him to carry out any such fell intention—you, yes, I say, *you*, have taken away from me the power of preventing him."

"You have said," remarked Fitzgerald, "and you have said truly, that I have already done you mischief which I cannot repair, and that no repentance on my part could efface. Believe me—alas! you have no reason, but the contrary, for believing me, but still, I say, if you can believe me—here, at least, is the proof that my wishes were not fulfilled, and that my orders were disregarded— here, Miss Lawson, is a small dagger. It is sharp and well-tempered, and so small, that you can conceal it in your dress. With it in your possession, and with your courage to use it, you can no longer say you are absolutely defenceless."

The weapon which Fitzgerald placed in the hand of Judith was about six inches in length, including the ivory handle; the blade was broad, narrow-pointed, and with two edges, each as sharp as a razor, thus making it a very dangerous instrument in the possession of one resolute and determined.

Whilst Judith was examining this dagger with the practised eye of a connoisseur, she felt a new spirit of courage pervading her; and certain that she possessed the means of punishing an aggressor, she looked with a less stern eye upon him who, though he had done her great wrong, had now given her the means of protecting herself.

Unpractised in deceit, unaccustomed to self-control, and unversed in the habit of suppressing the expression of any feeling she entertained, Judith looked at Fitzgerald; and as she hid the dagger in the folds of her dress, well fastening it beneath her girdle, she turned suddenly round upon him, and said:—

"What has brought you here? Wherefore have you come to me? Not to give me a dagger, I am certain."

"My purpose in visiting you," replied Fitzgerald, "was this, and this only. I wished, now that some days of captivity have passed away, to judge of your character by a personal interview. I wished to know whether you were what you had been described to me—a description which induced me to waylay you, and carry you off—or, whether you are, what I find you to be, and what your conduct subsequent to the capture first led me to suspect or suppose you might prove to be."

"Sir!" said Judith, "if I understand you correctly, you

had a description of my temper, and manners, and morals, which served as an inducement to you to treat me as I have been treated. I entreat of you, Sir, be frank. Let me know how I was portrayed to you. It cannot hurt my feelings now to be told anything which has had such a sad influence upon my present position and my future destiny."

"I entreat," replied Fitzgerald, "your patience and your pardon for mentioning matters which, however insufficient as a justification of my conduct, are still, I am sorry to say, the only extenuating circumstances I have to rely upon. You were described to me as a bold-spirited and ambitious girl; as one anxious to forget, in a marriage with any man of good birth, the lowly origin of your father, with whom, I was told, you were in a constant state of warfare; that you were sick of home, and that you were annoyed because offers of marriage were not made to you by persons your superiors in rank and fortune. I was told that the reason you dressed so richly, and, at the same time, so much at variance with the usual habiliments of women, was for the purpose of attracting attention towards yourself; and I was also informed that you had often spoken admiringly of me."

"Of *you!*" cried Judith, in amazement, "Why, I never heard of you, never saw you, until you were introduced to me by Lord Arran."

"I am sure you speak the truth," said Fitzgerald; "but you know not, young lady, how natural is vanity to our sex, and how ready even the most humble amongst us are to believe any one who tells them that their personal appearance has found favour in the eyes of a woman. I repeat to you what I was told over and over again, namely, that you had often spoken of me in the very highest terms, as one, such as you would wish to have as a husband; but it was added—and here was the worst and most diabolical part of the invention, of those foul lies whispered untiringly into my ears—I was told that whilst you said you would approve of me as a husband, still you were afraid I was a coward and a milk-sop, one who would not have the courage to carry off a fine woman for the sake of her fortune. I was told that you had said, that even if I was to propose for you, you were sure that your father would, on account of my want of fortune, refuse you; but that if, on the other hand, I had the bravery to seize upon you by force, to carry you away with me, conceal you for some days in some place where your father could not discover you, that then you would be in a position to give me willingly, not only your hand and fortune, but your heart also, whilst your father could not refuse to sanction our marriage. These things were dinned into my ears day after day, for months together. At length, I was fool enough to believe them, and knave enough to act upon them. It was with a view of carrying this long-thought-of project into effect that I was introduced to, and spoke to you on the race-course, and that I wished others to see me constantly near you during that day. As I was carrying out one plan, so did I fancy you were carrying out another; that your coolness to me was assumed; and when you had been taken prisoner, I ascribed the valour of your resistance, and the violence of your language, to an artful display of animosity, a cunning concealment of your real feelings, so that if my plan had failed, you should be held by your father and others perfectly harmless of the consequences."

"Am I awake or dreaming, that such things are told to me?" cried Judith, utterly amazed and confounded by the statements of Fitzgerald.

"Reflection upon the scenes and various incidents of that night, and certain words that have been unintentionally dropped, and circumstances that have since occurred, have all combined to shake my confidence in the truth of him who told such tales to me respecting you," exclaimed Fitzgerald.

"And who on earth," exclaimed Judith, "could have invented such fables concerning me; or, how came you to believe them? What reason had you for thinking there was a particle of truth in them?"

"The person who told me all those tales about you was Gerald Geraghty," replied Fitzgerald; "and the manner in which he said he came to know all about you, and your sentiments respecting me, was from his own daughter, Fanny Geraghty, your tire-woman and confederate!"

"Fanny Geraghty! my tire-woman! There never was any one of the name a domestic of any description in my father's household. My tire-woman is an Englishwoman. She was in attendance upon me at the race-course. She was made captive at the same time with myself. But, then, you say all those tales about me, so dishonouring to me, so degrading to me as a maiden, so calculated to render me an object of loathing, of scorn, and contempt, by all who prize honour, purity, and modesty in a woman; all those false, foul libels upon me and my reputation were, you say, told to you by Gerald Geraghty?"

"As I live and breathe, I speak the truth," said Fitzgerald. "The idea of committing an act so utterly base as that of taking away a young woman from the protection of her father's home, by brutal violence, never would have occurred to me. Bad I am, and wicked as I have been, my own vices have reduced me from a position in which I might have been respected to one in which I feel I am lowered and degraded; but still, the cowardly baseness of waylaying a woman, and forcing her into a marriage, never would be perpetrated by me. It is a monstrous act, which I am incapable of performing. Believe me, then, most deeply injured lady, that but for Gerald Geraghty this crime never would have been committed. You never would have been assailed, nor should I have been, at the same time, a dupe and a criminal. He first suggested this act to me, and never ceased to tell me—so completely did he pretend to know your sentiments, through his daughter—that you expected me to make this attempt at a sham abduction, and that, if I did not gladly comply with your wishes, you would regard me as deficient in moral courage. He thus assailed me on my weakest point; and, in the hope I was proving I was not a coward, I did, in fact, commit the basest, the cruelest, and the most cowardly act of which a man can be guilty."

As David Fitzgerald was thus speaking, and whilst he was so endeavouring to exculpate himself, he perceived that Judith, who was at first listening to him with attention, assumed, of a sudden, an abstracted air; that her face became flushed, then deadly pale; that her limbs trembled, as if with an ague; that then a film seemed to fall upon her eyes; and all her limbs relaxed, and she would have fallen wholly senseless on the floor, had he not caught her in his arms, and at the same time cried out to Mrs. Gregg to come to his aid, and bring some cold water with her.

It was with some difficulty that Judith was restored to consciousness. Her first impulse, upon feeling she had sufficient strength to move, was to cast herself upon her knees, and then, in a weak voice, to pour forth her feelings in prayer; and as she proceeded in the pious exercise, her courage seemed to revive, and renewed energy was given to her words.

"O Lord! I have been," she exclaimed, "as Thou knowest, a great sinner, and I have done evil before thee; and now is Thy time come to punish my transgressions, and to make me feel the bitter consequences of my own follies and great ignorance.

"Thou hast said, O Lord! by the lips of the wise man, '*The attire of the body, and the laughter of the teeth, and the gait of the man, show what he is;*' and I have trespassed in these matters; for it was my foolishness of attire, and my giddiness of speech, and my inconsiderate boldness of demeanour, that gave to my enemies the thought of weakness and wickedness on my part, and they have availed themselves of the advantage I thus presented them, and hence I am this day an object of reproach to my friends, and a subject of laughter to my foes.

"Such are the consequences of my own folly, and such, too, is Thy will; and Thy holy name be acceptable and blessed, now, and for ever more.

"Thou hast said, O Lord! '*Fodder, and a wand, and a burden are for an ass; bread, and correction, and work for a slave;*' and as one who has been, and who is, a slave to her own vanity, a slave to her own pride, I accept the degradation and the bondage that have been imposed upon me; and I accept them, O Lord! the more willingly, because Thou knowest my innocence in my intentions, and that no acts have been done by me unworthy of a maiden.

"I am punished, O Lord! in my weakness; I am punished by feeling the arrows of my enemy; his slanderous tongue, thrilling in the very vitals of my pride; penetràting me where I thought I was most strong, and impervious to every assault, in my virginal reputation.

"Be it so, O Lord! for it is Thy will; be it my duty to imitate, so far as weak mortal can, Thy submission, Thy patience, and Thy resignation, when Thy enemies cast reproaches upon Thee, and sought to slay Thee by false accusations.

"Patience, resignation, charity, these are the things I have to practise. This is the work I have to do. Give me strength and I will do it, for without Thee I am all weakness, all fragility, all corruption. Give, oh! give me strength, and I will do Thy work, looking with certainty to Thee for my reward; for this, too, hast Thou promised: '*Work your work before the time, and He will give you your reward in His time.*'

"'Our Father which art in heaven,'" murmured to herself Judith, as she still remained on her knees.

Whilst she was thus engaged in silent prayer, Fitzgerald pointed to Mrs. Gregg to leave the room, and the good woman did so without attempting to quarrel with him: the example of Judith, it is to be supposed, having for the moment a tranquillizing effect upon that bellicose disposition which the widow always manifested upon coming into collision with one of the male sex.

Judith rose from her knees, and again resuming her seat remained for some time without speaking. She seemed to be lost in profound contemplation. At last, looking up at Fitzgerald, she said:—

"Can you, Sir, account for Gerald Geraghty's conduct with respect to me? I never saw the man until I came here; I never heard of him—nay, I do not recollect having ever even heard the name of Geraghty at all, until I first saw him; and yet he pursues me with a malignity that is not only awful to think of, but is actually incomprehensible. I find him not only telling gross and scandalous falsehoods to you about me, but I find him telling stupid and monstrous falsehoods to the old woman who is in the next room; and when he spoke to me, and he never did so but once, he told me the most malignant and the most wicked falsehoods about my own father? Can you account for all this?"

"There is but one way of accounting for it," replied Fitzgerald: "the devil is the father of lies, and those who have dedicated themselves, as I believe old Geraghty has, body and soul, to the enemy of mankind, delight in practising sin, because it is sin. As to this wicked old man, I was, when I called upon you, suspecting that which I now know, namely, that I was made use of by him as a vile instrument to accomplish his malignant designs. I see now more plainly than I ever did before, the trap into which I have fallen, by lending myself to his wickedness. It was to further my plan with respect to you, and to facilitate your capture, that I pretended to be a witness in the Popish plot, and so got the aid of associates that I could not otherwise command. And what is the consequence? The toils which I had laid to gain my own ends, now surround me on every side, and hands stronger than my own control, and check, and guide me. I sought for my purposes to make a compact with the devil; and now, having baffled me, withheld from me the prize I had hoped for, he is using me for his own purposes, and such vile purposes too——"

A loud knocking at the outer door interrupted Fitzgerald.

"I must leave you. I am, as you may perceive, suspected; and our conversation, if it has not been overheard, and I trust it has not, has been sufficiently prolonged to make Geraghty fear we have come to an explanation, by which his villany has been discovered."

The bolts of the door were withdrawn, and Geraghty came into the room. He did not appear to notice Judith; but handing a paper to Fitzgerald, said:—

"Honoured Sir, your presence is required instantly at the Castle. Here is an order from the Council for you to appear and give evidence against the Popish conspirators. A party has been despatched for the arrest of one of their leaders—Dr. Plunkett, the Popish Archbishop. We, loyal Protestants, should be lost, if Ireland had not discovered saviours and witnesses in such brave and fearless swearers as yourself."

Fitzgerald received the written order from the hand of Geraghty, and he turned pale when the wicked old man stated openly for what purpose he was required at the Castle.

"I take my leave of you, Madam," said Fitzgerald, "and if you do not—as I trust you will—speedily leave this prison, I intend to have the honour of again waiting upon you."

"To be sure!—to be sure!" said old Geraghty, as he followed Fitzgerald from the room, speaking aloud, but still as if he was unconsciously giving expression to his own thoughts. "To be sure!—to be sure!—the handsome lover will be pining until he sees his brave lady-love again. What a handsome couple they are to be sure! What a hard-hearted father that Ebenezer Lawson must be, if he could think of keeping separate a pair of beauties that nature seems to have formed for each other! Well! well! but that love is a mighty queer thing entirely. It will break through bolts and bars, I am told."

And as the old man was still speaking, the harsh clashing of the chains outside the door was heard by Judith, who was again left alone.

CHAPTER XIV.

THE WILLING MARTYR.

"EVER since the proclamation of the 16th of October, 1678, persecution raged furiously against the bishops and clergy of the Catholic Church. Vast numbers of them had been shipped off to foreign countries; and those who remained did not dare to come near the great towns, but lay concealed in the bogs and mountains. The Primate, however, did not desert his country, or even his diocese; but he left his usual residence of Ballybarrack, within a short distance of Dundalk, and took up his abode in a small house in an obscure country-place called Castletown-bellew, within a few miles of Drogheda. It was here he held his last ordination."

In the lone little house, or rather cabin, which is thus described, the Catholic Archbishop was sitting alone one evening, when the noise of a body of cavalry approaching was heard by him.

"The will of God be done in all things! *Deo Gratias!*" exclaimed the Archbishop. "The sacrifice is to be made, and the victim is not only willing but joyful. Here are those who seek my life. They are welcome."

Whilst he was thus speaking his thoughts aloud, he heard the word of command given, and the cavalry halted; and in a moment afterwards the room was entered by the same man who had been called "Mr. Brown" by John Elliott, and who afterwards acted as second to Vincent Fitzpatrick in the duel with Lord Arran. This man's dress, however, was somewhat different from that which he wore when in Dublin, for now he had a bright steel cap on his head, a polished, glittering steel cuirass on his breast, and his dark green military coat was richly embroidered with gold, whilst on his feet and legs were the high, heavy boots of a cavalry officer.

The moment this man made his appearance, he bowed low to the Archbishop, and kissed, with apparent devotion, the episcopal ring that was extended to him.

"What, *you!* Redmnod O'Hanlon; why come you here, and wherefore in soldier's attire, and accompanied with a military array?"

"Because, my Lord Archbishop," answered Redmond O'Hanlon, "I desire to perform a soldier's service ; because I wish to defend my Archbishop against his wicked enemies, who are now coming, as I am well assured, to this your poor and humble retreat to arrest you. Yes, to arrest your Grace, with the intention of depriving you of life. As an Irish Catholic gentleman, I will not permit this outrage to be committed in a district in which I have influence; and, as an Irish soldier, I feel bound to resist to the death the commission of such a crime."

"My son! my son! this cannot be," replied the Archbishop. "My enemies act with the authority of the superior powers, whom God in his wisdom and mercy has placed over us; and it is the duty of the Christian to submit to them. Thus acted the Christians in the early ages of the Church, and Heaven was thereby crowded with martyrs, and sinners thereby converted into saints by their example. And as Christian bishops acted when the throne of Empire was filled by a Nero, a Diocletian, or a Julian, so will I act, and no man shall prevent me."

"But, is your Grace aware that the men who are your persecutors are so, not because they are ignorant, or prejudiced, or misled, as pagans and idolaters were when they martyred the first Christians? Do you not know that they have collected against your Grace a number of witnesses, who will swear whatever their malice can suggest?" asked O'Hanlon.

"I know well, perfectly and minutely," replied the Archbishop, "the allegations that are to be made against me, and I know also the names of the witnesses. I am indebted for this information to your friend, Colonel Fitzpatrick, who, neglectful of his own and his son's interests, in order that he might watch over mine, has traced these unhappy men (who are prepared to swear against me) into all their haunts, and has made himself acquainted with all their secrets. Now, what do the accusations of these men amount to? That I, who you well know, never had for my maintainance more than sixty pounds a-year, have been collecting thousands of pounds to promote an invasion of the country! They also accuse me of being busily engaged in surveying Irish ports, such as might be suitable for the landing of a large force of invaders, and of my having at last fixed upon Carlingford for the debarkation of the French army! that is, that I had, with a full knowledge of the country, selected that spot which, beyond all others, would be the most unfit for the French to approach; because, to get there they must come by the narrow seas all along Ulster, thus choosing for them the most dangerous voyage they could encounter! And, to that improbability my enemies and false accusers have superadded an impossibility! namely, that I was to be ready, with seventy thousand men, to join the French the moment they landed; the fact being, as you and every man in Ireland must be aware, that in all the province of Ulster, take men women, and children of the Roman Catholics, they would not make up seventy thousand. Remember, my son, that however desirous these men may be to take away my life, they cannot do so but by the verdict of a jury. They can summon no jury in Ireland that does not know me and the quality of my adversaries. Most willing, then, am I to put myself upon my trial to-morrow, without any witnesses, before any Protestant jury that know them and me."

"But, my dear Lord Archbishop," said O'Hanlon, "you forget the character of the men you have to deal with. The instigators of these proceedings know thoroughly well there is not one particle of truth in the allegations made against you, and yet they urge on a prosecution—not for the purpose of testing the truth of such allegations by a fair trial, but with the fell intention of finding a sanction for them, through an unjust conviction and a cruel death. They, therefore, will take care—how they will do so I cannot imagine—but sure I am they are wicked and clever enough to contrive the means of preventing you being tried by an Irish jury, whether they are Catholics, or such as you suppose, and I am willing to believe are not difficult to be found—honest Protestants."

"That baseless story which my enemies have invented is, of necessity, laid in Ireland; they could not, if they would, place the *venue* elsewhere," replied the Archbishop. "Now, such being the case, all the alleged facts occurring in Ireland, I must of necessity be tried in Ireland, and if in Ireland, then by an Irish jury. Such being the case, all I ask is that I may have time to bring my records and witnesses, and then I will defy all that is upon the earth and under the earth, to say anything against me."

"But, my Lord Archbishop," earnestly urged O'Hanlon, "you forget that the determination is to give you not a fair trial, nor a fair jury, nor to allow your witnesses to be heard. What is resolved upon is to murder you. Remain here, permit your enemies to arrest you, to bear you to prison, and then your fate is finally determined. If they cannot slay you in Ireland they will in England. There is but one sole mode of saving your life. It is by an immediate flight from this country. I have prepared all things to secure it. I have with me a sufficient force to defend you from any attack; and your enemies are on their way here to capture you. Permit me, then, to escort you to Drogheda, where a vessel is prepared to bear you to France. The storm of persecution that now rages with such violence will, in a short time, have abated. When it does so, you can then return, and resume, for the benefit of religion and your country, the administration of your great functions."

"It may not," answered the Primate, "it cannot, and it ought not to be. The good shepherd lays down his life for his flock, and I am prepared to yield up mine a willing, and, as I trust, not through any merits of my own, an acceptable sacrifice. My hope, then, is, if, as you expect, my enemies prevail against me, that I be unfairly tried, and unjustly condemned, still, I say, that my hope is, that God will give me, though unworthy of it, the grace to have *fortem animum mortis terrore carentem*, (a courage fearless of death.) I have many sins to answer for before the Supreme Judge of the high bench, where no false witnesses can have audience. But as for any human tribunal before which I can be arraigned, and by which I may be condemned, then I can truly affirm, I am not guilty of any crime there brought against me. I would I could be so clear at the bench of the All-powerful. *Ut ut sit*, there is one comfort that He cannot be deceived, because He is omniscient, and knows all secrets, even of hearts; and cannot deceive, because all goodness; so that I may be sure of a fair trial, and will get time sufficient to call witnesses; nay, the judge will bring them in a moment, if there will be need of any. I am thus, you see, Redmond O'Hanlon, prepared, thoroughly prepared for whatever may befall me. If it please God to accept my life, my consolation will be, that it has been taken because I was fearless in the performance of my duty, as a Christian Archbishop; that I would connive at no abuse, and tolerate no scandal. If I now stood upon the scaffold, I would say, looking back upon my episcopal career, and the manner in which I endeavoured to act towards all under my jurisdiction: I, by preaching, and teaching, and statutes, have endeavoured to bring those of whom I had a care to a due comportment, according to their calling; and though, thereby, I did but my duty, yet some who would not amend, had a prejudice for me, and especially my accusers, to whom I did endeavour to do good. Yes, if this were my last moment in this world, I would, even as one of the seven deacons, holy Stephen, did pray for those who stoned him to death, so do I for those who, with perjuries, spill my innocent blood, saying as St. Stephen did, ' *O Lord, lay not this sin to them.*' I do heartily forgive them. Urge me then, no more, Count O'Hanlon, for here will I abide, and not the hair of one man's head shall be injured on my account. I will not permit it. I solemnly forbid it."

"Alas! my Lord Archbishop," replied O'Hanlon, "I know my duty but too well, in the circumstances in which you are now placed. I dare not act in defiance of your Grace's prohibition. I leave you, by your own command, to be seized upon by your bloodthirsty enemies. The consequences of this sad determination of your Grace can be already foreseen. You will be their victim; for you choose to win the bright red crown of martyrdom. Farewell! my Lord Archbishop, we meet in this world no more. Bestow upon me, then, your blessing, and pray—oh! pray for me whilst you are on the earth, and still more fervently pray for me when you are associated with the saints in heaven."

The jewelled hand of the Archbishop was laid upon the unhelmetted head of O'Hanlon, and after a short and fervent prayer motioned him to depart.

In a few minutes afterwards the tramp of horses was heard, and then succeeded a still and solemn silence.

The Archbishop knelt down in prayer—a prayer which continued for many hours; and ere that supplication had concluded, his house was surrounded by emissaries from the Castle, and he was in the hands of his enemies.

On the first day of July, in the year 1681, the most Reverend Oliver Plunkett, Archbishop of Armagh, and Primate of all Ireland, was barbarously executed at Tyburn.

CHAPTER XV.

REDMOND O'HANLON.

At the time that Redmond O'Hanlon was engaged in conversation with the Primate, and urging in vain that illustrious prelate to save himself by flight from the fell designs of his enemies, there was advancing from Dublin a body of horsemen despatched for the purpose of arresting the Archbishop, and conducting him as a prisoner to Newgate.

No opposition to the contemplated arrest was calculated upon, and not the slightest resistance anticipated. The body of horsemen then marched without the slightest regard to military regulations, and without adopting the usual precautions to prevent a surprise. They proceeded in the same wild, noisy, and boisterous manner, as if they had started for a day's sport from Dublin; or, rather, as if each was on his way to the hunting-ground at which a fox was to be unearthed, or a deer let loose.

Of all this tumultuary gathering there were but three who did not appear in the same hilarious spirits as their associates; and these three rode behind the rest, two of them keeping constantly together; the third, who appeared from his rich military garments to be the leader, holding himself aloof, and seldom speaking to the two who rode near him, and never, but on some point connected with the expedition in which they were all engaged.

The two companions who rode side by side, and whose gloomy looks and downcast countenances, contrasting so strongly as they did with the rude mirth of those who rode before them, might make them be mistaken for prisoners but that each wore by his side a sword, and there were no guards around to keep watch upon them. Side by side had these two men ridden for more than four hours, and seemingly becoming more sad the nearer they approached the object of their journey. At last one of them, stooping down to the side of the military saddle on which he rode, drew up with a thick leathern strap a flat stone jar, which dangled at the horse's side, undrew the cork, and, putting his nose to the neck of the jar, he inhaled the odourous vapour it emitted, and said, as he handed it to his companion:—

"It *is* the real stuff, and every drop of it more precious than a pearl. After all, John Elliott is like his own usquebaugh—genuine, pure, unadulterated. Taste it, David; it will do your heart good, and, if your spirits be as low as mine, help to elevate them."

"No, thank you, Mr. Murfey, answered his companion; "my tippling days are over. That accursed passion for drink has, with other vices, been my ruin; and I now see, what I before this I could not believe, that the man who indulges his passions may end, as I have done, in becoming not only the slave of them, but the continued slave of wretches that, in the days of his youth and innocence, he would scorn to know—that are born and bred so much below him, he would not allow them even to tie the latchet of his shoes."

Murfey put the jar to his lips, took a long, long draught, then corking it up again, and giving with his open hand a loud slap to the cork, so as to fix it tightly in the neck, he let the jar gently down to the position from which he had taken it, and then, but not till then, did he bestow the slightest notice on the observations made to him.

"David Fitzgerald, late of Drumsna, in the County of Limerick, Esquire, said Murfey, as he smacked his lips, "that is, I can tell you, a most celestial liquid—the quintescence of inebriety, the poetry of potations. Abuse yourself, abuse myself, abuse my father and my mother—thank heaven! you cannot abuse my wife, nor my children, for I never had, and never intend to have them, or the like of them; abuse the King, the Queen, the Duke of York, or the Duke of Monmouth; abuse Lord Shaftesbury and the Popish plot; abuse the Duke of Ormonde; abuse Cromwell's Scout-Master-General, the Bishop of Meath, or abuse him who was my Archbishop—that *Oliverus Cromwellus* of the clergy, Dr. Plunkett; abuse, if you like, the whole world, and everybody in the world, and everything about the world; but one thing let alone. Don't, as you love me, say one word against one drop of John Elliott's usquebaugh, for it is the only friend I have left: and from nothing else, and by nothing else, and through nothing else, do I ever receive consolation, satisfaction, or gratification, an hour's pleasure by day, or an hour's sleep by night. Respect my feelings, then, David Fitzgerald, and say not one word against drinking."

"Can you be serious, Murfey, for one moment?" asked Fitzgerald.

"I have done drinking; and if it will please you, I will not drink another drop for six hours," replied Murfey. "And to make such a resolution as that, with the intention of keeping it, is enough to cause any one to be serious. I am always very serious when I am sober."

"Then listen to me, Mr. Murfey; for, of all the persons with whom my late sad course of life has brought me to associate, you are the only one," said Fitzgerald, "in whom I have been able to detect one spark of feeling. All the rest of them are clumsy hypocrites, who have not the skill to conceal the wickedness they nurture in their hearts."

"Go on, Mr. Fitzgerald. I appreciate the compliment

you intend to pay me, although it is very clumsily expressed."

"I have one or two questions to ask you, Murfey."

"Go on, Mr. Fitzgerald; I will, as they say in the schools, answer you to the best of my skill and ability."

"The first question, then, I would ask you is, what is, in your judgment, the position of that most audacious old villain, Gerald Geraghty; he who you must know by this time entrapped me, by a most artfully contrived story, into the abduction of Judith Lawson? What is, do you think, his precise position? And how comes he to have a place like Brass Castle placed under his sole control? And what, think you, has been his object in obtaining the capture of Miss Lawson, and what are his ultimate purposes with respect to her?"

"Drunk or sober, Mr. Fitzgerald," replied Murfey, "wet or dry, I have always and at all times my wits about me, can tell what is doing around me, and remember every syllable of it right well afterwards. Now, as to that old fellow, Gerald Geraghty, I was not three times in his company until I came to the conclusion, and every day's experience justifies my first conviction, that of all I ever met, conversed with, heard, or read about, he is, before all and beyond all, the most thorough-paced scoundrel; competent to invent any falsehood, and capable of committing any wickedness to attain whatever purpose he aimed it. I had not seen him three times when I took a fancy to study him; because it is not easy in a century to meet with such a perfect specimen of a rascal. And yet, entertaining this opinion of him, and desiring to comprehend him fully in all his varieties of villany, I must admit that I find it most difficult, if not impossible, to give a categorical answer to all your questions. Perhaps you would dispense with my vow not to taste another drop for six hours, and let me take one more pull at the usquebaugh, just to give a flavour, strength, and richness to the epithets I desire to apply to a miscreant, who is like to Sejanus, because his will is in wickedness: '*Neque Sejani voluntas, nisi scelere quærebatur.*'"

"Not another drop, if you please, Murfey. The questions I ask you respecting that terrible old man deeply affect me," observed Fitzgerald.

"Deeply affect *you!* aye, and *me*, too; aye, and that proud, dull, dry Cromwellian, Captain Ludlow, who rides behind us, and thinks himself too proud to hold conversation with us; even he," observed Murfey, "for aught I know, may be, like ourselves, nothing more than the instrument of that scoundrel Geraghty in going upon this expedition."

"Oh! that is an absurd supposition of yours, Murfey. There cannot possibly be any bond of union between the rich Ludlow and the poor Geraghty. I have some reason for supposing they have never seen each other."

"Mine is only a supposition, I admit," replied Murfey; "but your suggestion is no answer to it. What did you know of Geraghty when a message from him brought you to listen to his lying stories about Miss Lawson? and what did I know of Geraghty, when I first quarrelled with my bishop? And yet he found me out; and supporting, or rather getting support for me, so incited me to carry on the war against the bishop, until bad became worse, and at last I was excommunicated; and then, to revenge myself, became a witness, and now am on my way to see the man, who was once kind as a father to me, arrested like a felon. The Lord forgive me!"

"True—true—most true," said Fitzgerald, sighing;

"it was Geraghty suggested to me what evidence I was to give as a witness, in order that I might, as a witness, have the means at my disposal of effecting my marriage through an abduction. But why has a man in Geraghty's condition all this influence and power, and why is he using both for some personal purpose of his own?"

"Why did you or I grasp at influence and power, and then seek to employ both for purposes of our own; you, to promote your marriage with a rich young woman; I, to gratify my hatred and revenge against my archbishop? The puzzle to me is," said Murfey, "not that Geraghty should employ the influence he has obtained and the power he wields, for the attainment of his own personal ends, but what these ends can be. There, I confess to you, I am completely baffled. How he has gained influence is easily seen. He is one of the agents in this country of that party in England, who have resolved, *per fus aut nefas*, to keep the Duke of York from the throne; and, as I think, setting that Duke aside, either to establish a republic, or what will be the same as a republic, retaining all the powers of government in their hands, putting upon the throne the Duke of Monmouth, giving to him the name of a 'King,' and so through him, and in his name, ruling over the three kingdoms. Now, I think that Geraghty is a trusted agent of that party—the same party that have got up the Popish plot. It is through Geraghty— his very obscurity rendering him unsuspected—that Lord Shaftesbury and his lordship's agent, Hetherington, are stirring up a Popish plot in Ireland. If I am right, and I am pretty sure I am, in this conjecture, then you have at once the reason given to you for Geraghty's power and influence, the motives for his aiding to entrap me, the motive for his trying to entrap you. That he is more astute than both of us he has already proved by his suggestion to us, if any attempt was made to rescue Miss Lawson when you seized her, to declare she was a party in the Popish plot."

"But then, why keep the girl in custody?" impatiently asked Fitzgerald. "The purpose has been accomplished for which the outrage was committed upon her. Why not restore her to her father?"

"Well," added Murfey, "if you will force a reason from me, whether I will or not, I must endeavour to give one. None of us are so wise as to foresee all the consequences of our own acts, and Geraghty, with all his cleverness, may be in that position with Miss Lawson. She may be a burden upon his hands, and he does not know how to get rid of her. Either he may fear the consequences of sending her back to her father, for her father, you will observe, is no more a Papist than yourself, and, therefore, to commit an outrage upon a member of an English Protestant family may be a far more serious matter in these times, than if the girl and her relatives were Papists. You may be sure Ebenezer Lawson would punish with the law, or if the law would not do, with his own sword, the man who had acted, even for an hour, as the jailer of his daughter; or, the reason why Geraghty had her seized, and so befooled you into taking part in her capture, was with an ultimate view to the making money of her; that is, of getting a large ransom for her release. Avarice is the common vice of old men, and this may have been the great motive, beyond all others, for his conduct with respect to that young woman, whose tongue I can say, from experience, is as sharp as her arm is strong, and who, if you had married her, I have not the slightest doubt, would have led you the life of a dog."

The observations of the sage and sober Murfey were interrupted by a loud whistle, and before its shrill sound had ceased to vibrate on the ear, or a word could be spoken to inquire the cause, he was surprised to find that the horse which he rode had been seized by the bridle, and that a man without hat on his head, or shoes on his feet, had grasped the wrist of his right hand. Upon looking at his companion, Fitzgerald, he saw that he was placed in the same predicament, his bridle-rein seized, and the wrist of his right hand grasped; and on looking back he observed his leader, Captain Ludlow, arrested in the same manner; and on looking before him, he perceived the few of his party who were in view had in the same manner been detained by wild, savage-looking, half-naked men, who wore long knives in their belts.

The captors and the captives were alike silent.

The captives were silent, for they were horror-stricken at the suddenness of the surprise, and the consciousness that the men who held them could by a single movement plunge their long knives, that had not yet been unsheathed, into their bodies.

The captors were silent, because they acted under the orders of a strict commander.

This terror-inspiring silence lasted for full five minutes, when it was interrupted by the following words, spoken in a tone of command: "Remove the prisoners right and left from the centre of the road, in order that their number may be ascertained."

No sooner had this order been obeyed than Murfey and his companions heard the noise made by an advancing body of horsemen. A portion of them appeared to be halted in front; and then they saw a gentleman in a rich, green, military uniform, with cuirass and helmet, advancing, and at a few yards behind him thirty well-mounted and fully-armed horsemen, who passed to the rere, and there halted.

"May I never sin," whispered Murfey to his companion, "but we are surrounded on all sides—back, front, sides, and rere. We are caught as completely as a fox in a trap, a fish in a net, or a fly in a bottle."

"If you want a knife put into you, before I'm ordered to do it, you will dare to speak another word," whispered the rough-haired man who held Murfey's wrist.

"Who is in command of the prisoners? Who is their leader?" asked the commander of the captors.

"I am," announced Ludlow.

"Bring the gentleman forward," said the commander. "Now release him. I wish to speak with him alone."

The prisoners were withdrawn on one side, and the cavalry of the captors fell back about a hundred paces on the other.

The following conversation then passed between the two leaders :—

"Your name and rank, Sir?"

"Edward Ludlow, formerly a captain in the army."

"In the Cromwellian army?"

"Yes."

"And nephew to Lieutenant-General Ludlow?"

"The same."

"Look at me well, Mr. Edward Ludlow; for there are reasons you should never forget me."

"I have seen you before, I am sure, but where I do not recollect."

"I will remind you. I once stood upon the ramparts of Dublin Castle; that was the first time we met. A second time I stood before you in a coffee-room in Dublin."

"Ah!" exclaimed Ludlow, with a yell of frantic rage,

"I do remember you—well—well—oh! how well. It was your accursed hand inflicted upon me this horrid wound in my face. It was you who dashed a wine glass at me, and sought to provoke me to a tavern brawl. Yes, miscreant, I do remember you."

"Moderate your language, Mr. Ludlow, unless you are prepared to abide on the spot the consequences of your own words. Once we met as strangers, a second time we met as enemies, a third time we meet as mortal foes. We are here now face to face. If you have the courage of a man and the spirit of a soldier draw, I say, draw at once. You are challenged to conflict by Redmond O'Hanlon."

"Redmond O'Hanlon!" said Ludlow, and as he repeated the words, his lips trembled with terror at that fearful name, although he did his utmost to conceal his apprehensions by a blustering tone. "Redmond O'Hanlon! a Rapparee! a tory! a highway robber! a cattle-stealer! challenges an English gentleman to fight a duel with him! You may assassinate me with your Rapparee's knife if you so please, but never shall you be able to boast that a man of my birth, rank, and position met you as his equal."

"Oh! I see," replied O'Hanlon. "Mr. Edward Ludlow is fastidious on the point of honour. He compares his life with mine, and he finds his past career so pure, and mine so dishonoured, that he will not cross swords with me! Come, Mr. Ludlow, we must see which of the two can best boast himself to be a gentleman. I have the time to spare to do so, for I own I have sought this interview with the purpose of fastening a quarrel upon you, of compelling you to meet me as a mortal foe ; having it in my power, by a word, to rid the world of such a base villain, but still preferring to do so by my own hand, because encountering you on equal terms, with equal weapons, and with no undue advantage on either side.

"You have," said O'Hanlon, sheathing his sword as he spoke, "chosen to apply various opprobrious epithets to me, and you have in the same breath boasted of your birth, your rank, and your position. If you know anything of my past career, and I believe you do, then you must be well aware my birth is equal to your own. As to your rank, you have been an officer in the Cromwellian army, and I have been an officer in the service of a foreign sovereign, as well as the ever-faithful adherent of my king, whether that king was a prisoner, a victim, an exile, or on the throne; and for my services I have been honoured with the title of a count. And now as to your position in society. What is it? In what respect is it superior to my own? The estate of my ancestors—that which should be mine, as it was theirs—was taken away, not on account of any vice or crime on their part or on mine, but by a band of rebels and of robbers, who, gaining possession of the government for the time, took from us our lands, because we were loyal to our sovereign and true to our God. And what have I done? and wherefore is it that you brand me as a Rapparee, a tory, and a cow-stealer? For no other reason than this: that I will not tamely and patiently submit to the wrong that has been done, that I will not allow the thieves who are the receivers of stolen goods, who hold possession of our lands, to have quiet and undisturbed enjoyment of the produce of those lands; that where I can, and when I can, I take that produce from them of which they have not the honesty to make restitution, nor the courage to defend. That I wage a war of life and death against these spoliators of our property; and that as long as I have life I will, with my own right hand, and my sword, vindicate our rights and punish our wrong-doers. Is it because I do this, you and your republican gang of invaders apply injurious and opprobrious epithets to us? but, at the same time, in your craven fear, and in the hope of being allowed to retain a portion of the spoil you have unjustly gained, you are forced to pay me tribute, and although you have what you call law courts in Dublin, still, in the midst of your abuse, you tremble at my name, aye, and shrink from a conflict with me. You abuse me privately, though you dare not denounce me openly; and sure I am, that if you find the opportunity of destroying me, the wicked purpose will be attained by base means, and the hand of an assassin effect what the sword of a soldier would not venture to attempt, nor the arm of a partial and unjust Government have the power to execute.

"I seek, by open, undisguised war to recover what is my own; to punish trangressors, to aid the helpless, and to protect the weak, and for doing this you call me a Rapparee, a tory, and a cow-stealer.

"You know that you are telling falsehoods of me, but these falsehoods your party purposely circulate to disguise from the world their own iniquitous spoilations, and as a palliation for cruelties which innate cowardice urges you and them to perpetrate.

"This, then, is my position; by open hostility I am seeking to recover what is my own.

"What is your position? Born to no fortune in England, you have acquired a large fortune in Ireland. But by what means has that been accumulated? I speak not of the wholesale confiscation which such scandalous and bloodthirsty hypocrites as Cromwell, Ludlow, and Ireton effected. Confiscation of the property of the loyal, for the profit of rebels; the robbery of the natives for the benefit of foreigners. All these were the common crimes of the republican faction; and I am not desirous of making you individually responsible for them, however, much and undeservedly, as an individual, you have profited by them. But you, Sir, who now forgetful of who I am, and how much I know of your previous career, *you,* who claim a superiority over me, *you* have not been content with the commission of the usual crimes perpetrated by the great body of the caitiff republicans—you, in your desire to gain the Fitzpatrick estates, have brought an innocent woman, a lady of rank, to the stake, for *you* had much to do with the execution of that noble female of the house of Ossory, Mrs. Fitzpatrick, and thus, in your desire to destroy all claim of the legitimate heir to the estate, you have hunted the child from one part of Ireland to another, seeking, in your base ambition, to imbrue your hands in the innocent blood of an unoffending boy. That brand upon your countenance is a memorial of your misdeeds. It was the same hand that now beckons you to a mortal combat, which, in defending the life of a helpless child, so marked you, his cowardly persecutor, with infamy. Remember, base villain as you are, the massacre in the death-cave of Dundalk; remember, *you* are responsible for that too; that the knives that were then unsheathed to destroy the lives of unoffending infants, were unsheathed with the hope that one of them might have reached the heart of the young Fitzpatrick. Think you, Sir, if heaven permits you now to escape from my hand, unpunished for these most atrocious crimes and murders, that you will be permitted finally to pass, even from this world, unscathed by the vengeance of an All-just and All-protecting Omnipotence.

"And now, the murderer in fact, as well as the murderer in intention, the spoliator of the orphan, the slayer of the widow, whose vile avarice has been impervious to all the stings of conscience, and deaf to all the claims of humanity, tells me he is an English gentleman! and that because of his rank, his birth, and his position, he will not cross swords with me!

"Base poltroon! orphan-butcher! woman-executioner! Twice I met you before to-night. First, in defending the life of a child, I struck you with an arrow; second, in defending an old man from the brutal and unprovoked attack of your associate ruffian and fellow-murderer, I wounded him and struck you. That old man was Colonel Fitzpatrick."

"Colonel Fitzpatrick, the old man in the tavern!" cried Ludlow, unable to suppress his feelings of surprise.

"Yes," continued O'Hanlon, "the father of him you had tried to slay in Dublin Castle. But I have done with them. The son is now by his father's side, and able to protect both from all your future schemes. I have done with them, but it is not so with you, if you now escape from my hands. But you shall not do so. I have called you poltroon! coward! orphan-butcher! woman-executioner! Will you bear these names patiently?"

"I have told you, Mr. O'Hanlon," said Ludlow, "that I will not fight a duel with you. I have stated my reasons. It is not necessary to repeat them."

Ludlow well knew the peril in which he stood by using the disparaging language he had done towards O'Hanlon; but he perceived that of the two dangers to which his life was exposed, there was, by declining a combat, a chance of escape, whereas by fighting with O'Hanlon his death was inevitable. He adopted, therefore, that course which afforded even a small chance of escape, to that which would lead to his speedy, almost instantaneous loss of life.

O'Hanlon turned to his followers, and said: "Advance, soldiers; let all the prisoners be brought in a circle around me."

These orders were instantly obeyed, and O'Hanlon, standing with Ludlow in the centre of the circle, said:—

"Soldiers, whether friends or enemies, I wish you to be the witness of a scene I would, if I could, have avoided. This man, Ludlow, your commander, is a villain, who has done great wrong to some of my friends. The mark you see upon his face my hand inflicted upon him thirty years ago, and when he was seeking to destroy, by means of a cowardly murder, the infant son of one of my dearest and most intimate friends. By accident I heard he was coming this way, and for reasons of my own, which I purposely do not mention, I desired to have a personal conflict with him—with him alone, and with none others that are here; and hence I adopted the expedient by which his adherents have been made captives. I did so, in order that I might propose to him in private that which I now propose to him in public, namely, to encounter me in single combat. That combat he has declined—that satisfaction he still refuses. He has wronged my friends, he has used insulting language to myself, and yet a soldier, and calling himself a gentleman, he declines a fair field and equal terms when they are tendered to him to repair a wrong, and to give reparation for injuries that have been done. What, then, are my means of redress with a man who acts so vilely, so basely, and so cowardly? There is but one; to treat him as a poltroon, and to inflict upon him a degrading punishment—so degrading that henceforth no man who respects himself can associate with him.

"There," said O'Hanlon, pointing to the two men who held Ludlow and his horse, "drag him to the earth, strip from him his officer's habiliments, bind him to a tree, and inflict upon his naked back twelve stripes with a rope; and as the blood follows each blow, let him think of the ramparts of Dublin Castle, and the blood shed by him in the cave of Dundalk."

* * * * *

The captors and prisoners had separated, and of the latter not one man, with the exception of their leader, Ludlow, had received the slightest personal injury from Redmond O'Hanlon or his followers.

"With your leave, Mr. Fitzgerald," said Murfey to his melancholy companion, "I must take an infinitesimal drop of comfort, consolation, and courage from my jar of usquebaugh. Oh! dear me! what a lucky thing I was not recognised by that bloodthirsty homicide, O'Hanlon. If he has punished so ignominiously a gentleman for only *speaking* ill of him, what would he have done to me, who have not merely spoken, but *written* abuse of him, and published it in a pamphlet? he would, I dare say, have hung me up, or scarified me alive!"

Poor Murfey! he was in the position of many an obscure and contemptible libeller. Redmond O'Hanlon had never heard of Murfey's paltry and ill-written pamphlet; and if he had, would have regarded the abuse, from such a source, as on a level with its author, and, therefore, alike undeserving of notice, and unworthy of resentment.

CHAPTER XVI.

PROMISES OF MARRIAGE.

Four persons—and four persons only—were seated in the splendidly-furnished drawing-room of the Lady Diana Massey, at Palmerstown. They consisted of the hostess and her guest Major Harvey, and her niece and Mr. Vincent Fitzpatrick; but although in the same room, they were so far apart as to form two distinct companies, it being impossible for the one party to hear what the others might be saying in a low tone of voice.

Whatever the subjects of conversation might have been between these two distinct parties, they seemed to interest both very much; for a stranger entering the apartment and seating himself in the centre, that is, the point the furthest removed from both, would have fancied he had come into a meeting of "the Society of Friends," and that each was awaiting the moment for the spirit of dialogue to move him or her with the disposition to speak aloud, and in such a tone as might be audible to all present.

For a full hour there was this silence in the same apartment, with sweet whispers and soft murmurs at either end, when it was at last broken by Lady Diana Massey. Starting up and striking with her spangled fan the jewelled hand of her companion, as it rested on the back of her chair, she exclaimed:—

"For shame! Major Harvey! how could you think of such a thing! Me! to marry again. Oh! monstrous! I'll expose you, Sir, this very instant."

"I defy you," said Major Harvey. "Tell what I have

just said to you, if you dare, to this company, and I will take my revenge upon them and on you."

"Well," said lady Diana, "there is nothing in this world, I do believe, can exceed the audacity of an old soldier——"

"Except it be," chimed in Harvey, "the courage of a young and handsome widow."

"There it is again, my dears," said Lady Diana. "Really this man can be no longer tolerated as a guest in this house."

"Then make him the host," said Harvey, whispering in her ear.

"Lud a mercy! there he has said it again," cried Lady Diana. "Kathleen! Vincent! niece! my dearest Kathleen! I say, I am speaking to you, children."

Kathleen and Vincent, whose heads were close together, started apart at the same moment, and, as if with one voice, replied:—

"My dear aunt!"

"Lady Diana!"

"Why, what on earth is the matter with you; or what can you both be talking about for this hour past?"

"Talking of! what were we talking of?" said Vincent, somewhat puzzled at the question. "Why, Madam, we we were talking of—of—let me think. Oh! aye, of fishing; was it not of fishing that we were last speaking?"

"Yes, yes, dear—Vincent, I mean," answered Kathleen, blushing at the mistake she was near making, "we were talking of fishing."

"Yes, I am sure you were," observed Harvey; "and you, young lady, I have no doubt, were showing Mr. Fitzpatrick how your aunt *ties on a fly.*"

"I see—I see what you mean, Sir," said Lady Diana; "but I'll expose you, Sir. Now, just listen to me, my dear children, and hear how this gentleman has been behaving. Whilst you, good, innocent dears, were harmlessly descanting upon the infantile sport of fly-fishing, this gentleman has been taking advantage of your minds being so properly engaged, and he has been—I really blush to say it—he has been actually making love to—*me !*"

"Oh! my poor, dear aunt!" cried Kathleen, in a voice of deep commiseration.

"Oh! for shame, Major!" cried the horrified Mr. Vincent.

"Yes, my dears! but that is not all, he has been actually proposing marriage to me!"

"Oh! poor, dear Aunt!" cried Kathleen.

"Oh! wicked, wicked Major!" cried Vincent.

"Alas! my dear, innocent babies, you know not the wickedness of these old soldiers; he has been doing something even worse than making love, or proposing marriage to me," cried Lady Diana.

"Worse than making love, and proposing marriage," cried Kathleen; "what a terrible man!"

"And what an awful Major!" exclaimed Mr. Vincent Fitzpatrick.

"Yes, my dears," continued Lady Diana; "something far worse than either making love or proposing marriage; for men may, as I well know, only make love to pass away the time—indulging themselves thereby with as idle a sport as fishing; and men, too, may propose marriage, and afterwards repent of having done so; but this awful man has asked me to do that which is irrevocable and irreversible. He has asked me—Oh! dear, only to think of it makes me tremble so, I can hardly speak—he has—yes, I will expose him—he has actually urged me, pressed me—almost forced me to—to—to *name the day !*'

" To name the day ! Oh ! my dear Aunt," said Kathleen.

" To name the day ! Oh ! brave-hearted Major !" cried Mr. Fitzpatrick. " Well, and what answer did you give to so plain a proposition ?"

" What answer did I give him!" replied Lady Diana. Really, Vincent, you have no idea of the state of my feelings. If you had been, as I have, twice married——"

" Which I hope I never shall be," said Vincent, as he looked at Kathleen.

" Well, but, Vincent, if you had been in that position, you could appreciate the delicacy of my sentiments, and you would feel yourself in such a situation that you could not reply to so monstrous a proposal ; but you would do, as I am now doing—you would consult your friends, as I am consulting you, and ask them—what do *you* think is the proper answer I ought to give ?"

" Do you ask for my opinion ?" asked Vincent.

" I do—of course I do," replied Lady Diana.

" And, dear aunt, do you ask for my opinion also ?" asked Kathleen.

" Yes, my dear niece, and wish above all things to have it."

" Then, as you have asked the opinion of us both, I think we ought to consult together before we give it," observed Vincent.

" But, remember," said Major Harvey, " that whilst consulting on a matter in which I feel so deep an interest, you do not lose a moment in talking over your own favourite amusement of—fly-fishing !"

Vincent and Kathleen whispered together, as if in solemn consultation, and then both coming forward, hand in hand together, the gentleman remarked:—

"I am commissioned to deliver the judgment of your arbitrators—your own chosen arbitrators—Lady Diana."

"Ah! I am almost afraid to listen to you," cried, in a tone of great alarm, the tender-hearted widow.

"The solemn judgment of your chosen arbitrators," continued Vincent, "is, that Major Harvey having made love to you, having proposed marriage to you, and having urged you to name the day for marriage, you are bound to name the day; and we, moreover, declare, that you are bound, not only to name the day, but also that the day you should name ought to be—next Saturday!"

"Oh! dear!—oh! dear!" cried Lady Diana, as if greatly afflicted, "what is a poor, lone, helpless, unprotected woman to do, when her friends and kinsmen decide against her? Major Harvey, you wicked old soldier, come here. Take my hand—I submit to the award;" and as the lady so spoke, she covered her face with her fan, and extended her hand to the Major.

"Lady Diana," said Major Harvey, "you have made me the happiest of men. And now, as your affianced husband, permit me to make one request—it is the first favour I have to seek for in the new relation in which I stand towards you."

"My dear Major," said Lady Diana, looking up and smiling, "ask what you please, and if in my power, consider it as already granted; for having given to you myself, I cannot refuse you anything else."

"Then, as the guardian of Kathleen, consent to her marriage with my friend Vincent, on the same day that you and I are united together. That Vincent's father approves of the union I know from Colonel Fitzpatrick himself. All, then, that is required to complete the happiness of these piscatorial lovers is your approval."

"My dear Major," replied Lady Diana, "not only do I give my consent to the proposed marriage, but with your permission I will present the bride with a gift of ten thousand pounds, which I always intended for her."

"You are an excellent woman!" cried the enraptured Major; "and with your goodness of heart, and my equanimity of temper, I am quite sure that even Kathleen and Vincent cannot be happier than we shall be."

Vincent and Kathleen were about giving expression to their feelings of gratitude to Major Harvey and Lady Diana, when Lord Arran rushed suddenly into the room; but stopped as he looked at the Major and Lady Diana on one side, and Vincent with Kathleen on the other.

"Ah, Major, Major!" cried Lord Arran, "I see how it is; neither my friendly warnings nor all the wisdom you brought from Continental wars, and that you concentrated in a Spanish proverb, has preserved you unharmed from the wiles and fascinations of the most lovely widow in Ireland. Benedict is already written in your face, I see it in your smiles, and I detect it in the rosy dimples of Lady Diana. Come, no secrets with an old friend; when are you two to be made happy?"

"On Saturday next; and I invite you as my bride's-man," replied Harvey. "These Spanish proverbs are, my lord, full of wisdom; and there is one of them has made a deep impression on me since I came here."

"What is it?" said Lord Arran. "Plainly, not that cautious, ill-natured, or prudential one which says, 'Before you marry, think well of what you are about to do.' *Antes que cases mira lo que hazes.*"

"No, no," replied Harvey; "the proverb that has influenced my destinies for life, and has made me the happy man you see, is one much more just, true, and good-natured— *Un alma sola, ni canta ni llora*—'One soul alone neither sings nor weeps.' My selfish, solitary bachelorhood will speedily expire."

"And you, too, my young friend," replied Lord Arran, as he turned to Fitzpatrick, and the smiling, blushing Kathleen, "you, too, I perceive have succeeded in your suit. Believe me, I wish you joy, for I believe you to be worthy of your happiness. My wishes, I assure you, Mr. Fitzpatrick, are not the less sincere, because, if circumstances had favoured me, I would have desired to be your rival, and would have contested against you for that prize, which you have fairly won. But, pardon me for my forgetting, in the contemplation of so much happiness, the important, and, I may add, serious, if not dangerous business that has brought me here."

"Dangerous!" shrieked Lady Diana, "you terrify me to death! What can you mean by using such a dreadful word?"

"Come, Lady Diana," replied Lord Arran, "you are about to become the wife of as brave a soldier as ever yet drew sword in the field of battle. I hope you will prove, when the occasion arises, that you are worthy of the name you are about to bear."

"Speak plainly, my lord," said Lady Diana, "for that which is most terrific to a woman is an impending danger that involves itself in mystery, and the extent and nature of which she is not permitted to appreciate."

"It is a just observation," replied Lord Arran, "and my belief is, that men are considered more courageous than women, mainly because men know what perils they have to encounter; and women are timid, because they have not the same amount of knowledge. I will, then, briefly as I can, explain to you why I am here unexpectedly, and even unannounced.

"That mean and monstrous villain, Ludlow," continued Lord Arran, "has, it seems, been driven to desperation by the last act of Redmond O'Hanlon. That celebrated partisan, it appears, encountered Ludlow when in command of a party to seize the Popish Archbishop, Dr. Plunkett; and wishing to avenge some personal wrong done to him, O'Hanlon challenged Ludlow to meet him in single combat, in presence of the followers of both. This challenge Ludlow refused to accept, and the consequence was, that O'Hanlon had Ludlow's back bared, and stripes inflicted upon him with a hangman's rope. Ludlow, for submitting to this degrading punishment, has been, since then, shunned by society. He has been refused admittance at the Castle, and at the house of every private gentleman. The consequence of this treatment is, he has determined upon leaving Ireland; but before doing so, he has resolved upon securing to himself the Fitzpatrick property, by the forcible abduction of Miss Kathleen Fitzpatrick."

Kathleen shrieked, and threw herself into the arms of Vincent. "Save me, Vincent; save me, my beloved, from such a villain."

"With my life," replied Vincent.

Lord Arran looked at the young couple, thus expressing their affection and devotion to each other; and, as he did so, there was a flush upon his cheek, and his voice trembled perceptibly as he resumed the discourse which had been so unexpectedly interrupted.

"The time fixed upon by Ludlow for carrying out this

diabolical plot is this very night. He has hired the services of six of the ruffians who were with him when arresting Archbishop Plunkett; and as he believes Lady Diana has not more than three men servants in the house, he considers that this number will be sufficient to effect his purpose."

"How has your lordship gained a knowledge of his secrets?" inquired Lady Diana.

"Through Colonel Fitzpatrick, who is stopping in the same inn at which resides this Ludlow's confidant, a man named Lawson, who was wounded in the hand a short time since by Redmond O'Hanlon."

"Redmond O'Hanlon!" exclaimed Major Harvey. "Redmond O'Hanlon again! Why, the man appears to be ubiquitous. What description of man is he, if he be, indeed, a man at all?"

"Ah! Major, Major," replied Lord Arran, laughing, "what a cunning, sly old rogue you are! I do not wonder you inveigled this innocent lady into a promise of marriage. Well, you know that Redmond O'Hanlon was the friend of our young hero here, on an occasion of which we need say no more in the present company."

"A secret told to me is a fact forgotten but by the teller," observed Harvey. "But this night you say the attack is to be made on this house. I am glad of it. The most grateful of all odours to me is the fume of gunpowder, when I have a chance of lodging a bullet in the brain of a vagabond. I trust the plan of defence will be confided to me. If it is, I promise you that there is not a man who enters Lady Diana's park to-night, with a hostile intention, that will not be carried out of it a corpse to-morrow."

"Oh! Major, my dear, dear, dearest Major," cried Lady

Diana, "do not talk in that horrid manner, or you will frighten me to death on the spot."

"Listen to your intended bride, Major, and be guided by her advice," said Lord Arran, "if you would not avoid the worst of all punishments, as I am told, of marriage folk, a curtain lecture. I have a plan to propose, somewhat different from the battle-scene you are already dreaming of."

"What is it?" asked Harvey. "No chance of escape, I hope, for such cowardly villains."

"Not the least," replied Lord Arran; "the only difference between your plan and mine is, you would not, if you could, let one of them escape with life, and what I propose is to entrap them all alive."

"And how will you do that?" asked Harvey.

"Mainly by your assistance, and wholly, I might add, from my confidence in your skill as a veteran campaigner—as one practised in all the arts and devices of war—as valiant in a forlorn hope, as you are astute in contriving an ambush. Now, what I propose is, that you leave the defence of the ladies to the men who are at present in the house, for without reckoning at all upon the male attendants, I am quite sure that Fitzpatrick and myself would be able alone to withstand the attack of two dozen such riff-raff as Ludlow can gather round him."

"And as to me," said Major Harvey, somewhat impatiently, "what do you propose for me to do?"

"As for you, the all-important part of the affair will devolve upon you. Fitzpatrick and I are to be entrusted with the defence of the house from within; but its exterior defence is to be your charge."

"What! put my dear Major out of the house to be fired at by murderers!" exclaimed Lady Diana. "Oh, my lord! my lord! how could you propose anything so dreadful, and that in the hearing of a lady who is to be married to the Major this very next coming Saturday?"

"My plan," said Lord Arran, smiling, "is to secure such happiness the very next coming Saturday to two such tender lovers as you and the Major."

"Yes, and two other such tender lovers as Vincent and Kathleen," added Lady Diana.

A slight frown contracted for a moment the brow of Lord Arran, but it dispersed as quickly as it had gathered, and he resumed: "What I propose is, that Major Harvey should depart this very instant, procure, as he easily can, such a number of his own dragoons as he deems to be sufficient for the purpose, and when he knows that the hour fixed upon for the attack is eleven o'clock, so dispose his troopers about the grounds that he can have every one of his assailants arrested the moment that the first hostile movement is made by them."

"Admirable! admirable! my Lord," cried Harvey, in an ecstasy. "I see it all now. I have studied every inch of ground about the house and park as earnestly, and know it as completely as if it had been a chosen field of battle. Even as I talk to you, I have laid out my ambush so thoroughly that the assailants will be prisoners before they are aware they have a single enemy outside the house to contend against. Farewell, my Lord, when you next see me, tonight, Ludlow and his gang will be in my custody as captives. Lady Diana, I kiss your hand. Kathleen, with my consent, no man but Vincent shall ever call you 'wife.'"

The information of which Lord Arran was the bearer proved to be correct.

The night was pitchy dark, when Ludlow, followed by ten men, crossed the wall of Lady Diana's park, and advanced with stealthy steps towards the front. No light shone in any part of the house to indicate that any one was on the watch.

Ludlow and his followers ascended the steps leading to the hall-door, and a single blow with a sledge-hammer had shivered the lock to pieces, but that was the only noise heard, for, at the same instant, the hall was filled with lights, showing Lord Arran, Fitzpatrick, and the three servants, armed with matchlocks, and the same light shone upon the uplifted sabres of forty soldiers, who surrounded the steps by which Ludlow and his gang had ascended.

"Down with your arms instantly. Surrender at once, or I will cut every man of you to pieces," cried Major Harvey, from the rere.

"Surrender! surrender, Mr. Ludlow, at once," cried Lord Arran, "or I will blow your brains out."

"Lay down your arms, men," said Ludlow. "It is in vain to contend against such numbers. Some one amongst you is a traitor, and I am in the hands of my enemies."

"Not your enemies, Mr. Ludlow, but the friends of your destined victim. Major, let the prisoners be bound outside. I will speak with Mr. Ludlow in a private room," said Lord Arran; and Ludlow was conducted into a small room leading from the hall.

"My Lord Arran," said Ludlow, when he found both were alone, "you have the reputation of being a generous man. Grant me, then, one favour. Give me, for I have been disarmed, some weapon by which I may take away my life, and no longer survive the dishonour that has befallen me."

"Mr. Ludlow," said Lord Arran, as he looked with undisguised contempt at the base man before him, "this is not the time nor the place to talk to any gentleman about your being apprehensive of dishonour. Had you preferred your honour to your life, there was an opportunity afforded to you for making a selection between the two, when Count O'Hanlon challenged you to single combat. On that occasion you submitted to personal degradation to save your life."

"My Lord, I am in your power," said Ludlow, whose distorted features showed the agony he was enduring whilst thus addressed by the son of the Lord Lieutenant. "I am, I say, in your lordship's power. I own that I have been apprehended by you in the commission of a crime, that there are sufficient proofs to convict me of an attempt at burglary. What does your lordship propose to do with me?"

"I have desired to speak with you alone, Sir," said Lord Arran; "and you may perceive by the preparations that were made to receive you, that I have not arranged for such an interview without having certain terms to offer you."

"Name them, my Lord. They must be very hard, indeed, if I do not prefer them to the fate which otherwise awaits me—the death of a common malefactor on the gibbet."

"I know much of your past career, Sir, in connexion with the Fitzpatrick family."

Ludlow's face became suffused with purple when Lord Arran mentioned the name of Fitzpatrick.

"I believe," continued Lord Arran, "from what I have heard, that the offence which you tried to commit this night, cruel, base, cowardly, and unmanly as it is, was but trivial when compared with those you have tried to commit, as well as those you actually have committed, in the attempt to gain possession of the Fitzpatrick property. Some of the wrongs done by you are irreparable; others are not so. One of the first conditions, then, which I have to impose upon you is, that you will restore to the Fitzpatricks such portions of their estates as you unrighteously retain."

" Restore the property!" cried Ludlow, horror-stricken at this proposition. " Restore the property! to whom? Who is to claim it?"

" The Fitzpatricks: to Colonel Fitzpatrick, or to his son Vincent, or to Kathleen Fitzpatrick. Do you agree to this condition, Sir? It is easily arranged to whom the restoration shall be made. Do you agree to this?"

" I do, I do, because I must," replied Ludlow.

" And this restitution you promise to make within a month?"

" I do, I do, because I must," again answered Ludlow.

" The second condition is, that within two months you leave Ireland; and within six months his Majesty's dominions, with the promise during your life never to return. Do you agree to this condition also?"

" I do, I do, because I must," replied Ludlow.

" Very well, on these conditions your companions and yourself shall be at once set at liberty."

" Thanks! thanks! my Lord, I take my leave of you. You are a truly generous conqueror," said Ludlow, his looks of hatred contradicting the flattering words he expressed.

" Stop, stop, Mr. Edward Ludlow; not so fast. I know whom I have to deal with. I cannot take your spoken word, Sir, for anything. If I were to let you off so easily to-night, you would laugh at me to-morrow morning, and deny all the transactions of this night, and perhaps threaten me with an action for slander, if I repeated them. Your spoken word, Sir, is that of a disgraced poltroon, and no man could place the slightest reliance on it. Here, Sir, is something more tangible, more substantial, and more lasting. It is a declaration to this effect: 'I, Edward Ludlow, of Monkstown, Esquire, late a captain in the army of the Commonwealth, having been detected in an attempt to commit a base, cruel, cowardly, and unmanly offence, and having obtained pardon, conditionally, for that offence, do hereby promise to fulfil the conditions imposed upon me, which are as follows.' The conditions, as I have stated them, are then set forth in this paper. Here, read them, read them attentively, and then say if you are prepared to sign the document I now place in your hands."

Ludlow took the paper with a trembling hand, and his eyes became first glazed, and then were filled with tears, as he tried to read its contents.

"I have read the paper," said the crest-fallen villain, "and am prepared to sign it."

"Here, Major Harvey, come into this room; I wish you to be a witness to this person's signature."

Harvey came into the room. Lord Arran placed pen and ink in the hands of Ludlow, who at once signed the paper.

"One word more, and then I have done with you for ever. Is this your proper name and signature?"

"Yes."

"Are the contents of this document true?"

"Yes."

"You have heard these acknowledgments made, Major Harvey, by Mr. Edward Ludlow; now sign that paper."

Major Harvey signed with a dashing hand and a flourish

that was as complicated as a grand military manœuvre—a contrast in itself to the small, creeping, feeble signature of Ludlow, by the side of which it stood.

"And now, Major Harvey, be so good as to conduct that man and his associates outside the gate of Lady Diana's park; and when outside, let his followers be unbound, and permitted to proceed without further molestation."

"Do not you think, my Lord," asked Harvey, "that they ought to be one and all horsewhipped out of the gate?"

"No, no: let them go as they came. Let their own shame be their punishment. If they cannot feel that, then a horsewhip would be dishonoured by being placed on the shoulders of the best of them."

Lord Arran's orders were literally obeyed, and upon Major Harvey returning to the room, the paper signed by Ludlow was placed in his hands.

"I am an old soldier," said Harvey, when he had read the document through, "but until this moment I never thought there was to be found in the whole race of mankind so much baseness and cowardice as that scoundrel, Ludlow, has concentrated in his own person. A gibbet is too good for him. Why let him escape so easily, when the gallows was waiting for him?"

"Because," answered Lord Arran, "he could not be brought to the gallows but by a public trial, and at that trial there should of necessity be introduced not only the name of Kathleen Fitzpatrick, but also of Lady Diana, and their virtues should not be contaminated by a connexion, however remote, with such a miscreant."

"A very satisfactory reason for not hanging him," said Harvey, "and one with which, for Lady Diana's sake and my own, I am perfectly content."

CHAPTER XVII.

JUDGE DONNELLAN.

"ALL things are advancing in accordance with my wishes," said Gerald Geraghty, as he proceeded towards the apartment in which Judith was confined, with no other companion than the ever-discontented Abigail Gregg. "Ludlow and Lawson are now inseparable companions, and can, therefore, be both entrapped by the same lure. Fitzgerald, who cannot stir a step without some spy dogging at his heels, must, with his associate Murfey, be got rid of and sent to England. And now to take from this unhappy girl the only person in the world who might have power to tell what had become of her."

"Good! dear! sweet! handsome Widow Gregg!" said Geraghty, as he knocked at the outer door of Judith's room, "I wish to have the happiness of looking at your fair countenance, and of whispering a word in your virtuous, matronly ear."

"Eh! is that you, you old villain?" said Mrs. Gregg. "What new piece of scoundrelism is now afoot?"

"Gently, gently, most loquacious of antiquated widows," said Geraghty; "take care of using such words as 'scoundrelism' in connexion with any act of one of his Majesty's justices of the peace. Take care! take care of your precious life, widow, and that he who is the awful dread of all malefactors, Mr. Justice Donnellan, is not told that you have been calling him 'a scoundrel!'"

"I!" said Mrs. Gregg, in amazement—"I call Judge Donnellan a 'scoundrel!' Why, you old villain, what has caused such a notion of wickedness to come into your diabolical brain?"

"What has made me think of such a piece of wickedness?" replied Geraghty, in an assumed tone of astonishment—" why you, you woman you ; for was it not a woman that put into a man's head the first notion of any wickedness that ever was committed in this innocent world? Why here—here am I, not thinking of any harm at all—a poor man, meekly performing his duties ; and here I come with an order from good Judge Donnellan, commanding me on my allegiance to the King and my attachment to the Church, as by law established, on the receipt of this warrant—there, look at it, Mrs. Gregg, it is duly signed and sealed—to produce before him the body (and an ugly body it is) of Abigail Gregg, widow, to answer such charges as may be made against her by one Edmond Morfey, a divinity student ; and yet the moment I am seen with this commission in my hand, from the model of magistrates and the purest of judges, Mr. Justice Donnellan, you, Mrs. Gregg, —yes, you did, ma'am, and I'll swear it—you, alluding to my business, and to that self-same judge, asked me ' what new piece of scoundrelism is now afoot?' These were your very words, and I'll take my affidavit you used them. But come, hasten, hasten, widow ; put on your hood, until I have the high honour and the immeasurable satisfaction of producing your body—I hope he won't be frightened—before Judge Donnellan."

Poor Mrs. Gregg was so horrified by the intelligence thus conveyed in his usual bantering and triumphant manner by Geraghty, that she was unable to reply to him.

"Oh, dear! oh, dear!" she exclaimed, rushing back to the room, to Judith, "here is another of the vile acts of that demon, Geraghty. He has brought an order for me to appear before Judge Donnellan. I see what he intends by this: it is to take me away from you, and to have me placed in some prison, where I could neither give you any assistance, nor convey information to your friends of the place of your confinement. He can do me no harm; and for myself, I defy his malice; but it is not so with you. God help and protect you, young lady! I am forced to leave you."

"Farewell! farewell!" replied Judith. "If I am ever freed from this captivity, you shall find in me no ungrateful friend; meanwhile, take with you this poor memorial of my regard."

As Judith thus spoke, she placed a glittering diamond ring upon one of Mrs. Gregg's fingers. Neither the words nor the gift of Judith had escaped the watchful observation of Gerald Geraghty.

Never in all her long life was the widow Gregg so much astonished as when she appeared in front of the prison, leaning on the arm of Geraghty, who held her hand as tightly as if it was in a vice; and when she saw not only a coach waiting for her, but fifty mounted cavalry encircling it, and that there was a loud shout, as if in triumph, from the rabble at seeing her a prisoner, and observing her placed in the coach, and all the guards with drawn swords before and behind and by the side of the vehicle in which she was enclosed.

"What is the meaning of all this?" cried the widow Gregg to Geraghty, who sat opposite to her; "or who in the world do they take me for?"

"They take you for Abigail Gregg," answered Geraghty; "and as to the meaning of it, you will soon learn all that from Judge Donnellan, who is the cutest man that ever yet was seen at unravelling a plot."

"A plot! a plot! cried Mrs. Gregg, still more mystified, —"what have I to do with plots? I am an English

Protestant, and, therefore, hate, detest, and abominate all Papists—yourself in particular—and all their hellish plots and damnable contrivances for destroying our King, and uprooting our glorious Constitution in Church and State."

"Augh, bother, widow, don't be going on with that sort of *raumash* before Judge Donnellan, or he'll stop your examination, and put you in the ducking stool, until you come to your senses. Sure! any one—I myself, that you call a Papist, can say the same words that you do. That's the way all the plotters go on till they are found out. Lord Danby, a born Protestant, tried the same game in England, but the patriotic Lord Shaftesbury was too clever for him, and hit him, notwithstanding all his sham zeal for Protestantism, with a Bill of Attainder; and so it will be with Judge Donnellan and you, if you try to bamboozle him with prating about your being an Englishwoman and a Protestant, and all that sort of stuff. Just take a friend's advice, widow : listen patiently to what is said against you, and answer it if you can, and for my part I don't think you'll be able to do so. But here we are at Judge Donnellan's. Please to get out, Mrs. Gregg, and do it willingly, and at once, or you'll be dragged before his worship like a horse's head to a bonfire."

A loud shout from the rabble in the street announced the re-appearance of the widow Gregg from the coach. The moment her foot touched the earth, she found twelve soldiers with matchlocks about her; and thus, with Geraghty holding her firmly by the arm, she was ushered into a crowded court, and the presence of the formidable Judge Donnellan.

Judge Donnellan was a very old, a very bloated, and a very red-faced man. For forty long years he had given all his zeal and his abilities to the service of the oppressors of

Ireland; and had laboured with an untiring energy to aid in the affliction and persecution of his own countrymen. Selfish, cold-blooded and remorseless, he had spared neither age nor sex, rank nor condition, but had dipped deep his ermine in the blood of the innocent. He had laboured so hard for promotion, as to render it impossible for any parties he had served to gratify his ambitious desires; for he had made himself far too odious and too detestible, for those who wished to preserve the peace of the country to elevate him to one of the highest positions on the bench. He was made use of, he was trusted by the anti-Irish interest, but he was not promoted; and instead of being, as he had hoped, when age had come upon him, a Chief Justice of the King's Bench, he found himself taken from the judge's seat to act as a magistrate.

Judge Donnellan, therefore, regarded himself as an ill-used man; as one whose sacrifices to advance what he called " the *English* Interest " had not been appreciated by his *masters ;* but still he consoled himself with the opportunities afforded to him, by his office, to tyranize over his countrymen, and he endeavoured to conceal the venom that festered in his heart against his fellow-creatures by an indulgence in bad puns and worse jokes; so that he was at the same time, when on the bench, a buffoon and a hangman.

It was before this magistrate, one of the worst instruments in the hands of the Cromwellian tyrants, during their reign in Ireland, that Mrs. Gregg was now brought to undergo an examination.

"Put the prisoner to the bar, in order that the court may have her recognised," said Judge Donnellan.

" Remove your hood, woman; if you are handsome it will be a pleasure to see you; if you are ugly your face will help to condemn you,—and so it does! There is a plot in your eye, and a conspiracy in your nose; what is your name?" continued the judge.

"Abigail Gregg," replied the widow, indignant at the observations that had been passed on her personal appearance.

"Abigail; it should be Jezabel. And then Gregg, a very Popish name; we shall soon hear the Greg-orian chaunt from you, I warrant," observed the judge.

"Please your worship," said the prisoner, "I am an Englishwoman and a Protestant"

"Then the more shame for you to be conspiring against your country and your religion, if you speak the truth. But I don't believe one word of it; because you have the most unmistakable brogue I ever heard in my life."

"I!!! a brogue! I who speak with a pure English accent."

"Yes," answered the judge, "a brogue so thick it would blunt a strong knife to cut through it. Your's an English accent! I have been in London once in my life, and I ought to know how the English speak their own language. Why, if you were a genuine Englishwoman, instead of saying, 'I am an Englishwoman,' you would have said, 'Hi ham han Henglishwoman.' Go to! ugly impostor as you are, if justice is said to be blind, no one ever described it as deaf. But I won't hear another word from you. Call the witnesses. Here you, Mr. Murfey—you are one of the principal props of the state to preserve us all from Popery and slavery—what have you to say about the Jezabel Gregg? Say the worst you can; and I will think you are understating the case against her. A woman so confoundedly unsightly must be an undoubted Popish conspirator. Go on, sir; you know the Testament so well it would be a waste of piety to swear you."

Gerald Geraghty stood by the side of Murfey, who was

much intoxicated, and slipping five golden coin into his hand, he said: "You shall have twenty more when you see her lodged in Newgate; observe, she has a diamond ring on the little finger of her left hand. There is *a fact* for you, make use of it."

"*Thigum*," said Murfey, as he winked at Geraghty, and pocketed the gold.

"Please your Worship, and all good loyal Protestants who hear me," said Murfey, clearing his throat for an oration, "that woman at the bar is the most awful, wicked, dangerous, and detestable Papist that ever stepped in shoe-leather."

"I knew she had a Papist *soul*," said the judge, "when I looked in her face; but according to your account of her, she has two Papist *soles*."

"Please your Worship, and all good loyal Protestants," resumed Mr. Murfey, "you all know that I aided in the arrest of the Popish Primate."

"And a *prime* thing it was for you to be *at* such a good piece of work," added the Judge.

"Well, your Worship, from that day to this, the prisoner at the bar never stopped abusing, and vilifying, and annoying, and aggravating me."

"Oh! dear, dear!" said Mrs. Gregg: as I am an honest woman, I never saw nor spoke with the man in my life."

"Don't mind her, your Worship," said the unabashed Murfey; "she would swear a hole through a ladder."

"Yes, and not leave a Protestant a *step* to stand upon; and then she says she is an honest woman; she is no more an honest woman than I am Chief Justice Scraggs. But go on, Mr. Murfey. I cannot allow the dignity of the court to be trifled with by this arch-Papist at the bar."

"Please your Worship, and all good loyal Protestants,"

continued Murfey, " I did not mind the abuse of a Papist for doing my duty to king and country; but what has caused me to bring this woman here is, that she said his most Gracious Majesty was in his heart a Papist, that his Excellency the Lord Lieutenant, his Grace the Duke of Ormonde, was a sworn Papist, and what is more and worse than all, that even you, your Worship, Judge Donnellan was a Papist."

"Me! me! Did she accuse me of being a Papist?" asked the Judge, fuming with rage.

"She did, your Worship, and that you had been born a Papist, bred a Papist, and that you only *turned* in the hope of serving your own interests."

"Oh! monstrous! monstrous! most monstrous!" exclaimed the Judge puffing and blowing, and almost breathless with passion, for in these statements, there was, he well knew, a repetition of accusations that had been made against him thirty years previously.

"And I must say," added Geraghty, here stepping forward, "that when I shewed her your Worship's warrant for bringing her here, she asked me, ' What new piece of scoundrelism was now afoot?'"

"I'll *foot* her off to prison," said the Judge. "Hallo! you Jezabel Gregg. What! do you deny that you so spoke this very day to Mr. Geraghty?"

"I said the very words he has repeated; but I did not commit myself by——"

"I'll *commit* you, never fear. Don't dare to say another word to me, you audacious, scarlet-souled feminine fright."

"But will not your Worship hear one word in explanation?" asked Mrs. Gregg.

"Not a syllable," replied the judge. "*Scoundrelism*— a nice word to apply to a Judge in the execution of his office. Expl*a*nation, indeed! But we shall have more than one nation with you by-and-bye, Jezabel Gregg, for as well as your expla-*nation*, there shall be my condem-*nation*. But go on, Mr. Murfey; the country owes you a deep debt of gratitude."

"Ah! your Worship, and all loyal Protestants that hear me," added Murfey, "if you were but to know the tempting offers this woman made me."

"Stop, stop," Mr. Murfey," said Judge Donnellan, "I do not think it is in the power of the prisoner to be tempting in any way. Her face is like a physic-bottle, and the look of her enough to turn a man's stomach."

"Ah, but your Worship! she made me such offers if I would only aid in the escape of a French prisoner, now confined in Brass Castle."

"Oh! villain! villain! you are at last caught in a glaring falsehood," cried Mrs. Gregg, triumphantly. "There is no French prisoner in Brass Castle."

"Eh! eh! what's this, Mr. Murfey? No French prisoner in Brass Castle! What say you, Mr. Geraghty, you have charge of Brass Castle? Is there a French prisoner there?"

"There is, your Worship," said Geraghty, "a French Prisoner—a young woman arrested in the vaults of the Popish Primate's palace in Drogheda, a Mademoiselle Josephine de Lauzun. The prisoner has been in constant attendance upon her."

"Oh! dear, dear, dear me!" cried Mrs. Gregg; "why the young lady that he calls a French prisoner is an English woman and a Protestant."

"As much an Englishwoman and a Protestant as you are yourself, I suppose," said the Judge.

"Exactly so," said Mrs. Gregg.

"Exactly so!" retorted the Judge. "It is as I guessed. Go on, Mr. Murfey, every word this woman says confirms the truth of your statements."

"Please your Worship," continued Murfey, "it was by my assistance this Frenchwoman, now in Brass Castle, was first arrested; and the prisoner at the bar was always urging me to aid in her escape; and it was no later than yesterday she took a diamond ring off the little finger of her left hand, and wanted me to accept it as a pledge I would support the hellish Popish plot."

"Is that diamond ring forthcoming?" asked the Judge, as his eyes sparkled with an unwonted light when the ring was mentioned.

"Here it is," said Geraghty, "still on the little finger of the left hand of the prisoner."

"Hand it up, in order that it may be inspected by the court," observed the Judge. "Upon my word, a very large and a very pure brilliant—and worth, at least, fifty pounds. This is too important a piece of evidence to be parted with by the Court. When the prisoner is brought to trial before a jury, she will have to show how a person in her condition of life became possessed of an ornament of such great value."

"And when she is brought to trial," added Murfey, "I shall be able to swear that the very ring that Abigail Gregg offered to me to aid in releasing the French prisoner, I saw at one time worn by Pere La Chaise, the confesser to the Popish King of France."

"Phew! this ring will then help to *wring* the neck off Jezabel Gregg," added the Judge. "But it is a waste of time to hear any more of this case. Here, clerk, make out a committal of this woman to Newgate, as an aider and abettor of the hellish Popish plot—and with strict orders she is to have communication with no one but in the presence of the jailer. Whilst you are writing out the committal, I may as well listen to what she has to say. Do you hear, woman, now is your time to speak. What have you to say for yourself?"

"What have I to say for myself?" said Mrs. Gregg; "well I say first I am an honest woman."

"Well, and it is my opinion," answered the Judge, "that honesty and you might be married, for you are not the least akin."

"Next, I say, I am a Protestant."

"Yes, but it is against the Church by law established you are a Protestant."

"Next, I say, I am an Englishwoman."

"Aye, an Englishwoman that was born and reared in the bog of Allen, and is as indigenous to the soil as the *prasha bruie.*"

"Next, I say, that the lady I was attending on is, *like myself*, an Englishwoman and a Protestant."

"That is the only thing you have said I believe."

"Next, I say, that I never saw nor spoke with, and never offered a diamond ring to the villain, Murfey."

"'That is a Popish equivocation, and all turns on the word '*villain ;*' you might not have done any one of these things with '*a villain*' called Murfey, and yet have said and done everything that is alleged against you with '*an honest man,*' called Murfey. It is a shame for an old Papist like you to be trying to impose on the Court with mental insinuations and equivocations, and such stale Jesuitical tricks."

"The next thing I have to say is," said Mrs. Gregg, raising her voice and losing all command of her temper, "that I do most firmly believe that there has long been hatching a Popish plot for the extermination of all true, pious, good, and loyal Protestants. I believe that Popish plot is fostered and encouraged by persons calling themselves Protestants, but who in their hearts are Papists, and they subservient slaves of the Pope. I believe that some of these false Protestants, but sworn Papists, hold high and influential offices; that some of them are judges; and from your conduct to me this day, I believe in my heart, you, Mr. Donnellan, are one of them."

"Oh! you traitress!" cried the Judge, giving way to his fury, "is not this another proof of the truth of honest Mr. Murfey's allegations against you? He averred that you had so spoken of me; you denied it; and yet now, the very thing you denied you not only admit, but voluntarily declare. Oh! these Papists! these Papists! when will this poor country be well rid of them! But I will teach one of you, at all events, a *New-gait* of going. Here, commit her at once to prison, Geraghty and Murfey: there is the warrant for you. See her safely lodged in Newgate.

CHAPTER XVIII.

TERRIFIC VISIONS.

"Is your friend and associate here, Mr. Fitzgerald?" said Gerald Geraghty, as he ascended to the upper rooms of an obscure dwelling close to St. Nicholas' gate. "He did me good service yesterday before Judge Donnellan, in ridding me of a troublesome old woman, and I have called to pay him the twenty *Louis d'or* I promised. There is nothing like paying what you owe, Mr. Fitzgerald, especially if it has been honestly earned."

"Murfey is at home, in his apartment, but I am greatly afraid not in a condition either to recognise you or to receive the money you have brought with you."

"What can be the matter with him? Not ill, I hope. Yesterday he appeared in excellent health and spirits."

"And he was so," replied Fitzgerald, "but, unfortunately, he went, from curiosity, through the various cells of Newgate, and in one of them he unexpectedly encountered his old Archbishop, Doctor Plunkett. What passed between them I know not, but on his return, Murfey appeared like a man distracted; commenced drinking usquebaugh, and never ceased so long as he was able to move his hand to his head. He fell asleep drunk, snored in such an awful manner as to frighten every one in the place, and to be heard even in the next house. He awoke this morning to demand more usquebaugh. Some has been given him, but I greatly fear, from the way he is going on, that he is insane. I was on the point of going out for the purpose of bringing to him a person he is very anxious to see, a Mr. John Smith, a doctor, I believe."

"I should like to speak with him," said Geraghty. "It is very probable this is nothing more than the passing result of an extraordinary drinking bout."

"Come this way," said Fitzgerald, as he conducted Geraghty to Murfey's bed-room.

Upon a wretched bed, on which he had flung himself in his clothes, Murfey was now seen lying, shivering from head to foot, as if he were in an ague fit; his hands and legs trembling, and his eyes wildly staring constantly about him, as if he was endeavouring to discover either where he was, or as if under the apprehension of being attacked by some enemy.

"Good morning, Mr. Murfey," said Geraghty, as he

approached the bed, and looked down upon the unhappy man. "I am sorry to find you are not well this morning."

"Well, well, well, very well, I thank you, Mr. Geraghty," replied Murfey, speaking in a rapid manner, as if it were a relief to him to utter, in one breath, all the words he wanted to say.

"I promised yesterday to give you twenty pounds in gold," said Geraghty.

"Yes, yes. Have you got them? Where are they? Give 'em to me at once—this minute—instantly; d'ye hear?"

"Here they are," said Geraghty, "twenty shining jolly yellow *Louis d'or*, as fine a coin as ever came from the King's mint."

"Thank you! thank you," answered Murfey, stretching out his hand, but instead of lifting the coin, which Geraghty presented him, his fingers, as if it were in despite of him and beyond his control, clutched at the bottle of usquebaugh! he relaxed his gripe of the bottle, again tried to lay hold of the gold, and again his fingers clutched at the bottle!

"Strange! strange! my own hand won't do what I want it. Even it is turning against me. But hang it—I *ill* force it to obey my wishes. Give me another chance at the gold, Geraghty."

"Here," said Geraghty; "I wish you to take it. I brought it to you."

"Thank you! thank you heartily. There, Fitzgerald, take the bottle out of my way, lest my fingers play me another trick. Let there be nothing between me and the money. Now, now, now, I will die or have the money. Ah! ha! I have it! I have it! You see I did force my hand to take it. At last—at last—yes, at last I have it—money—gold,

I love usquebaugh much; but I want gold more. Oh! I do want it so very badly at this present time."

"And why want it so very much at present?" asked Geraghty.

"I'll tell you, I'll tell you. No, no, I'll whisper it to you. Go away, go away, Fitzgerald. I don't want you to hear what I am saying. Is Fitzgerald gone?"

"Yes," answered Geraghty, "he is gone out of the room; and, I believe, out of the house. Now you can speak aloud."

"No, no, no, he might hear me outside the door. It's a secret; such a secret! Listen! Are you listening to me?"

"To be sure I am," said Geraghty. "Whatever be the secret, you may depend upon it I will never mention it again."

"Now, mind, you have promised to keep what I am going to say to you, as a secret."

"Yes."

"As a dead secret."

"Yes."

"As a state secret—a secret of the greatest importance."

"Yes, yes."

"Well, then, I'll whisper it to you—listen."

"Go on."

"Are you listening?"

"I am."

"Well, then, the secret—the great secret is this—mind, you are not to mention it again, without my leave."

"You may be sure of that."

"Well, then, the great secret I have to tell you is this. David Fitzgerald—you know David Fitzgerald, of Drumsna, in the County Limerick, Esq.?"

"I do."

"Well, then, the great secret I have to tell you about him is, that that same David Fitzgerald is a great rascal."

"Indeed!"

"Yes, and I am another great rascal."

"Is it possible?"

"It's a fact—a fact—a downright fact; but I have not yet told you all. You are Gerald Geraghty?"

"Yes."

"Well, you are the greatest rascal of us all."

"I am, I suppose, to keep that a secret also?"

"Of course, of course, of course you are. It would not do to go publishing it to the world. The world, you may be certain, will find it out soon enough. Meanwhile, what are you, and I, and poor David, and all the other witnesses to do?"

"The best thing for you to do, Mr. Murfey, is to keep quiet."

"Keep quiet! keep quiet! how am I to keep quiet? Look at me; my hands are always going as if I was playing the spinet; my feet are always going, as if I was dancing a hornpipe; my eyes are always going, as if they wanted to see everything at once; my tongue is always going, as if it never would stop; my head is always going—turning, turning, in despite of me, as if one was whistling a reel inside my skull; and my heart is always going beat, beat, beating inside me, as if it was determined to break through one of my ribs. Quiet! quiet! quiet! How is a man ever to keep quiet who can never sleep? How do people go to sleep, Mr. Geraghty? If you know the secret tell it, and I'll give you back, though I am sadly in want of them, the twenty *Louis d'or* you have just handed me."

"The reason you cannot go to sleep, and the reason why you cannot keep quiet, Mr. Murfey, is this, and nothing else: you have got wrong notions into your head."

"Wrong notions! wrong notions! What notions of mine are wrong? Answer me that, and say it quickly, for I am in a hurry! Oh! such a hurry."

"Humph! I'll ask you by-and-bye, *why* you are in such a hurry, my fine fellow," said Geraghty, considering he had to deal with a half lunatic, and from whom it would be easy to worm any secrets he had to tell. "You ask me what wrong notions you have. Why your own bad opinion of yourself?"

"I deserve it."

"Then your bad opinion of Fitzgerald?"

"He deserves it."

"Then your bad opinion of me?"

"You deserve it."

"I deserve it! why do you say so?"

"Why do I say so? Eh! Why do I say so? Why do I think badly of you? Why, simply and solely because you are the most remorseless old villain I ever met, saw, heard, read, or thought of. Hercules, who slew a Nemæan lion, a Lernæan hydra, an Erymanthian boar, a Cretan bull, Arcadian vultures, and such monsters and robbers as Geryon and Cacus, yet never rid the world of a greater pest, plague, abomination, and monster, than yourself, Gerald Geraghty."

"Oh! Mr. Murfey, this is all vague abuse, without a single fact to justify it. Why do you think so badly of me? What have I done?"

"What have you done? Eh! eh! Is that the question you are putting to me? Ah! but it's I that will give you an answer, and that answer will be comprised in one name, and two words—Judith Lawson."

"Judith Lawson!" exclaimed old Geraghty, and though he fancied he was talking to a downright madman, still, that name coming so unexpectedly to his ears, from the lips of the raving wretch before him, made drops of cold perspiration burst from his withered brow; and his limbs, for a moment, trembled like those of Murfey.

"Ah! ha! I knew I could give you an answer. But see me now!—see me now!—just mind me, Gerald Geraghty, and what I am going to say to you—it's as true as the Gospel. You know very well my early history; you know I was a divinity student; you know I intended to enter into holy orders; you know that I broke my vows, and you know the life I have been leading ever since. Well, Geraghty, that much you know; but there's something I'm going to tell you that you don't yet know, and that is, that the man who acts as I have done cannot do so with impunity; that the devil gets a hold of him— and once the Old Boy has a grip of a man like me, it isn't a single sprinkle of holy water, nor ten *Paters* and *Aves* that can get rid of that chap. No, no, no, he is a cleverer fellow than you or I after all. Now, the devil has got his paw upon me. Do you doubt it? Look at me; there *he* is quivering in every limb, shaking in every joint, jumping in the pupils of my eyes, capering on the tops of my fingers, playing *cutchy cutchoo* with my legs. He has made *an object* of me; but it is an old saying, 'we should give the devil his due,' and therefore I'll tell you a truth about him. If he has taken from me a power over my own body, he has made me some compensation—he has sharpened my senses, and he has given me faculties I never before possessed; and, therefore, I see what you can't see, and I know what you don't know; and, therefore, I say, Gerald Geraghty, don't do what you are thinking of doing, with Judith Lawson, or before another week is out you'll be dead and damned."

"Then you can tell," said Geraghty, with a sneer, "my intentions with respect to Judith Lawson."

"Tell your intentions! to be sure I can; would I be bothered speaking with you at all, and I in such a hurry, if I could not tell them?"

"Well, what are they?"

"You intend to kill her."

Geraghty winced for a moment under this reply, but considering he was only conversing with a lunatic, he endeavoured to hide his emotion under a forced laugh, as he said—"Oh! fie! Mr. Murfey, what could put such a horrid notion into your head? Why should on old man like me think of killing a nice young lady like that?"

"Ah! ha! The devil, I tell you, is cleverer than the two of us put together. He only lets one know a bit of the truth, not all the truth. If I knew your reasons for wanting to massacre Judith Lawson, I might be able to show you why you ought to forego so base and cruel a design. I only know what you intend to do, not the reason, nor the cause for your intention. But now I tell you, don't do it; for, as sure as you and I are talking together, if you do make the attempt, she will slaughter you; yes, you will die by the hand of Judith Lawson. Even whilst I am speaking to you, I see, as plainly as I see yourself, a little devil, not as high as my knee, standing by your side, and he has a coffin on his back, and he is grinning at me, and pointing his finger in derision at you, as much as to say, ' There is no use in talking to him, for I shall soon have him packed up in this; you see it is intended for him.' And as the weary limb of Satan in indicating so much to me, he turns his back that I may see *whose name* is on the coffin: as I am a living creature with eyes in my head, it is *your name* is on the coffin-lid. There it is as plain as I could read my A.B.C. 'Gerald Geraghty, aged 72 years, three months, and —— days.' There is a *blank* for the number of days, as if, whether you did well or ill, you should not outlive the month; the actual number of days depending upon the exercise of your own will for good or for evil."

"Accident has helped you to the exact knowledge of my age," said Geraghty, "but allow me——"

"Don't let the devil cheat you out of your soul, by fancying accident has anything to do with any, even the simplest thing that occurs in this life. If I can, he shan't cheat me, and that's the reason I am in such a hurry. Accident, indeed! Is it an accident that enables me to see what's going to happen to you, and how you will come by your death? Why, whilst I'm speaking to you, I see your white beard becoming red with blood—aye, and it is your own blood, too! If you are a wise man, you will let Judith Lawson alone, and send her home to to her father. She never did you any harm *yet*. Drive her to desperation, and she will be the death of you. Mind what I say, and I repeat it, before the week is out you'll be dead and damned."

"I'm much obliged to you for the warning," answered Geraghty, upon whom Murfey's words made not the slightest impression; "but now let us say one word about yourself. Why are you in such a hurry? Where do you want to go to?"

"Why am I in such a hurry? Where do I want to go to? I don't know where I want to go to. I only know I want to go somewhere out of this. Oh! I am in such a hurry—such a hurry."

"Wherefore?"

"I am in such a hurry—such a hurry—such a hurry to get away from—you."

"From me."

"Yes, yes, yes, from you. I am *such* a tool in your hands. I was with that other rascal, as great a rascal as myself, but not as great a rascal as you: I was with Fitzgerald when Judith Lawson was seized upon; that was bad enough, and I added to the poor girl's sufferings by my own bad language. I was your tool then, but what is worse, I was your tool yesterday. I did not know that Abigail Gregg was the only attendant on poor Miss Lawson in Brass Castle; and you told me you only wanted to frighten the old woman, and to keep her from annoying you, by sending her to Newgate; but instead of that (the devil, you see, has told me some of your secrets), your real purpose was to take from the young woman her only protection, so that you might carry out your plan for killing her, without any let or hindrance; but, again, I warn you, let Judith Lawson alone, or she will be the death of you. But why say the same things over again, and I not having a minute to lose, for I am in a hurry—such a hurry? I want to be out of your hands. I want to be away from you, and Fitzgerald, and Hetherington, and Mayer, and, and—and all the other witnesses to the Plot."

"But why, Mr. Murfey, wish to get away from such company? You always appeared to me to be the merriest man amongst them."

"Ah, Lord help me! merry! merry! yes I was, but all is not gold that glitters, Geraghty; and the heart is often ill at ease when there are smiles on the lips and laughter on the teeth. But what says the Scripture? '*Sand, and salt, and a mass of iron, is easier to bear, than a man without sense, that is both foolish and wicked.*'

And I have been without sense, and foolish, and wicked, and, therefore, intolerable in the sight of earth and heaven, and my punishment has come upon me. Do you doubt it? Look at me now; but I'm in a hurry—such a hurry to get away from it. Oh!" cried Murfey, sitting up in his bed, and extending his outstretched hands as wide apart as he could, and then vehemently clapping them together, "Oh, the sight, the sight, that I saw yesterday! Listen to me, you poor, weak, miserable, wicked old man—listen to me, may be it's for your good I am telling it. I was in Newgate yesterday; I was through its cells, its dark, filthy, foul, miserable cells—this sordid chamber is a palace compared to the best of them—and there I saw my Archbishop, and when I opened his cell he was on his knees, and he was kneeling before, before—but it's not right for my lips to mention IT; and I saw—yes, I saw as plainly as I see your withered face at this moment—I saw from IT shining rays of light, and they all fell upon the head and neck of the Archbishop, so that his face, and hair, and head seemed to be encrusted with diamonds, that is, all his head was one sparkling brilliancy, as if, whilst living, heaven had chosen to shed upon him a portion of its splendour, whilst his black cassock was changed into the colour of blood, and he so looked as a martyr who was rising to be glorified out of his sufferings in the cause of truth. And as I looked at him, I remembered I was one of the witnesses against him. There will be a muster of these same witnesses one day; it will not be before a human court, but all will be called upon to answer for what they said, and what they did, and what they swore; and I'll take right good care I shall not be one of them. I'm in a hurry, such a hurry to get away from them and from you. Yes, Geraghty, watch me as much as you like, still I'll baffle you all. I tell you I will not swear what I said I would. I'll get away from you—away—away—away from you! Oh, I'm in such a hurry to get away!"

And as Murfey so spoke he fell back again upon the bed, seemingly insensible, the quivering of his limbs being the only indication that he was alive and suffering.

"He is mad, raging mad, with drink," remarked Geraghty as he looked at the prostrate body before him. "Now I must take care, however, he does not carry his intention into effect. I will, at once, procure an order for his removal from Ireland. I must do the same for his friend, whose footsteps I hear ascending the stairs."

"Oh! I am glad to see," said Geraghty, as Fitzgerald, accompanied by two other persons, entered the room, "that you have brought physicians with you. I cannot stay longer, but I shall call or send this evening, to hear how our friend goes on. To me he appears to be, at present, stark, staring mad; utterly unable to speak one word of common sense."

The two persons who entered the room with Fitzgerald, as Geraghty departed, were John Elliott, and the old gentleman that Murfey called by the name of John Smith.

"Who is that old man?" asked Elliott.

"His name is Geraghty," replied Fitzgerald; "and from all the ravings of Murfey this morning, I conjecture that his main reason for wishing to speak with Mr. Smith——"

"There is no longer any necessity for concealing my real name," said the old gentleman. I am Colonel Fitzpatrick; the warrants issued for the arrest of my son and myself have been cancelled. I am not, however, known to this unhappy man here by my real title or name."

"It is my belief, that Murfey's principal desire in wishing to see you was first to talk to you about the best means of his avoiding to appear as a witness against Doctor Plunkett; and next to it, the thing he talked most of was a young lady named Judith Lawson, who was in the power of the old man who has just left the room."

"A young lady named Lawson, and an old man named Geraghty! oh! poor Murfey must indeed have been raving; I know nothing of any such two persons," observed Colonel Fitzpatrick.

"Lawson is a name that ought to be very well known to you," remarked John Elliott. "It is the name of one who was an instrument in the hands of Ludlow, when that person was seeking after your son, then a boy, to slay him."

"Oh! that Lawson I know very well," replied Colonel Fitzpatrick. "We both know him. He was the same fellow who was punished by Redmond O'Hanlon, when seeking to engage me in a tavern squabble; but what connexion is there between such a person and a young lady, and a man named Geraghty?"

"Do you know," asked Elliott of Fitzgerald, "what is the name of Lawson's daughter?"

"I do very well; it is Judith."

"Lawson—the Lawson who was, at one time, engaged in seeking to deprive your son of life—was my fellow-soldier. I therefore know him as well as my own brother, and I am aware he had a daughter, and her name is Judith," remarked Elliott.

"Be it so," observed Colonel Fitzpatrick; "but what connexion can there be between that Lawson and this old man, Geraghty?"

"Lawson, Lawson—Geraghty, Geraghty," repeated John Elliott, musing over past occurrences, once well known to him, but that had for years disappeared from his memory.

John Elliott walked about the room for some time in deep meditation, and then suddenly stopped. "Ah! I have it, I have it! I see it all now. Your foster-father, your son's foster-mother, and brothers, in seeking to escape from Ludlow, fled for refuge to the North. They were attacked in a cave, most of the persons there were massacred; and the principal family then destroyed by Lawson and Ludlow, were named Geraghty. One of the Geraghty family has, I suppose, got hold of the daughter of Lawson——"

"He is going to kill her, to kill her, to kill her. I know he is," cried Murfey, suddenly starting out of the stupor into which he had momentarily fallen. "I charged him with it whilst he was here; is he here still? No; but I told him he was going to kill her, and he did not deny it; and then I told him what I tell you, that as soon as he makes the attempt, she will slaughter him, for she is a brave, stout-hearted girl. Save her, oh! save her, Mr. Smith; John Elliott, most magnificent, most generous, most perfect of inn-keepers, save her, save her, save her, and——give me another bottle of usquebaugh."

"Here, here, my poor Mr. Murfey,' said Elliott, producing from one of his capacious pockets a bottle of usquebaugh. "You must swallow a hair of the hound that bit you. I know well what is the matter with you, and I hope, with judicious treatment, to see you yet perfectly cured."

Oh! such liquor! such liquor! there is music in its gurgle, there is beauty in its gleam, and there is a celestial soothing balm in its taste. He who drinks usquebaugh imbibes immortality! exclaimed the enraptured Murfey, forgetting in his animal enjoyment of the moment, all the terrific visions that had haunted his imagination.

"We must not take Murfey's words as literally true,"

observed Fitzgerald. "He only expresses what he fears; but this I know, that much artifice was employed by Geraghty to get Miss Lawson into his power. For what purpose he did so I cannot divine."

"I tell you, it was to murder her, and, for all I know, he left this room to carry that plan into effect, Sir," cried Murfey, again trembling in every limb, and his hair standing up with affright. "There he is, there he is, listening to you all outside the door."

John Elliott rushed to the door and threw it wide open, so that Murfey might see he was mistaken.

"Ah!" said Murfey, "that is one of his old tricks, rendering himself invisible, that is, his body invisible; but it is not so with his spirit. I can see what you don't see. I can see his dark spirit brooding over the contemplated murder. I can see him, in revenge for my telling on him, getting a band of thieves to murder me—they are coming, they are coming, I hear the heavy stamp of their iron-studded boots on the stairs; there it is, there it is, stamp! stamp! stamp! Oh! I must fly from them—hurry, hurry, hurry——"

And as Murfey so spoke, he started from his bed, threw open the window, and was on the point of flinging himself outside into the street, when he was caught by Elliott and Fitzgerald, and by main force dragged back to the bed, the clothes placed over him, and then tied down about him, so as to prevent him from doing himself or others any injury.

"I thought to escape, I was in such haste to do so, and now you have tied me down, so that old Geraghty can come in upon me at any time and cut my throat, and he'll do it, he'll do it, I tell you. Still, I will not hold my tongue. I say old Geraghty is going to murder Judith Lawson. Will none of you do your best to prevent him?"

"There may be truth in the ravings of this poor fellow," observed Colonel Fitzpatrick, "and we are bound as men, and as Christians, to protect the daughter of Lawson. Where is her father now to be found, Elliott? I think you told me he left the hotel unexpectedly this morning."

"And so he did," replied Elliott. "He and Ludlow were closeted for a long time together yesterday, and—now I remember one of the drawers telling me that a very curious looking old man was for some time in the same room with both. Can that visit have had anything to do with the dreadful surmises of Murfey?"

"In such a case, we must lose no time in vain surmises. Do you, Elliott, see if you can trace out to their present abode either Lawson or Ludlow. I will betake myself to the Castle, where, through Lord Arran, I hope to be able to get, backed with all the powers of the Government, the means of preserving Miss Lawson from any harm that may be concocted against her."

"No good—no good—no good," cried Murfey, from the bed. "Geraghty is determined on doing the devil's work, and the devil always takes care of his own."

"Poor man! poor man!" said Colonel Fitzpatrick, as he looked with compassion upon Murfey. "I must send my own physician to him. I never saw such a strange case of madness. I suppose his disease has some peculiar name?"

"It has, Colonel," replied John Elliott; "and I am very sorry to say it is one but too well known in this country. It is...*Delirium Tremens.*"

Elliott had stated, as a report to which he had not paid much attention at the time, that Lawson had been visited on the previous day by a strange-looking old man. Elliott then asked a question to which none of had been able to give an answer—namely, whether that visit had anything to do with the dreadful surmises of Murfey?

The inquiry may be in some measure an interesting one, Let us see if we can throw any light upon it.

CHAPTER XIX.

A LURE.

JOHN ELLIOTT's memory had served him well. He stated what was correct, when he mentioned that on the previous day there had been a long conversation between Ludlow and Lawson, and that an old man had called and had an interview with them.

Lawson was recovering but slowly from the wound inflicted upon him by Redmond O'Hanlon. The pain of the body was aggravated by severe affliction of mind; and the grief endured by him for the loss of his daughter had served to render a slight injury dangerous: its cure slow and protracted.

So entirely was Lawson's heart absorbed with the thoughts of Judith, that Ludlow perceived it would be useless to consult him upon any matter not connected with her. All then that had befallen Ludlow; the degrading punishment inflicted upon him by O'Hanlon; his subsequent capture, exposure, and the conditions on which he had been released from the house of Lady Diana, were utterly unknown to Lawson.

In connexion with the latter, there was, however, one matter—the restoration of the Fitzpatrick estates, a part of which were held by Lawson—on which it was necessary to speak with his confederate, and to determine what should be done—whether he acted in accordance with the condition into which he had entered, or should endeavour as he was disposed to do, to evade it.

With this view Ludlow called upon Lawson, who had not removed from John Elliott's inn, "The Cock," in Cook-street, from the night he had been wounded.

"I hope, said Ludlow, as he entered the room, "that I find my old friend better than when I last saw him."

"Yes yes," sighed Lawson, "better in health—much better. I feel no pain now, though I have not yet recovered the use of my hand; but as to my spirits—alas! my child!—Judith!—no tidings!—no tidings of her!—not even a trace of her!"

"Keep up your spirits, Lawson; you are sure to hear of her. All this pain is inflicted upon you for no other purpose than to enhance the price of her ransom. You will have her back; be sure of it, sound and safe, heart-whole as she was taken from you. But you will have to pay a swinging price for her."

"Oh! to have my dear, dear child once more in my arms, the same as when she left me. Let me but have that happiness, and I would assign to those who so restored her to me all of the Fitzpatrick lands I hold, as well as all I hope, by virtue of your bond, yet to possess."

"The Fitzpatrick estates!" said Ludlow; it was with respect to them I called upon you. I wished to have a consultation with you about them."

"It is in vain to consult me about anything of the sort, until I have news of Judith. Be you, Ludlow, the means of restoring her to me, and I will make you a present of your bond, and the lands to boot."

"But what if the bond be valueless—not worth the paper it is written on, and the lands are no longer your own; then your promised reward for the restoration of your daughter would amount to nothing?"

"What mean you? I cannot understand you. How come you to say that your own bond is worthless, and the lands I hold not my own to dispose of to whom I please?"

"I will not trouble you, Lawson, in your present enfeebled state, with a detail of the many misfortunes that have lately occurred to me. Sufficient is it for me to have to tell you the sad result: I was out-manœuvred by older, better, and more cunning campaigners than myself. The consequence has been I was driven into so false and so untenable a position, that I had to surrender at mercy. I had, in fact, to choose between the gallows and conditions which bound me to quit this country soon; and before doing so to abandon to one of the Fitzpatrick family all the portions of their estate, which at any time came into my possession. A portion of the restitution thus required to be made by me includes, of course, property many years ago assigned by me to you."

"And which of the Fitzpatricks is it that is to be thus endowed with the lands so long held by us?"

"Kathleen Fitzpatrick. The Colonel and his son, Vincent, have, for the purpose of avoiding any future disputes as to title, transferred all their rights to her."

"And she is," said Lawson, frowning at his companion, "to be married to you."

"Married to me!" cried Ludlow, as his limbs shook with passion. "Married to me! married to the ——. Oh! but I forget you are not aware of my disasters. No; she is to be married to Vincent Fitzpatrick."

"Vincent Fitzpatrick!—you do not—cannot possibly mean the son of the Colonel!"

"I do; and I am pressed by the lawyers of the Fitzpatricks to fulfil the conditions of the surrender, because it is deemed advisable that the transfer of the property to the lady should be made previous to the marriage; and Vincent and Kathleen are alike impatient for the ceremony to be over. We are," said Ludlow, with a bitter sneer, "in the way of the young couple, and by our delay an impediment to their happiness."

"And you come here, Captain Ludlow," said Lawson, rising from his chair, and stamping his foot indignantly, "you, of all men living! come here, knowing how much I have suffered—how much I did to put you in possession of that property—you come here to propose to me that I should rob my own daughter! Judith! of a portion of her dowry, to endow the wife of Vincent Fitzpatrick; that boy, whom I have hunted from childhood to this hour, in the hope I might cut him off from the inheritance, it seems he is now not only to enjoy, but towards the increase of which I am to be called on—by you, too—to contribute. Arrange your affairs as best you may, I will have nothing to do with them."

"My dear old friend," said Ludlow, "you are a little too hasty with me. I have told you enough of my affairs, to enable you to appreciate the difficulties of my position. One of the misfortunes consequent upon it, is the abandonment of that wealth I had so long regarded as my own. If I cannot retain it for myself, I would wish to transfer it to you, because there is the chance, at least, you would act generously towards me if I dispossessed myself of the property for your benefit; whereas, in resigning it to the Fitzpatricks, I yield to those who hate and detest me, and who are, of all other mortals, the most abominated and the most odious to myself. I wish to evade the conditions for your benefit—your certain benefit in the first instance. My desire is to consult with you as to the best means of carrying out such a project in such a manner—I mean by legal forms—as may baffle the efforts of the common enemy."

"Oh! I see now," replied Lawson, " what you mean; to transfer to me, in accordance with all the necessary forms, the absolute right over this property, but with a secret understanding between us that I, in accepting that transfer, shall be, in fact, nothing more than your trustee."

"Precisely so," replied Ludlow; "but with this understanding, also, that I will give you twenty per cent. on all sums received by you and paid over to me."

"It is a very fair," replied Lawson, "and, in my judgment, a very honourable proposition, and I can see no difficulty in——"

"What's this?" exclaimed Lawson, as a waiter entered the room, and placed a small parcel in his hand.

"An old man waits below; he desired me to give you this, and to say he wished to speak with you," replied the waiter.

"Good heavens! send the bearer of this up directly," said Lawson, in the same breath, the moment he opened the parcel, and recognized what it enclosed—the silk kerchief of his daughter, with the initials of her name embroidered in gold.

Lawson had sufficient command over his feelings not to allow the waiter to perceive how deeply he was agitated by the sight of this memorial of his lost child; but the moment he was alone with his associate, he burst into tears as he covered the kerchief with kisses, and exclaimed :—

"At last!—at last!—at last! Ludlow, there is hope of tidings of my beloved child. This tiny article of dress belonged to *her!* It was one of my own gifts to her. See where the darling has embroidered her own name upon it. Oh! I would not give this tiny, tiny kerchief of Judith for all the wealth we have been talking about. But I hear the heavy steps of an old man on the stair. He has been the bearer of this precious treasure. Now—now—oh! now for some certain tidings of the lost one. But, I must try and master my feelings. Aid me, Ludlow—aid me in my inquiries of this old man, for I know and feel I am not myself; I scarcely know what I am saying; and am incapable for the moment to account for what I am doing."

Gerald Geraghty entered the room!

The old man had evidently prepared himself with great care for this interview. His habiliments—he was clothed from head to foot in deep mourning—were those of a wealthy citizen, and he looked in presence of the two men before whom he now stood, as a rich usurer who is about to have dealings with two cavaliers of whose solvency he is not perfectly certain. He bowed, upon entering the room, proudly and stiffly, and then said—"My business is with a Mr. Ebenezer Lawson. I thought I should have found him alone."

"I am Ebenezer Lawson; this is my most particular friend, Mr. Edward Ludlow, from whom I have no secrets. Will you please to take a seat?" said Lawson, as he handed a chair to the old man.

"Ah! Sir," said Geraghty, "you are the father of the young lady? You know what it is to be deprived of the society of a beloved daughter—to know that some rude and ruffian hand has torn away from you one of the joys of your existence."

Lawson tried to speak, but there was a choking at the throat, as if the words he wished to utter were each a knotted substance, impeding the power of breathing and stopping the flow of blood. He gasped as if for air, then beat with his left hand his breast, and found at last relief by a copious gush of tears.

"Ah, poor dear gentleman!" said Geraghty, "he seems to have suffered greatly. Believe me, Sir," he added, turning to Ludlow, "I can appreciate what he has gone through, for I, too, lost a daughter."

"Lost a daughter!" said Lawson; "lost a daughter! Oh! yours has been, I suppose, a common loss. Had my darling been taken from me by the slow process of disease, or even by the violence of an unforeseen accident, I could have borne such a grief like a man. My heart would have bled, and my tears would have flowed, and I should have felt day by day the void made in all my future life by such a loss. But to suffer as I have suffered: that *has been*—that *is* the intolerable grief, not knowing whether she is living or dead, but knowing this thoroughly well, that she was taken from a home where she was mistress, to be placed I know not where, and treated I know not how. Oh! speak, good Sir, and by one word, at least, take from me a burden that is killing me—is Judith living?"

"She is."

"And well?"

"And well."

"Thank heaven!" said Lawson, again bursting into tears.

"Ah! Mr. Lawson," said Geraghty, "you may well indeed, say 'thank heaven,' for your child is, at least *still*, living; but such is not my case. You seem such a kind, good-hearted gentleman, I cannot refrain from telling you something of my sad misfortune; and I am the more disposed to do this, because there is some similarity, indeed it is very slight, between the grief you are now enduring, and that which has embittered my life for many a long year. So far as I understand your case, your daughter has been taken away by some villain; but as yet that villain permits her to enjoy health, and it can, with truth, be told of her, 'she is well.' Now, in my case, my daughter also was taken away by a villain, and the moment he laid hands on her, he slew her."

"Was there ever heard of such an atrocity!" exclaimed Lawson, whose thoughts were not of himself, but of his daughter. "To run away with a young woman, for the purpose of murdering her."

"A villain so treated a girl, and that girl my daughter, the same age, I think, of Miss Lawson, that is about five-and-twenty years of age," added Geraghty.

"Oh, Judith! Judith! Judith!" exclaimed Lawson, as his affrighted imagination pictured to him his daughter in the gripe of a murderer.

"You have described Miss Lawson as being about the same age as your daughter," observed Ludlow. "Then you have seen her since she was removed from her father's house?"

"To be sure I have, why else am I here? Or how could I have sent her kerchief to her father, and tell him she was in health? or how let him know that I possess her confidence, and that it is my hope, if my advice be taken, that I shall, before many hours, bring father and daughter both together?"

"Bring Judith and me together! Place the joy of my heart, the jewel of my life, the pride of my soul, once more within my arms. Do that, Sir, and on the instant I will, with thanks bestow on you two thousand pounds," cried Lawson.

"I am much obliged, Sir," replied Geraghty, "for your generous offer. Miss Lawson said she was sure you would give a thousand pounds. She appreciated your affection, but underrated your munificence. I do not want your money, Sir. I never will touch a farthing of it. Affections, family affections are, I think, far too precious to be bought, or sold, or chaffered about. If I can accomplish the design I have in hand, in bringing you and your daughter together, believe me my main reason for doing so will be the recollection of what has occurred to myself and my family, and of which I may tell you more at a more fitting time. Here, Mr. Lawson, if I may judge of your feelings by my own, is something for you which you will prize much more than a patent of peerage from the King. You have offered me a gift I will not take. Let me, however, have that small gold ring on your finger, and I will present you with something you will prize."

As Geraghty thus spoke, he presented Judith's letter to her father.

Lawson looked at it, and then exclaimed with rapture: "Judith! a letter written by herself. O precious! precious! thrice precious letter! Here, here, take the ring. I wish it was all one diamond. It was Judith's, but I give it in exchange of her most welcome handwriting."

Lawson read the letter over rapidly, then more slowly, then re-read it for a third time, and then with a cheerful voice and a smiling face he turned to Ludlow and said:—
"Huzza! good news! good news, my friend. Here I have some very important facts from Judith; the all-important one is, that my darling child is now as she has left me; that the villain who carried her away in the hope of

forcing er into marriage has not yet dared to present himself before her; that she does not, therefore, know his name, and has seen so little of him that she is unable to give me a description of his person. She says also, that the bearer of the letter, this good old gentleman she must mean, will give me such information as may ensure her release, and tell me that which he must best know, whether any force will be required to ensure her freedom. These are the material points in the letter, what say you to them?"

"That I am rejoiced to hear them," replied Ludlow. "The important matter now is to ascertain where Miss Lawson is, and what we are to do to release her? This old gentleman is, I suppose, prepared and willing to afford us so much information."

"It is with that view I called on Mr. Lawson," replied Geraghty. "The story I have to tell you is rather curious, and the motive for Miss Lawson's abduction rather a strange one. It has not been, as she supposes, merely from a sordid motive alone she has been seized upon, but it was as a means of taking revenge, as I am informed, upon Mr. Lawson."

"Revenge," exclaimed Lawson and Ludlow at the same instant.

"Yes, from a revengeful motive," added Geraghty. "You, Mr. Ludlow, may not have heard, but Mr. Lawson, probably, very well knows a rebel named Colonel Fitzpatrick."

"Colonel Fitzpatrick! Ludlow and I knew him very well; but what can he have had to do with Judith?" asked Lawson.

"Listen to me patiently," replied Geraghty. "This Colonel Fitzpatrick and his son, it seems, conceive themselves, for what reason I know not, to have been,

not merely aggrieved, but deeply injured by you, Mr.
Lawson. And, I suppose, as they had no other means
of revenging themselves, when they could not assail you,
they resolved, it seems, to wound your feelings, by inflicting an injury on your daughter. They, therefore,
as I am told, hired Redmond O'Hanlon's gang to seize
upon her, to hold her in custody for some time, and then
to force her to marry a low and debauched spendthrift,
named David Fitzgerald, a man who has reduced himself
from an ample fortune to sordid beggary by an indulgence in all sorts of vices. That diabolical plan they have
not, as yet, been able to carry into effect. But it is to be
attempted to-morrow night; but where, I am not, as
yet, quite certain. This, however, is arranged, that a
degraded parson (for Fitzgerald is, like Miss Lawson,
a member of the Established Church) is to be with the
two Fitzpatricks at a certain place, not yet fixed upon
(or rather which I have not yet heard of); and that there,
with such witnesses, the ceremony of marriage will,
with or without her consent, be gone through."

"The Fitzpatricks! father and son! both together!
and without any attendants! are you sure of that?"
asked Ludlow.

"Perfectly sure of it. There will be but the old man;
he is a great deal older, and not half as stout as I am,"
replied Geraghty. "And with him his son—that is,
you may say, but one man alone, for as to Fitzgerald, I
would be more than a match for him myself, he is so
broken down with constant intoxication. And then the
degraded parson—another miserable drunkard. Thus,
you see, if you wish to prevent this abominable marriage,
you will require no additional aid. I will go armed as
well as you, for I have an old grudge to settle, as it was
on account of these Fitzpatricks that I suffered that

calamity, the effects of which will last as long as my life."

" Right! right!" remarked Ludlow. " An additional force would be, in such a case, an impediment, instead of an assistance; and if I was—for I too have an old grudge to settle with these Fitzpatricks—if I was, in the endeavour to prevent this marriage, or in my desire to punish those who had planned it, to blow the brains out of one or both the Fitzpatricks, would you feel displeased at my doing so?"

" I am too much of a gentleman myself," replied Geraghty, "to interfere with another in the indulgence of his resentment, or the gratification of his revenge."

" Your sentiments do you honour, Sir," observed Ludlow. " What plan do you then propose for us all to adopt? for in this case, as I perceive, we have a common object to attain, and the same enemy to destroy."

" Precisely so," replied Geraghty. " We all wish to inflict summary and condign punishment upon those we detest."

" And to prevent my daughter from being married," added Lawson.

" Oh! certainly to prevent your daughter being married," added Geraghty. " Do as I bid you, and no such event can possibly take place."

" It is easy seeing you *are* a father," observed Lawson.

" *Have been*, Sir," replied Geraghty, "and you will be, I trust, afforded the proof how deeply I feel the loss that was inflicted upon me. But now, without making any other professions upon the one side or the other, listen to what I have laid down as a fitting course of proceeding for us all. You should, I think, leave this place either to-night, or at a very early hour to-morrow, and meet me to-morrow evening at the fortress-tower which lies on the right-hand side of the high-road, about three miles from Dundalk. The tower, if I mistake not, is the only relic left of a small fortification which was destroyed by the valiant General Ludlow, when he was making a progress towards the North."

"Oh! I remember it very well," replied Ludlow. "It is a low-square tower."

" The very same," replied Geraghty. "Miss Lawson is confined somewhere in that neighbourhood, and from her present prison will be brought to some solitary place where the marriage ceremony can be huddled over without interruption. Meet me at ten to-morrow night at the square tower on the road. Remember you come well armed; you are both men of courage. If you see your enemies then you know what to do—you know what claim they have on your mercy. I know my enemies have none on mine. Farewell."

The old man disappeared.

Lawson was engaged with the reperusal of his daughter's letter.

"Oh!" cried Ludlow, as he walked up and down the room with an air of triumph. " Oh! what a glorious opportunity for ridding myself of all my difficulties has this old man placed within my grasp! Father and son! both at my mercy; both within the reach of my weapon—unprepared to defend themselves—expecting to meet with no foe. To strike them down with one blow, and so attain the end of a life-long struggle; and so secure those possessions for which I have waded through the blood of the innocent and the unoffending. Lawson! arouse yourself. Think of to-morrow night—your daughter restored to you, the Fitzpatricks got rid of; my bond still available for your profit and advantage. Arouse yourself, Lawson!

Prepare your weapons for the short, decisive, and the last, the very last conflict in which we shall have to engage."

"And make you, Ludlow, all the preparations that you deem to be necessary. You know me of old—if I see an enemy, my blood will be up on the instant, and I am ever sure to strike a deadly and decisive blow. But now I can do nothing, think of nothing, but that in the course of a few hours I shall clasp to my heart my lost—my long-lost—ever-lamented, and ever most dearly beloved daughter, Judith."

CHAPTER XX.
A SNARE.

From the moment that Abigail Gregg had been so unexpectedly removed from her side, poor Judith Lawson had found herself to be completely deserted. Her meals were brought, and her apartments swept, by a young girl that appeared to be both deaf and dumb, and whose attention and curiosity Judith had in vain attempted to awaken and excite. The poor drudge seemed to be incapable of doing anything but her allotted tasks, and even these in a careless and slovenly manner.

Judith was thus thrown entirely and absolutely upon her own resources. Without books to read, or paper to write, or embroidery to work, she was left in her solitary confinement, with nought to occupy her mind but vain regrets for the past, and equally vain hopes for the future, whilst the present, the awful present, was a dread blank.

Hour after hour, and day after day passed, and from morning till night she might be seen in the same position, gazing wistfully at the window opposite where she had last seen "the imp," and wishing—oh! how many times wishing—that his frightful face might again present itself. She sat so long there that, at last, she took an interest in watching the movements of the furious animals in the court-yard below, even though she never could venture to lean out, and gaze down upon them, without their fierce muzzles and white teeth gnashing at her, and their impatient barks clamouring in her ears.

Ever furious, and mischievous, and malignant as they were, still they were living things, and to her poor tired eyes it was something to see life and motion, even though there was, in both, unprovoked hostility to herself untiringly exhibited. She looked so long, and so constantly at these odious brutes, that at last she was able to distinguish them, one from the other, and to give them, in her own mind, names by which she marked their identity; calling one "the lion," another "the tiger," another "the panther," and another "the hyæna."

Even these most odious and detestable animals became, each in turn, objects of interest to her, and she wiled away many a day, and many an hour of many a day, in bestowing her undivided observation upon some one or other of these in themselves most uninteresting objects.

Oh! the wearisome hours there are in this life, for many a poor sad heart, separated from those it loves, and neglected by those who are near. How it pines and how it throbs, with a longing desire for parents or kinsmen that are far away, and who, if near, would have sustained it with looks and words of deep affection; how it tries to delude itself by watching what it does not care for, while the gentle affections that are trodden under foot are thrilling with pain and quivering with agony; and then, how, at last, wearied—wearied and exhausted by its sad and solitary watching, its lonely horrors, and its desolate occupations, it rises in prayers to the All-merciful, and begs that He will take it to Himself, and, by the dear remembrance of His abandonment and forlorn Agony in the Garden, give to it what the world denies, or has taken away from it—love for love—everlasting peace—undying affection—the repose of the grave; the tranquil, soft, sweet, refreshing, never-ceasing repose of heaven.

Poor Judith! Her dreary occupation had been to watch the furious, detestable brutes in the court-yard beneath her window, until she knew them perfectly, and at last was able to observe that amongst them all there was one, that seemed to be always more infuriated than the rest at sight of her; this was a large white bull-dog, to which she had given the name of "the tiger."

One day, on looking down, she was astonished to perceive that when his fiery companions opened their mouths and gnashed their teeth, howling and grinning at her, "the tiger" appeared not to take the least notice of her, but lay curled up in his own kennel, as if an unusual fit of sullenness had come upon him. And so the brute remained for the entire day, changing his position constantly, fidgetty, and as if dissatisfied with himself, and yet not disposed to vent his ill-humour upon anything around him. The next day she remarked "the tiger" lay with his head between his paws, never varying his position more than once or twice during the day. A short time after this, the dog was looking wildly and strangely about him, as if he did not know where he was. Upon another day, "the tiger" would now and again spring up, as if he saw some strange object before him, at which he would give an angry look, and then plunging about with a savage howl.

All this time it appeared as something extraordinary that the dog never looked up at her, nor watched her as he used to do. A listlessness had fallen upon him; his food was neglected, and he lay crouching down, gnawing at straws, or licking with his tongue the cold stones of the court-yard into which the sun never penetrated.

As Judith was thus engaged watching the tiger, and speculating in vain as to what could be the cause for this sudden change in the usual habits of the animal, she was astonished at perceiving the window opposite suddenly open, and "the imp" again presenting himself, and making signals to her that she should stand back until he cast over the rope he held in his hand.

It was with a joyful heart, bounding with hope and pleasure, that Judith beheld the imp flinging the rope, that she fastened it for him, and she watched him speed, by its means, across to her, bearing her golden-handed riding-whip in his mouth.

"What news? what news? how is my dear father?" cried Judith, as the imp bounded into the room.

"Well."

"Has he received my letter?"

"Yes."

"When am I to get out of this prison?"

"To-night."

"Will my father come for me?"

"No."

"Why?"

"He cant."

"Then how am I to get out?"

The imp produced a ladder of ropes, and pointed with his finger down into the court-yard.

"What! to go down *there* amongst those frightful

dogs!" exclaimed Judith, turning pale. " What! to be devoured alive! Wretch! you have not seen my father. This is a plot to lure me to my own destruction."

The imp looked as if it were an enjoyment to him to witness the terror exhibited in the face of Judith. He then made a motion with his hand as if locking a door, and said:—

"Do it myself at night! I'm afraid of the dogs as well as you."

"What proof have I that you have seen my father? that you are not deceiving me?" asked Judith, whose fears were excited, and her apprehensions aroused, by the proposal she should place herself near to those ferocious brutes, that had so often barked in anger at her.

"Daddy sent you this," said the imp, as he placed in Judith's hand the ring which Lawson had given to Geraghty in exchange for her letter.

"Daddy sent this—so glad to get the letter," repeated the imp.

Judith kissed the ring a thousand times, and said, as she took from her purse some pieces of gold, "These are for yourself; I'll give you more when I am in my father's house."

"Won't have 'em," replied the imp; "give me usquebaugh."

"I have not, I am sorry to say, any," replied Judith.

"Augh!" cried the imp in an angry tone, "don't care for anything else; gold no good; can't drink gold —can drink usquebaugh."

"But why not make our escape through the door?" asked Judith.

"Grand-daddy watching there—not watching courtyard."

"Then there is no escape from this place but by the court-yard?" observed Judith.

"None."

"Very well; then into the court-yard I'll descend whenever the time has come for doing so. At what hour may I expect you?"

"At ten; pitch-dark then."

"I will be ready."

"Good," said the imp, pointing to the riding-whip; "take that—wanted."

"What! shall we have to ride a long way before I meet my father?"

"Yes," replied the imp, making a motion with his hand, as if he was whipping a horse to make it go on very fast.

"And who will be my companion on the road, and point out the way to me?"

"I."

"Are you certain you will make no mistake?"

"None."

As the imp thus spoke, he was about to dart out of the room, when Judith caught hold of him, and at the same time said—"Pardon me—I am sorry thus to stop you; but there is one question I wish particularly to ask."

The face of the imp changed as he felt Judith's hand upon him. There was the scowl of a demon on his brow for a moment, his right hand slipped into the breast of his jacket, as if he had a deadly weapon concealed there; but as he listened to Judith's words, the scowl relaxed and the hand was withdrawn, and he stood in his usual attitude before her—that is, looking at her whilst appearing to be listening for some noise in the distance.

"I wish, I say," observed Judith, "to ask you one question which has disturbed me very much."

The imp still listened, but said not a word.

"I wish," continued Judith, "to know how came you to be so long absent from me? Why did you not see my father at once? Why have you been such a time—oh! such a very long time—without bringing me some proof you had seen him?"

"Grand-daddy," said the imp.

"Well!" added Judith, as if waiting for some further explanation.

"Grand-daddy," repeated the imp.

"What has grand-daddy to do with it? How was he able to prevent your seeing my father?"

"Grand-daddy," repeated the imp for the third time, and then making the semblance of one person boxing and lashing another, and then of twining ropes or fetters around his arms and legs.

"Oh! I understand you now," remarked Judith; "your grandfather beat you, and then tied you down, and so made you a prisoner; and therefore you were neither able to see my father, nor to let me know what had become of you."

The imp nodded.

"Very well. Now you may go. I shall be perfectly ready to accompany you at ten o'clock."

At ten o'clock that night Judith was prepared fully to make that attempt which would, as she trusted, end in restoring her safe and well to her father.

With tremulous anxiety had she watched the progress of the hours, and with satisfaction noted the lengthening shadows, and the gradually declining day; mistiness, and gloom, and then night descending upon the earth, and concealing every object in a thick cloak of darkness.

Whether it was that her senses were rendered more acute by her anxiety, or that the thoughts that were whirling through her brain made her mistake internal sensations for the action of exterior things, she found it difficult to determine; but it appeared to her as if there was an ominous sound in the slightest motion of the air. There was, she fancied, a sigh in the slightest breeze that fanned her cheek, and a groan given forth as she heard the shutting or opening of a distant door, whilst the fierce howls of the dogs seemed to her the raging of a storm as it bursts on a rocky shore, and with it was occasionally mixed the unnatural, hideous, new-noted yelp of "the tiger," which seemed to come up to her from the court-yard as the agonized shriek of a dying wretch, whose last drowning cry is smothered by the foam of the relentless billow that is about to bury him down in the sea for ever.

Judith struggled with these feelings for a long time; bringing to her aid her resolute will, and native courage, and so occasionally conquering them—even though, after a few moments, they rose again in their strength to unnerve her. At length she believed she had overcome them completely, when a new species of terror assailed her—it was the dead, the awful, and the sudden stillness that she felt surrounding her. There was not a breath, not a motion, not a sound! It was as if nature or art had conspired or contrived that there should be such a complete absence of all motion, that the slightest noise made by her in attempting her escape could not fail to betray her.

Poor Judith! her long, sad, solitary confinement had

made a deep inroad upon her constitution in weakening her body, and numbing her mind, blunting her brave spirit, and undermining her powers of endurance. Ah, me! how many sad, sad hours are there in this dreary, weary world! How many a noble spirit it quells, and how many a generous being it destroys, whilst selfishness reigns supreme, and with a cold but sure hand crushes to death many a loving heart! Who can tell the effects on an ardent spirit and an impulsive nature of coerced inactivity and compulsory lassitude? Its results may be calculated by gravestones; its sufferings can never be known but on that Day when shall be unfolded to an appalled universe a record of ALL that each of us had *said*, and *done*, and *thought*.

Poor Judith!—she was young, unaided, unadvised, and she was about to accompany, she knew not where nor for how long a period, a half-witted boy, whose imbecile mind, like his dwarfed body, appeared to place him beyond the pale of humanity. Who can be surprised to hear, under such circumstances, that the once valiant Judith was, for the moment, exposed to vain fears and baseless apprehensions, or that when she detected the slight noise made by opening the casement in the tower opposite to that in which she sat, an unaccountable feeling of deep awe fell upon her? Her spirit was abated, but her will was firm; and therefore it was with a steady hand she fastened the rope by which "the imp" could pass over to her.

The noise made by flinging across the rope aroused the vigilance of the dogs beneath, and their loud barks and yells were renewed with the same clamour as when they observed Judith looking at them in the day time.

Judith's lips trembled as she heard this outburst of

canine ferocity. She looked down into the court-yard, but could discern nothing beneath. She only knew the raging brutes were below by their untiring howls.

This clamour continued for some minutes, when she observed a lighted lanthorn moving beneath in the darkness, and heard words spoken in soothing tones to the dogs. She was sure she could remark "the imp" carrying some food along with his lamp, and the dogs following him; then there was again darkness for a minute or two, and at last, the lamp reappeared, and was borne about to different parts of the yard, as if he who carried it was in search of something. It appeared to Judith as if one of the dogs was missing, and the person with the lamp was looking for it, and tempting the animal to come to him; for she was sure she heard the words, "Come, Sir,—hi, hi! here, good dog, come here!" This continued for a minute or two, and the lamp again disappeared; and then again there was a deep, solemn, and profound stillness; and in the midst of it, and whilst still looking down into the dark court-yard beneath, Judith perceived "the imp" was beside her. Pulling her dress, he whispered in a low voice:—

"Ready?"

"Yes—what have you done with the dogs?"

"Locked up."

"Go on, I'll follow you," said Judith.

The imp cast the rope ladder into the yard, and then, getting outside the window, he said: "Follow me; I'll guide your feet; hold your whip in your mouth; you'll want both hands to hold fast."

Judith did as she was directed. She scarcely ventured to breathe as she felt herself in the air; her feet guided from step to step by the imp until she was sure she was near the earth, when her foot was let go, at the same instant that her conductor cried out:—

"Oh, God!—jump, jump to the ground at once; one of the dogs I thought I had put up is out; he has a fast hold of me. Strike him on the head with your whip, or he will crush the bone of my leg to pieces."

"Where is the brute?" cried Judith, as she bounded to the earth, forgetting all her fears, the moment that a struggle was impending, and that a human creature appealed to her for assistance. "Where is the brute? and where are you?"

"Here! here! oh! I'm destroyed."

"Where?" said Judith, as she grasped the whip in her nervous right hand, and stretched out her left to find the boy, and so turn where she could inflict a death-blow on the dog.

The hand of Judith, in searching for the boy, lighted on the head of the dog, and it released its hold of the imp to make a snap at her hand, its fierce teeth touching the flesh, and tearing away a particle of the skin that covered the lowermost joint of the little finger. The brute thus missing its snap, tore the clothes of Judith in the endeavour to reach her feet; but before it could effect its purpose a blow from her whip had stunned it, and "the imp," with a single pull of a short knife across its throat, deprived it of life.

This conflict with the dog did not last half a minute, and beyond the noise made from the crushing blow of Judith's whip on the dog's head, not the slightest sound was to be heard. The dog uttered neither bark, nor cry, nor yelp, whether in making his attack, or in succumbing to the death-blows received by him.

"I hope you are not much hurt," said Judith, as she rolled a handkerchief around her left hand, to stop the blood which she felt to be flowing quickly.

"Lamed for a month," cried the imp; "it does not bleed much—but I don't care—I won't feel it when granddaddy gives me my bottle."

"Bottle! of what medicine does your grand-daddy give you a bottle?" asked Judith.

"Usquebaugh, nice usquebaugh," said the imp, smacking his lips, though his leg was ringing with pain. "Come haste, you make haste."

"Will you not stop to bind up your leg?"

"No! no! no! not time—haste, haste, haste. This way, give me your hand. Ha! he has bit you I see— more sorry for you than myself! Brave girl! tried to save me! Come, come, come! haste! Pity you haven't usquebaugh. Come, come, come. I want my bottle to stop this pain."

Judith gave her hand to the boy, and he led her through what was to her impenetrable darkness. All she could ascertain was, as she wound her whip about, that for some time they were going through narrow passages; and then that they were at last in the open air, and as the darkness seemed to recede from her view, that they had passed beyond the walls of the fortress, and were walking upon grass: at last she heard the pawing of a horse, and then felt that such an animal was at her side.

"Mount," said the imp, "I'll ride before you."

Judith felt that a pillion had been provided for her, and in front of it was a small saddle for the imp.

"This is," observed Judith, as her practised hand ran along the horse's head, neck, and shoulders, "a very powerful horse. Have you the strength to manage him?"

"You'll see," answered the imp.

Judith at once mounted. The imp clambered into the

saddle before her, and then uttering the ejaculation "Hi, Sir!" away dashed the animal as if it had started for a race.

"The horse cannot long keep to that pace," remarked Judith.

"Then another will."

"What, a relay of horses!"

"Yes."

"Who has provided them?"

"Daddy, I'm told."

"Who told you that?"

"Hi, Sir!" shouted out the imp, either not hearing, or pretending not to hear the question.

Judith tried again to speak, but each time that she began a question, the imp, upon hearing the first word spoken, again burst out, with his usual cry to the horse of "Hi, Sir!" and so baffled all her attempts to keep up a conversation with him.

And all this time the horse was going on at a mad gallop. At last its pace began to weary, and scarcely did Judith note this change, than the imp cried out, "Another horse! then another—then mount again! Jack-spur-and away."

And so, four different times in the same night, were horses changed for Judith; but on no occasion could she perceive any one either in attendance with them, or to take care of those that had been used; but at each stage into which the journey was broken, there was a saddle and pillion ready prepared, with a fresh horse, on which to start her and her strange companion.

At last day came, and disclosed to her a portion of the country in which she could not recognize a single feature with which she had been previously acquainted. Before her was an old ruined square tower, for a long time discernible ere she reached it; but when she came opposite to its half-covered moat, the imp sent the horse, with a leap, bounding across it; and the next instant stopped, dis-, mounted, nodded to Judith to do the same, and then, with his finger, directed her to go inside the tower.

Judith acted upon the intimations of the imp. She perceived, upon entering, there was but a single room in the base of the tower—if that could be called a room which was without a roof, except a small portion covered over with a wooden shed, directly underneath which were trusses of straw, on which were stretched clean blankets. On a table, in the centre of the room, were two pitchers of milk, and two loaves of bread.

"For you," said the imp; "breakfast, dinner, bed—sleep till night; I'll then be with you—bring you to daddy."

As he uttered the last word he rushed out of the place, and in a minute afterwards she heard the words—"Hi, Sir, alive!" followed by the quick galloping of a horse.

The imp had vanished!

Judith was again alone. She hastened, as she heard the noise of the horse's feet, to the door in front of the tower, and when she sought to discover the imp he had disappeared. She walked all round the banks of the moat, and then perceived she was in the very midst of a desolate country, with moors and bogs on all sides, and not the smallest appearance of a living thing within her view. The bleak prospect was alike destitute of man as of beast; no human habitation by the side of the rough paths, for they were unworthy the name of roads, and no animals feeding in the fields.

"Again left to myself! again without a companion!— a solitude as complete as that of my late prison; but, oh, how superior! for here are God's own works around me; but there were not only man's works, but man's iniquities. Ah!" said Judith, "how sudden and severe a pang, and from so slight a wound too!"

As Judith thus spoke, a tingling, torturing pain, that seemed to thrill in every nerve, shot up from her little finger to her arm, and made her tremble for the moment with the agony it caused her.

"This is strange! what can be the reason for it? I must look to an injury on which I never fancied I should have to bestow a second thought."

With these words, Judith unloosed the handkerchief she had bound around her hand the night before. She perceived that there had been but a slight discharge of blood once the handkerchief had been tied; but although the incision of the teeth was scarcely perceptible, and the small piece of flesh removed from the hand almost insignificant, still all the hand around the slight wound was red and swollen.

"Ah!" thought Judith to herself, "if I were in my usual health, this slight cut would be nothing; but now my long anxiety—my fears of being overtaken last night—the fatigue to which I was unused, and the long ride, have all inflamed my blood, so that the scratch of a pin would, I suppose, afflict me as much as the small nip given to me by that wicked, ill-conditioned brute. I must ask the imp which of them it was. Now, with a good bathe of my hand in fresh water—with this kerchief steeped in cold water around it—and with a sound sleep, I hope to be able to meet my dear father to-night, almost as well as ever I was."

The shades of evening were beginning to fall, when the

imp stood by the side of Judith, who lay in a profound sleep. He touched her with his hand, and said:—

" Time to go."

" I'm ready."

The imp looked with surprise at the table, as the food lay on it untouched.

Judith remarked his surprise, and then said—" I was not disposed to eat, but I have slept almost ever since."

" Sleep! I'll never sleep again."

" Why ?"

" Oh ! this leg !—this leg !"

" What, is it paining you ?"

The imp pointed from his hip to his toe, and cried as if in intense agony—" Pain—pain—all pain !"

" Which of the dogs was it that attacked us ?"

" The white dog."

" Ah ! the tiger," thought Judith to herself.

" Why did you not shut him up at the same time with the other dogs last night ?"

" I thought I did—but he hid himself. For some days back he did not come for food, and when I thought I had been tempting them all out of the yard, he must have stayed behind—hid his eyes from the light—and then, not knowing me in the dark, he bit me; and you he bit, because he did know you."

" I have noticed," said Judith, " that same dog going on in a very strange manner for the last few days. Have you heard what is the matter with him ?"

" Oh ! yes."

" What is it ?"

" Mad !"

" Mad !" exclaimed Judith ; " the dog mad ! Good heavens ! Then you and I are both lost."

T

"Not at all!" answered the imp, with seeming indifference.

"Not at all! What do you mean?" asked Judith, hoping she had misapprehended the meaning of the imperfectly informed being before her.

"No harm can overtake him who has plenty of usquebaugh. I'll soon have plenty. What do I care for mad dogs?—mad dogs cannot do me any harm. Oh! this leg! this leg!" cried the imp, as he hopped about. "But come, no more time to lose. We must be off to meet daddy."

"Come! come! come speedily. If what you say of the dog be true, there is indeed no time on this earth for me to spare. First to see my father—that one last, sole happiness the world can give me; and then—to meet that other Father, who, seated in Heaven, looks down with the unceasing vigilance of ever-watchful love upon His erring, poor, weak, mortal children."

"Come! come for the grand cure," cried the imp, as he mounted the saddle in front of Judith. "For the cave, and then—for such an everlasting drink of usquebaugh!"

CHAPTER XXI.

A TRAP.—THE DEATH-CAVE.

"What a strange! what an awful! and what a gloomy-looking place is this!" said Judith, as, having crept upon her hands and knees through a long passage, she at length stood erect in a cavern, which looked like a natural hollow in a mountain side, dimly illuminated through a few crevices of the rocks of which it was composed.

"In what a strange place I am to meet my father! How unlike our last parting to our next greeting! Then I knew no sorrow—then health was rioting in every vein; and now—death is upon me! Yes! yes! that poor semi-idiot has told the truth. The dog *was* mad; and the poison that was in his foul body he has infused into mine, and it burns and chills by turns this poor wounded limb. Be it so! be it so! It was well received. It has fallen upon me in a good cause. I was injured in the effort to save another from injury; and better—far better—that life should be so taken from me, than that I should lose it when sinning, or thinking of sin. Yes; God is very merciful, and I must prepare myself to meet Him; but then, my father— my poor, poor, dear father. What tidings are these I have to tell him! Oh! death! death! there is thy bitterest pang. Leave me, boy, leave me,' said Judith, turning to the imp, who had followed her into the cave, and who stood watching her, whilst she was thus soliloquising with herself.

There was a new and a strange expression in the face of " the imp."

So new and so strange was this expression that, despite of the sad and absorbing thoughts that filled the mind of Judith, she could not refrain from taking notice of the youth. Instead of the malignant grin, which at all times and upon all other occasions distorted the countenance of the imp, it was now marked with profound sorrow, an anxious care, and a deep gloom; whilst sighs issued incessantly from his lips, and he moved, not as he had been wont, with the agility of a baboon, but with the slow, hesitating, and halting step of a wounded animal. It was as if suffering and affliction, for the first time acutely felt, were awaking in the intellect of this poor young creature faculties and sentiments that had previously lain dormant.

"Alas! alas!" cried Judith, as she looked upon him. "I see in your face a confirmation of my fears. What can I do for you, my poor boy? In what manner can I assist you?"

"Noways," replied the imp.

"Then leave me here," said Judith.

"I do not wish to leave you."

"Then remain."

"I do not wish to remain."

"You do not wish to remain—and you do not wish to leave me here. What do you mean? Is it that I should not remain here?"

"Yes."

"But is it not here that my father is to meet me?"

"It is."

"Ah! then, be the consequences what they may, here I must—and here I will remain, until I see my father."

The imp's eyes filled with tears, and falling on his knees, and clasping her hands, he said to her, "I cannot, dare not tell all I suspect and fear; but—you—you were bitten by the dog in trying to save me. You tried to save me. I—I—I want to save you; there's but one way of doing it; leave this place before your daddy comes."

"My poor boy," cried Judith, deeply moved by this manifestation of feeling on the part of the imp: "Not all the world—the wealth of the world—or the medical skill of this world could save you or myself from impending fate—a horrible death! We are sad companions in misery. I understand you. There is danger, I suppose, hanging over my father by his coming here; there is danger to my life in my remaining where I am. Much better for me then, to stay where I am, because, by so doing, I may in time, give warning to my father of the peril that threatens him, and so prolong an existence that is dearer to me than my own."

"Come, come," cried the imp, catching Judith by her robe. "Come, come, or you'll be too late. Come, I say," he added, tugging impatiently, like a fretted and spoiled child, when one of its wishes has been unexpectedly thwarted. "Come! Oh! do come, or you'll be too late."

"Never—never," answered Judith. "Here my father is coming to meet me; and here, therefore, will I remain."

The imp started away from her, threw himself on his hands, and placing one of his horn-like ears to the ground, stayed in that listening position for a moment, then jumped up again, let fall his hands by his side, and howled rather than cried out, "Woe! woe! too late! too late! they are coming! they are coming!—they are—*here!*" And so speaking, he dashed into the narrow dark entrance, and disappeared.

"My father! my beloved father!" cried Judith, as she flung herself upon her knees.

Judith listened for the approaching footsteps; and, as she did so, she tried to pray, whilst her sense of hearing and her devotional aspirations were disturbed by alternate chills and flushes, which made her tremble now with cold, and then burn as if with a fever. A strange stiffness fell upon her neck, and there was the sensation as of a strong hand grasping her round the throat, and endeavouring to choke her.

Poor Judith!

Lawson and Ludlow were punctual in keeping the appointment made with Gerald Geraghty. At the hour fixed upon they were to the very moment in front of the old ruined square tower; and at the self-same moment Geraghty came from out of the tower, and greeted them from the mound surrounding it.

"You are welcome," said Geraghty; "not a moment too soon—not a minute too late; you, Mr. Lawson, to see your daughter, and you, Mr. Ludlow, to witness revenge for old wrongs fully satisfied."

"And too long delayed," remarked Ludlow.

"I agree with you, Sir—too long, entirely too long delayed; but that which is done completely at last, is still done in time," replied Geraghty. "I hope you are both well armed?"

"You may be sure of that," replied Ludlow.

"And you are not disposed, I suppose, to show the least mercy?"

"Mercy!" exclaimed Lawson. "Mercy! is it I show mercy to the villain who has laid his brutal hands upon my daughter?"

"It is a crime not to be forgiven," remarked Geraghty.

"Oh! never! never!" replied Lawson. "It is one of those wrongs that can never be appeased but in blood."

"So I say," drily remarked Geraghty. "But come, gentlemen, I have but to mount my horse, and then I shall be with you."

Geraghty withdrew to the tower. He there looked carefully to a small iron box he had brought from Dublin with him—saw that the matches, tinder, and fine powder were in due order—re-clasped the box—placed it beneath the flap of the saddle, and then, getting on his horse, rejoined Ludlow and Lawson in the high road.

"Have we much farther to travel?" asked Ludlow.

"Not more than two miles—scarcely two miles," replied Geraghty. "And now, to give you, gentlemen, the last directions, and to make our final arrangements. The place where the parties you are in search of are concealed, is in some sort of a hole, cell, cave, or cavern in one of these hills—I am not quite sure which it is; but a scout—a little boy, will be on the look out for us. When we have met this boy, what I propose is, either that I should enter the cave before you, or you before me—whichever you please; or let one of you go first, I shall then follow, and another of you can follow me— I am indifferent which is done. All I want is that we make our arrangements now, and act upon them when we get there; for when there it will be necessary for us not to speak one word until we are all safe inside the place, face to face, and standing before old enemies whose villainies are well known to each of us."

"A very proper arrangement, and a very wise precaution," remarked Ludlow; "and sure to lead to a most desirable result."

"Most desirable, indeed!" again drily remarked Geraghty.

"Well, what do you propose, Lawson?" asked Ludlow; "I will do whatever you say."

"I was at one time in a cavern in a hill side in this part of the country," answered Lawson; "and nothing but the hope of seeing my child would ever induce me to enter another. Let the old man, then, go first, I will follow, and you can bring up the rear."

"Be it so," replied Ludlow.

"I have taken care," said Geraghty, "to have the news conveyed to Miss Lawson that her father is coming to rescue her; she will be then on the watch for you, Sir; and there is the chance that in the hope of seeing you she may be able to make some excuse, so as to et for an instant, at least, from the Fitzpatricks, and so be able to see you alone for a few moments. If this supposition turn out to be correct, it would perhaps be better for you to enter first, for your friend to be by your side to sustain you, in case the Fitzpatricks are present; and then the most feeble arm in a combat—my own—would be the last to engage in it."

"It is the better plan of the two," said Lawson. "It is, too, the one most pleasing to me; for that which I most desire in this world is to see again my darling child—no matter how, no matter when, and no matter where."

"Now we understand each other perfectly," said Ludlow; "Lawson first, myself second, our friend here, last."

"And though last," added Geraghty, "not less anxious than either of you to see condign punishment inflicted by a father on one who has done him wrong. And now, gentlemen, from henceforth, silence. I will ride in front, so as to be recognized by the boy who is on the watch for me."

The old man, Gerald Geraghty, rode forward. The agility and the buoyancy of youth seemed to be restored to his withered limbs and wasted frame. There was a triumph in the manner in which he flourished his whip, and a species of waggery in the way he squared his elbows and turned out his toes, as he urged his horse to a more rapid pace than usual. Nothing but the powers of a daguerreotype, manipulated by a Claudet, could convey an accurate transcript of the mingled expression of ferocity and fun, of hate and mirth that corrugated his brow and smirked about the hard lines of his toothless mouth, every time his eye rested for a moment on the two men who followed him.

A complete—and it was felt by Lawson and Ludlow as an awful silence—fell upon the party of horsemen for a full half hour.

On a sudden, as the rough, steep road made a sharp turn direct into the hill, the old man was seen talking for a few minutes to one so diminutive, that he appeared to Ludlow and Lawson to be a very young boy. They could not, however, hear the conversation that passed.

The conversation between the imp and the old man was very brief; but very important. Those who followed had no idea with what terrible consequences to themselves it was fraught.

"Is the woman in the cave?"

The imp nodded assent.

"Does she suspect anything?"

The imp again nodded.

"Why?"

"She is ill—very ill—in great pain, and so am I."

"You! What is the matter?"

"Both were bitten in the court-yard."

"How was that? Why did you not secure the dogs?"

"I thought I had. The white dog would not eat food, and did not follow me. He first bit me, and then bit her in trying to save me."

The old man turned ghastly pale, and his lips trembled, as he said, with terror: "Unhappy boy! Hapless girl! bitten in trying to save the life of my grandson. Why is the miserable woman the daughter of such a villain? But there's no saving her now. She's already doomed. I could not save her if I would. But are you sure it was the white dog?"

"Sure!—right sure—I cut his throat."

"The white dog! Why he seemed for the last few days to be going——"

"Mad," answered the imp. "Sullivan, the keeper

told me so on Tuesday. But I don't care. Usquebaugh, you know, cures everything. Have you got it for me?"

"Here it is," said the old man, producing a large bottle from one of the wide pockets of a large outside coat.

The imp made a clutch at it, but the old man was too quick for him. He drew it out of the reach of the boy, and thrusting it into his pocket, said:—

"Not yet, not yet. Here is the fire-box. I have shewn you what to do with it. Now mind what I say to you. You are to keep your eye fixed on the place I shewed you: you can there see everything that is going on in the cavern. The people there, when they find me alone, may want to take *your bottle* from me, but I won't give it to them. In saving it I may be knocked down. If I am, your only chance to get your bottle is to take out the things from the fire-box, and to do what I told you. If they do not molest me, then I will leave them, and bring you your usquebaugh, and then———"

The old man smiled at the thought of being able, in safety, to complete the diabolical plan he had projected.

"Now, boy, away! Observe, if you see me struck or knocked down, then, but not before then, use the fire-box."

The boy nodded assent, made a motion as if he was striking a spark from a flint, and ran off towards the hills.

As the boy disappeared, the old man turned to his fellow-travellers, and said: "All right! Your daughter, Sir, is in the cave, and, you may be sure, anxious to hear your footsteps, because certain you will save her from her persecutor."

"That I will," replied Lawson, "or die in the attempt."

"So I expect," replied Geraghty. "Great caution, however, will be required. Let us dismount here. You can follow me on foot from this place to the entrance of the cavern. When there, you can easily find your way in, as the boy tells me there are a couple of lamps lighted. Their brightness in the midst of darkness will be a sure guide to you."

The horses of the travellers were tied together; and thence they proceeded by a precipitous path, through rocks, to the mouth of the cavern.

The night was dark; but still the path which Lawson was travelling seemed to be familiar to him, and when Geraghty pointed out the entrance to the cavern, he said in whispering accents, marked with some emotion: " I feel almost certain I have been in this place—certainly in one very like it—before now."

"Very probably you have," answered Geraghty, "but this is no time for talking. Your daughter is in there, if you wish to try and recover her."

Lawson said no more, but entered with firm and cautious steps into the mouth of the cave, closely followed by Ludlow. As they advanced, they found it necessary first to stoop, and finally, at last, to creep on their knees.

At last Lawson was able to discern, as he advanced by the light of the lamp, a woman on her knees, and, from her dress and figure, he felt not the slightest doubt it was his daughter Judith; still he said not a word, but kept creeping on slowly, slowly. He at last emerged into the cave, and then, bounding to his feet, and without waiting for Ludlow, he made the cave ring with the salutation:—

"Judith!—my beloved!—here! here is your father."

"Oh! my father! at last! my dear, dear——"

Poor Judith could say no more. She had started from her knees as she spoke, and rushed with open arms to meet Lawson; but before he could catch her she fell heavily, with her face to the earth.

"Oh! my child! my child! my darling child!" exclaimed Lawson, as with trembling hands he raised her from the earth, and covered her cheeks, eyes, forehead, and mouth with his kisses.

The unhappy man's short ecstacy of happiness was doomed to be of brief duration; for his daughter was awakened to consciousness by the fervour of his affection, and the ardour of his kisses. And as she opened her eyes, she flung her arms around his neck, and said, as she burst into tears, "Oh! father, father, do not venture to kiss me. Oh! do not, as you love me; dare not to touch my mouth with your lips. Oh! dear, dear father, make me happy, and say you have not touched my lips. Oh! father, father, forgive me if you have done so! for if you have I have slain you—slain you! Oh! God be merciful to me."

"My darling child!" cried Lawson, bewildered alike by his affection and the strange words of his daughter, "what mean you? Why talk so wildly? Has sudden joy at our thus meeting crazed you? Kiss you, my beloved Judith! Kissed *you!* aye have I, a thousand times. Wherefore not kiss you now as I ever have done?"

"Oh, father, as you love me, as you love your ever-true, ever-fond, and ever-darling child, make me happy by the assurance that your lips have not touched mine, which brun with a raging fire: oh! say that your mouth has not inhaled my breath, which is hot as a blast from the entrails of Etna."

"Good heavens! what is the matter with you, Judith? are you mad?"

"Oh! yes, dear, dear father, I am mad, mad, mad! Oh! the worst of madness is upon me. I have been bitten by a mad dog; and if you have kissed me I have poisoned you," cried Judith, as she flung again her arms round her father and burst into tears.

"My child, my beloved Judith, whatever strange fancy possesses you, this at least is certain, you are ill, very ill. But come, my child, I am here to release you from your enemies. Ludlow look to the entrance of the cave, that they may not escape us. Ha! there comes our old friend to assist us."

As Lawson spoke, Judith looked up. Her eyes gleamed at Ludlow for an instant, but did not rest upon him. It was not so, however, with old Geraghty, for, although he had his hat slouched down over his brows, and the cape of his riding-coat drawn up about his face, still he could not conceal from Judith's scrutinising gaze his large, staring, watchful, greedy eyes, with the red eye-lids and red eyebrows. Despite himself, there was a gleam of recognition in his malignant eyes, as Judith's look fastened on him.

Judith looked a second time at her jailer, then her eye wandered around the cavern—and then she looked at the old man again: it was a long, earnest, and painful look. At length she turned to her father, and suddenly asked him the question:—

"Who brought you here? Who told you that you would find me in this cavern?"

"It was I," said Geraghty, casting aside his hat, and letting the cloak he wore fall from his shoulders. "It was I—Gerald Geraghty, it was I, who——"

His speech was interrupted; for as he spoke, Judith's quick hand was inside her dress, the dagger that Fitzgerald had given her was withdrawn, and flung with desperate force and an unerring aim, it was quivering in the neck of Geraghty, who fell at once to the earth rolling in his blood.

Lawson and Ludlow were both horrified at this spec-

uncle, and gazed by turns at Judith, and at the old man as he writhed in agony upon the ground, trying in vain to speak.

There was silence for some moments in the cave, and the only interruption to it was the distant rapid clicking of a flint.

"What means this, Judith?" at last asked Lawson. "Why have you slain the good old man, without whose aid I never should have discovered your place of concealment?"

"Oh!" replied Judith, her eyes glowing with the fire of insanity, "that was my worst enemy. He it was who had me carried away from you; he it was who kept me in a prison; he it was who owned the animal. Oh! these fearful, fearful, dogs, who have made me mad, and why did he——Ah! the old wretch is dead! there he lies at last, slain by a woman! And why did he, dear, dear father, so persecute me? Because—oh the ruthless, false old villain—because he said—you heard him state who he was,—Gerald Geraghty—because, he said, in a cavern like to this, you, my own fond, loving father—you—only think of such a falsehood—he said that you had slain his wife, butchered his daughter, and all this for the sake of getting some property not yours, but that belonged to persons named Fitzpatrick; and finding him tell such atrocious tales of you, and seeing him here with you, I knew, for I saw it in his eyes, that he had brought you, and me, and this gentleman also, to murder us; and when I saw him, and remembered all he said, I was resolved that he, at least, should die before us—and so—and so I slew him. Was I not right, my beloved father, in so doing?"

The question so put by Judith Lawson was never responded to in this world; for as she spoke, there was a hissing sound as of many serpents, and then along the sides of the cavern, and over the floor, there came twisting, twirling, narrow lines of fire, running backwards and forwards, so that it was impossible for the dazzled eye to tell to which object they were tending, or whither they were going.

"A mine! a mine!" cried Ludlow, as he bounded towards the entrance, in the hope he might be in time to escape the explosion; but as he spoke, the earth yawned beneath his feet, and a sheet of fire arose, and in a moment there burst from the cavern's mouth a mass of heated rocks and scalding earth, which, striking "the imp" as he stood before it, sent his shattered limbs in fragments down the hill side—the only memorial that the eye of man ever looked upon of that dark and diabolical act of vengeance by which the wrong-doers and the wronged, the innocent and the guilty, were involved in the one common chaos of destruction!

A fearful, a cruel, and an unprovoked act of barbarity had, after the long lapse of thirty years, been fearfully, cruelly, and we may add, basely avenged. Great wrong had been done to Gerald Geraghty; but he was not content to leave the punishment of the wrong-doer to Heaven; for taking upon himself—weak, poor, short-sighted mortal!—that which is the office of Omnipotence, the result was that all his toil, trouble, fabrications, and schemes ended in his own perdition. He was cut off in the midst of his sins, without having that wretched satisfaction for which he had laboured—that of torturing Lawson, previous to slaying him, by the recital, in the presence of his daughter, of the base and unmanly deeds done by him in his youth.

The evil deed was punished; but the avenger was baffled even at the moment that all his plans were crowned with success. The sweetness of revenge was refused, and the bitterness of death was, by his own act, brought upon him.

Patience under his sufferings, and forgiveness, with prayers for his enemies, might have won for him heaven. He would not pardon, he could not forgive, and he dare not pray, and his end was the destruction of his own soul.

And so it was from the beginning, and so it will be to the end, whenever men assume to themselves the functions of the Deity, and, indulging in feelings of vindictiveness, seek to revenge, instead of pardon wrongs.

"*Before man is life and death, good and evil, that which he shall choose shall be given him.*"

CHAPTER XXII.

CONCLUSION.

THERE was a grand ball at the Castle of Dublin. His Excellency the Duke of Ormonde had resolved upon having in that ancient fortress one of the most magnificent entertainments ever displayed within its walls. He was desirous, when such a festival as that of "The Restoration" was to be celebrated, that the seat of government in the Irish metropolis should, by the munificence of the Chief Governor, the number of his guests, and the fervour of their loyalty, constitute a marked contrast to "*The Green Club*" of England, its ex-republican leader, Shaftesbury, and all anti-monarchical sympathisers in "the sister country."

The throne-room of the Castle was crowded. There were glittering uniforms and magnificent dresses, and noble-looking personages, and fat corporators in red, gaudy robes, intermingled with ladies remarkable, some for their great display of jewellery, and not a few attractive for their sparkling beauty. Amongst the latter there was not one more gorgeously attired than Lady Diana Harvey— the newly married wife of Major Harvey; and none more distinguished for her juvenile charms than the young lady who had been at that moment presented to His Excellency as the bride of Mr. Vincent Fitzpatrick.

It was with peachy cheeks, deeply flushed with pleasure at the compliments which had been paid to her by the Lord Lieutenant, that Kathleen returned, leaning on the arm of her husband, to take her place by the side of Lady Diana.

"Bless me, my love!" said Lady Diana; "I hope there is nothing the matter with you. You look greatly flushed. Your cheeks are entirely too red. I hope you are well."

"Well!" answered Kathleen; "I never was so happy before in all my life. That charming old gentleman, the Duke, has been saying such very kind things of—my husband."

"Your husband! indeed!" chimed in Lord Arran, as he appeared in a rich, full dress suit, with a diamond star on his breast. "Your husband, indeed! My worthy old father was thinking of you, and not of your husband, or perhaps he was like his son, wishing he was himself your husband. You know, Lady Diana, how little of a poet my father is; and yet, I assure you, such an impression did this saucy young bride produce upon him, that as she turned away, I heard the worthy, but somewhat antiquated beau, quoting Shakespeare, and saying as he looked upon her:—

> "' For where thou art, there is the world itself,
> With every several pleasure in the world;
> And where thou art not, desolation.'"

"I do not know, my Lord," observed Kathleen, "for which quality you are most to be admired—the readiness of your fancy, or the happiness of your memory. Come; say the truth; did you not invent that quotation and give it to your father, in order that you might so make an opportunity for reciting it?"

"No, on my honour," replied Lord Arran; "I only repeat the words he used. I believe myself to be utterly destitute of a poet's great faculty—fancy; but I do own to my taking some pride in my memory. I do assure you, Mrs. Vincent Fitzpatrick, I never forget an old love, nor an old friend; and as a proof, here is one for whom I have a great esteem. This is Alderman Elliot—Lady Diana Harvey; Mrs. Vincent Fitzpatrick—this is Alderman Elliot, an old friend of mine—the friend, too, of Colonel Fitzpatrick."

"Thank you—thank you heartily! my Lord Arran," said burly John Elliot, as he bowed with all the stiffness of an old trooper, though arrayed in the scarlet robes of an alderman. "It is a great satisfaction to me to be made known to the wife of a young gentleman whom I recollect a prisoner in this very Castle."

"My husband a prisoner!" cried Kathleen, surprised. "Strange! I never should have heard that before. Pray, upon what charge was he confined as a prisoner in the Castle?"

"He was about two years of age," replied Elliott, laughing, "when he was a prisoner. The charge against him was, being the son of Colonel Fitzpatrick; the offence of which he was guilty, being heir to large estates in Ireland. Had he not fortunately been rescued from his incarceration here, he would have been put to death."

"Put to death! oh! frightful!" exclaimed Lady Diana. "What monsters could contemplate a deed so barbarous?"

"Ah, madam!" answered Colonel Fitzpatrick, who, with Major Harvey, now joined the group, conversing together, "it is a long and a sad story, of which your valiant husband already knows most of the facts. Sufficient is it now to tell you, that all who were concerned in it have gone to their last and dread account. The worthy alderman, John Elliott, and myself, used our best efforts to save them. They were enticed into a cave by a wretch, whose family had been slain when they were seeking to murder my son. We got some clue to the plot, and I and the Alderman, with a large force at our command (given to us by Lord Arran here), were on our way to the death-cave of Dundalk to arrest all the parties, and when we had reached within a quarter of a-mile of our destination, a flame, as of an ignited powder-mill, was perceived, followed by the crash and noise of an earthquake, and then all was still. Upon an examination of the place, we perceived that the roof of the cave had fallen in, burying those who were inside under an impervious mountain mass of rocks, whilst outside, and at a considerable distance from the cave, were found the mangled limbs of some poor boy who was, I suppose, near to the place at the time of the explosion. There can be no doubt but in this case crime was followed by an awful punishment; but what is to be most regretted is, that with the guilty was also slain the innocent —a young woman—the daughter of one of the parties who was, at the time that Alderman Elliot stood sentinel on the ramparts, concerned in the attempt to kidnap and slay my son. That son, you know, is Vincent, who now stands before you, but who then was the lost heir in Dublin Castle."

"The lost heir in Dublin Castle!" repeated John Elliot. "Most truly may it be said, that 'the heir' would have been lost *in* Dublin Castle but for the bravery and gallantry of one, whose name would be considered now a species of high treason to mention."

" You refer to Redmond O'Hanlon," said Lord Arran.

" I do, my Lord," answered blunt John Elliot; " I remember, as if it were only yesterday, the tall, fearless, stripling youth, disguised with the helmet and cloak of my comrade, Lawson, and bearing the boy in his arms over the ramparts, well knowing at the time that every step he took exposed him to certain death; and I remember making the remark at the time, as I pondered over what I had witnessed, that he had done that brave deed for the sake of those who, perhaps, would live to forget it. I am afraid, as the Colonel made no reference to the part which O'Hanlon took in preserving his son from destruction, that my surmise was a prophecy."

"It is the way of the world, however, worthy Alderman," observed Lord Arran. " So it has been, and so it ever will be. Redmond O'Hanlon's generosity, his gallantry, his chivalry, and his disinterestedness, will be forgotten, whilst all that will be remembered of him will be that he was a Rapparee.

" ' The evil that men do, lives after them :
The good is oft interred with their bones.' "

" Such is not the case with me," replied Colonel Fitzpatrick. " I have endeavoured to procure Redmond O'Hanlon's pardon, and I am already promised one—a conditional pardon from the government. The conditions are such as I hope O'Hanlon may accept and act upon. If they are, then I shall be able to prove by my acts, how sensible I am of the inestimable benefit he has conferred upon me and mine."

"And so acting, Colonel," added Lord Arran, " you will prove that you are an exception to the general rules and maxims of worldly men. They are sincere in their enmities, and untrue in their friendships; they never forgive a wrong, and are seldom mindful of services conferred upon them. Thus will it be with Redmond O'Hanlon. Those on whom he has lavished benefits will cease to speak of him; those whom he has punished for wrong-doing will never pardon him; and they will seek a justification for their own misdeeds in calumniating his memory. He who, if he had lived in former times, would have been honoured by the nation and people in whose defence he fought as a Viriato, a Herman, or a Scanderberg, will, probably, be remembered in Ireland as nothing better than '*the Robber Chieftain :*' and should such an incident as this which has occurred in your family, Colonel, be told of him, it will be treated, perchance, as an idle story —'*a tale of Dublin Castle.*'"*

* See Illustration D., "Redmond O'Hanlon."

ILLUSTRATION A.

THE DEATH-CAVE OF DUNDALK—GENERAL LUDLOW'S NARRATIVE.

"From hence I went to visit the garrison of Dundalk, and, being upon my return, I found a party of the enemy retired within a hollow rock, which was discovered by one of ours, who saw five or six of them standing before a narrow passage at the mouth of the cave. The rock was so thick that we thought it impossible to dig it down upon them; and, therefore, resolved to try to reduce them by smoak. After some of our men had spent most part of the day in endeavouring to smother those within by fire placed at the mouth of the cave, they withdrew the fire, and the next morning, supposing the Irish to be made incapable of resistance by the smoak, some of them, with a candle before them, crawled into the rock. One of the enemy, who lay in the middle of the entrance, fired his pistol, and shot the first of our men into the head, by whose loss we found that the smoak had not taken the desired effect. But seeing no other way to reduce them, I caused the trial to be repeated, and upon examination, found that tho' a great smoak went into the cavity of the rock, yet it came out again at other crevices; upon which I ordered those places to be closely stopped, and another smother made. About an hour and half after this, one of them was heard to groan very strongly, and afterwards more weakly, whereby we presumed that the work was done; yet the fire was continued till about midnight, and then taken away, that the place might be cool enough for ours to enter the next morning. At which time some went in armed with back, breast, and head-pieces, to prevent such another accident as fell out at their first attempt; but they had not gone above six yards before they found the man that had been heard to groan, who was the same that had killed one of our men with his pistol, and who, resolving not to quit his post, had been, upon stopping the holes of the rock, choaked by the smoak. Our soldiers put a rope about his neck, and drew him out. The passage being cleared, they entered, and having put about fifteen to the sword, brought four or five out alive, with *the priest's robes, a crucifix, chalice, and other furniture of that kind.* Those within preserved themselves by laying their heads close to a

water that ran through the rock. We found two rooms in the place, one of which was large enough to turn a pike; and having filled the mouth of it with large stones, we quitted it, and marched to Castleblany, where I left a party of foot and some horse, as I had done before at Carrick and Newry, whereby that part of the County of Monaghan was pretty well secured."
—*Memoirs of Lieutenant-General Ludlow* (printed at Vevay, in the Canton of Bern, 1698), vol. i. pp. 422, 423, 424.

ILLUSTRATION B.

EXECUTION OF MRS. FITZPATRICK BY THE CROMWELLIANS.

" COLONEL FITZPATRICK was the first who submitted, on condition to be transported with his regiment into the service of Spain. * * *

"In Ireland, * * the number of those who submitted, on condition to be transported into foreign service, was so great, that they became a great burden to us before we could procure shipping for their transportation. * * *

"The Courts of Justice erected in Dublin and in other parts proceeded vigorously in making inquisition after the murders that had been committed. * * * The mother of Colonel Fitzpatrick was found guilty of the murder of the English, with this aggravation, that she said she would make candles of their fat. She was condemned to be burnt; and the sentence was executed accordingly."—*Ludlow's Memoirs*, vol. i. pp. 403, 408; vol. ii. p. 443.

ILLUSTRATION C.

CROMWELLIANS KIDNAPPING IRISH BOYS AND YOUNG WOMEN, AND SENDING THEM TO THE WEST INDIES.

"I RECEIVED yours of the 4th inst., and give you many thanks for your relation of Jamaica; and though we have met with some more than ordinary cross Providences in this undertaking, yet I doubt not but the Lord will smile upon it in the issue.

"I have endeavoured to make what improvement I could in the short time allotted me touching the furnishing you with a recruit of men, and a supply of young Irish girls. * * *

"Concerning the young women, although we must use force in taking them up, yet it being as much for their own good, and likely to be of so great advantage to the public, it is not in the least doubted that you may have such number of them as you shall think fit to make use upon this account. It will be necessary that care be taken for the clothing of them, which, if you allow money for, may be best and cheapest done here. All which is submitted to consideration."—*H. Cromwell, Major-General of the Forces in Ireland, to Secretary Cromwell*, September 5, 1655, in *Birch's Collection of Thurloe State Papers*, vol. iv. pp. 23, 24 (London, 1742).

"I shall not need to repeat anything about the girls, not doubting but to answer your expectations to the full in that; and I think it might be of advantage to your affairs there and ours here, if you should think fit to send 1500 or 2000 boys of twelve or fourteen years of age to the place afore mentioned. We could well spare them, and they would be of use to you; and who knows, but that it may be a means to make them Englishmen, I mean, rather, Christians."—*Ibid.* p. 40, Letter dated September 18th, 1655.

Secretary Thurloe to H. Cromwell.

"MY LORD,—I did hope to have given your Lordship an account by this post, of the business of causing young wenches and youths in Ireland to be sent unto the West Indies; but I could not make things ready. The Committee of the Council have voted 1,000 girls, and as many youths, to be taken up for that purpose, and that there be a sum of money for each head allowed for the clothing of them, and other necessaries, to the water-side. What that sum shall be, is left to the Council, to whom this will be reported to-morrow morning. Some speak of 13s. 4d., others of 20s. I should be glad to hear what you think of it in Ireland."—*Ibid.* p. 75.

H. Cromwell to Thurloe, (*Dublin, October, 16th,* 1655).

"SIR,—I understand, by your last letter, that the transportation of a thousand Irish girls, and the like number of boys, is resolved on by the Council; but as touching what you wrote for the charges you will be at to put them in an equipage fit to be sent, I have advised with some persons here; I know not what answer to return you to it; but it is thought most advisable to provide their clothes for them in London, which we think you may do better, and at cheaper rates, than we can here; we shall have (upon the receipt of his Highness's pleasure) *the numbers* you proposed, AND MORE if you think fit."—*Ibid.* p. 87.

Secretary Thurloe to H. Cromwell.

"I received your Lordship's, by Bradley, the Messenger, who arrived here this day; you know we are slow in all our business, which is all this reason that I can give your Lordship, that the directions concerning the transportation of some Irish girls are not sent herewith."—BIRCH'S *Collection of the Thurloe State Papers*, vol. iv. pp. 87, 88.

"The ships which are next to go thither (the West Indies), will be appointed to take on board them the Irish women or girls. It is agreed to provide their clothes here, and to put them in the aforesaid ships, to be ready for them, against such time as they come on board. So that all the charges that will be required further is the bringing them to the port where they are to embark, which, we think, will be Galway, and that we think will be very little. The time that they must be at the port will be about the latter end of December."—*Ibid.* p. 100.

H. Cromwell to Thurloe.

In a letter, dated Dublin, 14th November (1655), are the following sentences:—

"As for the Irish girls, you need not doubt of them, neither as to time or place.

"We have cleared the town of Galway of the Irish, and shall have a special care of that place."—*Ibid.* p. 198.

The number of persons transported is variously stated; some rating them at 6,000, others at 100,000.—See *Lingard's History of England*, vol. viii. pp. 175, 176, note 3, p. 175, with list of authorities. The following account of the treatment of European slaves in the West Indies, previous to Cromwell's project for transporting the Irish, and the actual state of circumstances in the West Indies when the project was to be carried into effect, cannot fail to be read with interest, as showing the *motive* in which this barbarous act originated.

SLAVERY IN THE WEST INDIES IN CROMWELL'S TIME.

The Governor of Barbadoes to the Protector.—(*Extract.*)

"Such as hitherto have been brought to this island from *England, Scotland, and Ireland*, have been landed on merchants' accounts, who, claiming a property in the persons being as servants, for their passage and disbursements on them, dispose of them here either for a term of years to serve, or for a sum of money, by which they free themselves from such servitude, either of which being performed, they have pardon to stay or depart hence by the law and customs of this place. For the future, such as your Highness shall please to command their stay here, I shall, to the utmost possibility of means to be used, labour *to keep them with us in pursuance of your Highness' commands.*"—BIRCH'S *Collection of the Thurloe State Papers,* vol. iv. p. 7.

CONDITION OF JAMAICA IN 1655.

Major Sedgwicke to the Protector.—(Extract.)
Letter, dated November 5, 1655.

" We landed 831, in Colonel Humphrey's regiment, lusty, healthful, gallant men, who encouraged the whole army. There are at this day fifty of them dead, whereof two captains, a lieutenant, and two ensigns, the colonel himself very weak, the lieutenant-colonel at death's door. I think all the captains sick; not above four commission-officers in that regiment now fit to march, and the men most part of them sick. Colonel Doyley is fallen sick again, and Colonel Carter very weak, as also divers other field-officers. Soldiers die daily; I believe 140 every week, and so have done ever since I came hither. It is strange to see lusty young men, in appearance well, and in three or four days in the grave, snatched away in a moment with fevers, agues, fluxes, or dropsies—a confluence of many diseases. The truth is, God is angry, and the plague is begun, and we have none to stand in the gap."—*Ibid.* vol. iv. pp. 153, 154. See also pp. 151, 152, 155.

ILLUSTRATION D.

REDMOND O'HANLON.

" THE Robber Chieftain," Redmond O'Hanlon, bears a double character: first, that which is given to him in publications issued at the time he lived or soon after his death, or that were, until a very late period, circulated amongst the poorer classes in Ireland: the second character differs in many essential points from the first, and while it does not disguise his faults, still loves to dwell upon his virtues; it is the character which *tradition* assigns to him.

It is in accordance with *tradition* that Redmond O'Hanlon is portrayed in the preceding pages.

To appreciate the character of Redmond O'Hanlon, we must have some knowledge of the times in which he lived, the circumstances in which he was placed, the difficulties he had to contend against, and the evils he sought to correct.

A few words from the pen of the ablest and greatest man that ever lived to labour for the well-being of Ireland, describes the times in which Redmond O'Hanlon lived.

" We are arrived at the Restoration—an event of the utmost utility to the English and Scotch Royalists, who were justly restored to their properties. An event which consigned irrevocably and for ever, to British plunderers, and especially to the soldiers of Ireton and Cromwell, the properties of the Irish Catholic people, whose fathers had contended against the usurped powers to the last of their blood and their breath.

" The Duke of York, afterwards James the Second, took, to his own share of the plunder, about eighty thousand acres of land, belonging to Irish Catholics, whose cause of forfeiture was nothing more than that they had been the friends and supporters of his murdered father, and the enemies of his enemies."

This is an accurate description of the times of Redmond O'Hanlon, so far as it goes; but it is not a full description of the injustice done to the Irish, nor of the oppressions to which they were exposed. Not only were the Irish robbed of their lands, but so merciless were the Cromwellians, that they constantly despoiled the poor Irish of the produce of the lands they still retained, and it was a common practice of the times for parties of the Cromwellians to make forays upon the lands of the Irish, and sweep away "the flocks and herds," to be found on them. The Parliament sanctioned the robbery of land, and the authorities afforded no redress for the spoliation of cattle.

Redmond O'Hanlon undertook the correction of both evils. At the time he lived there was no public opinion to appeal to, or rather " the public opinion" that then prevailed was a concentrated horror of " Popery," an immitigable detestation of "the Irish."

" They are," said an English pamphleteer, writing in the year 1647, "the very offal of men, dregs of mankind, reproach of Christendom, the bots that crawl on the beast's tail. I wonder Rome itself is not ashamed of them."

Petitions had failed, remonstrances were disregarded, and the only means of redress left were the sword, and an organization of physical force to correct evils that had become unendurable. Redmond O'Hanlon organized such a force. He was the leader of a band of armed men, that in a short time became the terror of the Cromwellians, and the English as well as Scotch settlers in the North of Ireland. He did that which the *Times*, so lately as the month of May, 1857, has praised one of the Napiers for doing, when commanding the military force of Great Britain at the Cape of Good Hope, that is, despoiling cattle-stealers of their own cattle. They who had robbed the Irish of their herds found themselves exposed to the incursions of Redmond O'Hanlon, and were unable to defend their property against him. Redmond O'Hanlon employed what was then considered one of the settled practices of war; he compelled "the enemy" to pay him contributions, and those who refused were punished, in accordance with the established usages of war, with the loss or the destruction of their property. Redmond O'Hanlon did something more in the correction of evils then existing. The "new proprietors" were, in many cases, "absentee landlords," and their lands were managed by "agents," who, in accordance with the instructions given to them, were merciless in the exaction of enormously high rents. In all cases where an appeal was made to O'Hanlon, he had those agents waylaid when they had received the rents, and despoiling them of their plunder, he re-distributed the money they were taking away amongst the tenants who had paid it; and the tradition is that he made no distinction in that redistribution between "English" and "Irish" settlers; between "Catholics" and "Protestants."

One circumstance connected with his career is indisputable, and is not only a matter of tradition but of written record, namely, that finding a fellow committing a robbery, and declaring at the same time it was done by his (Redmond O'Hanlon's) orders, he not only arrested the robber, but sent him to jail, in the custody of two of his men, and that robber was afterwards executed on the testimony of the injured person.

At another time, one of his followers, a man named Walter O'Casey, having been guilty of an unpardonable outrage, in which the victim was a young woman named Mary O'Rafferty of Westmeath, O'Hanlon gave O'Casey but three hours to prepare for death, and then ordered him to be shot by his comrades.

These two circumstances are sufficient to show that the force commanded by Redmond O'Hanlon was subjected to a stern and strict discipline, and are, in themselves, the proof that O'Hanlon was not that which books and pamphlets written by his enemies describe him as being—"a mere robber"—"the leader of a gang of robbers."

In the estimation of the peasantry not less than of most of the middle classes of the North of Ireland he was a hero, performing all those acts, in a state of society bordering on barbarism and anarchy, for which the knight-errants of old were celebrated, the protector of widows, the guardian of orphans, the foe to tyrants, the redresser of wrongs, the terror of the wicked.

Such is the character of Redmond O'Hanlon as it is known from the constant and firmly believed traditions respecting him in the North of Ireland.

But there is another and a far different character given of

O'Hanlon in the following extract from a very rare pamphlet published *in London* in the year 1681, and which, it will be perceived, connects together the names of Redmond O'Hanlon and of the martyred Archbishop of Armagh, the Most Rev. Doctor Plunkett:—

"The First occasion of Discovering the Plot carried on by Dr. Oliver Plunkett and other Treasons, was a difference that arose between Mr. *John Dermond* of *Castletown-Bedlow*, in the County of *Louth*, and one Ensign *John Smith*, as the Reader will understand in the perusal of the following relation:—

I.

"The Informant being Chanter of Armach, at which time the inhabitants of the said parish suffered great damage and losses by the Tyranny of one *Redmond Hanlon* and his Confederates; the said *Hanlon* being a cruel Murderer, Rebel, and Tory (which is apparent to the whole Kingdome of Ireland), against whom the Informant preached in open Assembly, and not only against his Associates, but also against all such as relieved and harboured the said *Redmond*, which he the said *Redmond* hearing, sent many threats to the Informant willing him to desist his reflections against him and his Companions, or otherwise the effect of the said Informant's preaching should prove bitter to himself in the latter end: for they protested to make him tread the same steps with sorrow back again to other Kingdomes, whence he came, upon default of not taking the advice aforesaid."

In another publication (one of the many *cheap works* sent forth at a particular period amongst the Irish people, *for the purpose* of infusing bad and pestilent principles, and which have happily been driven out of circulation by the cheap and good works issued by Mr. James Duffy), there was given under the title of "*The Irish Rogues and Rapparees,*" a considerable space to Redmond O'Hanlon, in which he was described as a low and debauched ruffian.

I only refer to that publication to remark that it is beneath contempt, and that it has justly become a work now difficult to procure, and when procured, unworthy of perusal.

In a far different, although not in a just spirit, will be found written the following passages from Carte's "*Life of the Duke of Ormonde,*" vol. ii. pp. 512, 513:—

"DEATH OF REDMOND O'HANLON.

"*From a Pamphlet, written by Sir Francis Brewster in* 1681.

"You have, I doubt not (says he) seen in the French, as well as our Gazettes, several relations of a famous Rebel named Redmond O'Hanlon, by the French called Count Hanlon. This fellow hath been out many years committing great murders, and being a scholar and a man of parts, managed his villainy with such conduct, that he became a formidable enemy, kept two or three counties almost waste, making the peasants pay continual contribution. So terrible was he in the northern parts,[*] that there was no travelling without convoys. In fine, since the general rebellion of Ireland, all the Tories in this kingdom have not done the mischief this fellow hath done, nor put the army to so much trouble in attending and pursuing as after him and his party, both in the Earl of Essex's and this Lord Lieutenant's Government. Various attempts have been made, and large rewards offered, for bringing in his head. The Earl of Essex employed several; the now Lord Lieutenant did the same; but all proving unsuccessful, the Duke of Ormonde took at last his own way, seeming quiet and giving the Court no disturbance; though at the same time his Grace was not idle, but laid the design without the privity of any but only two persons, whom he made use of in the affair. That there should be no room for the least discovery of the designs taking air, the Duke drew tho commission and instructions all with his own hand. These were as well pursued by the gentlemen (sic)[†] instructed, and succeeded so happily, that on Monday[‡] the 25th instant, at two in the afternoon, Count Hanlon was shot through the heart. Thus fell the Irish Scanderberg, who, considering the circumstances he lay under, and the time he continued, did, in my opinion, things more to be admired than Scanderberg himself. This relation I had from the gentleman's (sic) own mouth that the Duke employed. I saw his commission all written by the Duke's own hand; but he would not let me see the private instructions; only, he assured me, that all the army of Ireland could not have done it, nor was there any other way left but that which his Grace took."

The author of this tale has, through the kindness and labours of friends (whose names he hopes he may at a future time, and in another work, be permitted to mention), collected many interesting particulars respecting the life and fortunes of Redmond O'Hanlon. These particulars fully justify the character given in this book to " The Robber Chieftain;" but as they are personal in their details, he refrains from introducing them here.

For the present sufficient has been proved to show that justice has not yet been done to the memory of Redmond O'Hanlon.

[*] The Counties of Down, Tyrone, &c.
[†] Mr. W. Lucas.   [‡] April 25, 1681.

THE END.

www.ingramcontent.com/pod-product-compliance
Lightning Source LLC
Chambersburg PA
CBHW030000240426
43672CB00007B/761